Music Theory in Ethnomusicology

OXFORD THEORY IN ETHNOMUSICOLOGY

Martin Clayton, Series Editor
Martin Stokes, Series Editor

Music Theory in Ethnomusicology
Stephen Blum

Music Theory in
Ethnomusicology

STEPHEN BLUM

OXFORD
UNIVERSITY PRESS

Oxford University Press is a department of the University of Oxford. It furthers the University's objective of excellence in research, scholarship, and education by publishing worldwide. Oxford is a registered trade mark of Oxford University Press in the UK and certain other countries.

Published in the United States of America by Oxford University Press 198 Madison Avenue, New York, NY 10016, United States of America.

© Oxford University Press 2023

All rights reserved. No part of this publication may be reproduced, stored in a retrieval system, or transmitted, in any form or by any means, without the prior permission in writing of Oxford University Press, or as expressly permitted by law, by license, or under terms agreed with the appropriate reproduction rights organization. Inquiries concerning reproduction outside the scope of the above should be sent to the Rights Department, Oxford University Press, at the address above.

You must not circulate this work in any other form and you must impose this same condition on any acquirer.

Library of Congress Cataloging-in-Publication Data
Names: Blum, Stephen, 1942– author.
Title: Music theory in ethnomusicology / Stephen Blum.
Description: New York : Oxford University Press, 2023. |
Includes bibliographical references and index. |
Identifiers: LCCN 2023004621 (print) | LCCN 2023004622 (ebook) |
ISBN 9780199303533 (paperback) | ISBN 9780199303526 (hardback) |
ISBN 9780197683743 (epub) | ISBN 9780197683750
Subjects: LCSH: Ethnomusicology. | Music theory.
Classification: LCC ML3798 .B58 2023 (print) | LCC ML3798 (ebook) |
DDC 780 .89—dc23/eng/20230131
LC record available at https://lccn.loc.gov/2023004621
LC ebook record available at https://lccn.loc.gov/2023004622

DOI: 10.1093/oso/9780199303526.001.0001

Paperback printed by Marquis Book Printing, Canada
Hardback printed by Bridgeport National Bindery, Inc., United States of America

In memory of
Gilbert Rouget, 1916–2017
José Maceda, 1917–2004
Bruno Nettl, 1930–2020

Contents

List of Tables	ix
Acknowledgments	xi

Introduction: Theorizing as a Human Activity	1

1. Ethnomusicologists and Music Theory	**5**
The Scope of Music Theory	7
Outcomes of Theorizing and Genres of Theory	13
Roles of Researchers in Knowledge Production	16
Western Music Theory in Ethnomusicology	21
This Book's Agenda	23
Issues, 1: Theory and Practice	26

2. Communication and Transformation of Music Theory	**30**
Disciples and Apprentices	34
Discipleship	35
Apprenticeship	39
What can be taught, and when?	41
Transformation of Theories and Pedagogies	42
The Centre for Aboriginal Studies in Music	44
African musical arts	46
"Jazz musicians" and music theory	47
Continuing Issues	50
Issues, 2: Explicit and Implicit Theory	52

3. Making Music Theory for Modern Nations	**60**
Conferences	64
Arab music	64
Hindu music	66
Kurdish music	67
Notations, Scales, and Solfège	68
Japan	68
North Africa and West Asia	69
Institutions and Projects	72
Continuing Issues	75
Issues, 3: Systematization and Assemblage	78

viii   CONTENTS

4. Concepts, Models, and Metaphors   85
   Expansion and Internationalization of Musicological
     Concepts   86
       Mode   88
       Composition, performance, improvisation   90
     Models and Conceptual Models   93
     Metaphors and Conceptual Metaphors   98
     Continuing Issues   101
     Issues, 4: Variables among Interrelated Concepts   104

5. Relationships among Names and Terms   108
     Sets of Names and Terms   110
     Polarities, Complementarities, and Analogies   114
     Modeling Relationships among Terms   122
       Combinations and categories   123
       Configurations, constellations, and semantic fields   125
     Continuing Issues   127

6. Actors, Actions, and Outcomes   129
     Interaction of Participants in Musicking   130
     Multipart Vocalizing   132
     Interlocking Parts   134
     Ritual and Ceremony   137
     Process Models   139

Notes   141
References   163
Index of Names   213
Index of Topics   219

List of Tables

2.1a. Six topics for consideration in research on uses of music theory   31

2.1b. Six attributes that may enhance the value of a music theory   31

2.2. Some distinctions in ways of knowing, modes of consciousness, models, taxonomies, parameters, and the like   57

3.1. Projects of modernization calling for work in music theory   61

3.2. Some systems described or mentioned as relevant to musicking   80

4.1. Forty terms for musical resources   87

5.1. Common referents of names, terms, and metaphors in music theories   109

6.1. Variables subject to prescriptions in ritual (modified from Yung 1996)   137

Acknowledgments

Portions of this book originated in drafts for a study of musical production that I abandoned. Two lectures of 1991 came out of that work: "Music theory and the poetic imagination: Some Iranian examples" (Columbia University) and "How do we recognize theories, histories, and ethnographies of music?" (Brown University). Peter Manuel and I taught seminars on *Cross-cultural Studies of Music Theory and Musical Aesthetics* at the CUNY Graduate Center, most recently in 2009. Work on the book in its current form has occupied me off and on for more than a decade, with some sections presented as "Ethnomusicology in Relation to Music History and Music Theory" (joint meeting Rocky Mountain Chapter of AMS, Southwest Chapter of SEM, and Rocky Mountain Society for Music Theory, Tucson, 2010) and "Three Musicological Concepts: Mode, Composition, Improvisation" (colloquium honoring Anna Maria Busse Berger, University of California, Davis, 2020).

I am grateful for the privilege of discussing some of the book's concerns with authors of publications I mention and other colleagues, among them Kofi Agawu, Farzad Amoozegar, Mark Anson-Cartwright, John Baily, Gerard Béhague, Daniel Blake, Anna Maria Busse Berger, Alessandra Ciucci, Ruth F. Davis, Jean During, Catherine J. Ellis, Steve Feld, Charlotte J. Frisbie, Francesco Giannattasio, Giovanni Giuriati, Scheherazade Qassim Hassan, Ben Johnston, Margaret J. Kartomi, Ben Lapidus, Lee Tong Soon, David Locke, Bernard Lortat-Jacob, Ignazio Macchiarella, José Maceda, Tullia Magrini, Peter Manuel, Michael Morse, Bruno Nettl, Tony Perman, Ankica Petrović, David G. Pier, Amir Hosein Pourjavady, Harold S. Powers, Regula Burckhardt Qureshi, Evan Rapport, James Robbins, Gilbert Rouget, Miriam Rovsing Olsen, Nicola Scaldaferri, Amnon Shiloah, Marcello Sorce Keller, Nicholas Stoia, Michael Tenzer, Tom Turino, Rob van der Bliek, Matt Vander Woude, Robert Witmer,

xii ACKNOWLEDGMENTS

Richard K. Wolf, Ameneh Youssefzadeh, and Izaly Zemtsovky. Several of these, along with Sasan Fatemi, Eshantha Peiris, Stephen M. Slawek, and Tsukada Kenichi, have generously provided me with copies of their publications. I benefitted from Martin Stokes's gift for offering invaluable advice in the kindest way possible at a difficult time in my life.

Introduction: Theorizing as a Human Activity

The presence of music theory in ethnomusicology results from the socialization and theorizing of ethnomusicologists and of participants in the world's musical practices. *Theory* is produced by *theorizing*, a common activity among humans that sometimes produces theories retained for future use, just as results of *musicking* can be retained in various ways. Both activities are processes with potential relevance to remembered, current, and anticipated experiences.

Theories, or fragments of theory, are at once outcomes of theorizing and invitations or occasions for further theorizing. Though musicians who are content with the knowledge they have assimilated may ignore or decline such invitations, the creation, reorganization, and revision of knowledge presuppose theorizing. All humans theorize as we reflect on relationships we perceive or imagine in our various worlds and compare alternative courses of action, remembering or imagining their distinctive features and possible uses, and weighing possible reasons for unsatisfactory performances. We are theorizing when we analyze parts of a whole and reflect on their interrelations, when we recognize analogies or resemblances and ponder their implications, and when we evaluate new possibilities as ecological and social conditions change. Other words for activities treated as theorizing in this book include speculating, imagining, judging, and many more, each with its own implications in specific contexts. I do not assume that theorizing requires language: musicians can assess the potential effectiveness of different movement sequences, for example, without any words.

As ethnomusicologists encounter theories and theorizing that are not based on premises and concepts we take for granted, we must develop ethical and productive ways of responding to ideas and interests of our fellow theorists. Easier said than done, like so many challenges

Music Theory in Ethnomusicology. Stephen Blum, Oxford University Press.
© Oxford University Press 2023. DOI: 10.1093/oso/9780199303526.003.0001

2   MUSIC THEORY IN ETHNOMUSICOLOGY

of ethnomusicological research and teaching. One of those is to avoid what Johannes Fabian (1983) aptly termed *denial of coevalness*: those who help us learn about their practices are our contemporaries and just as capable of theorizing as we are. The evolutionary assumptions of comparative musicologists and musical folklorists active in the first half of the twentieth century led many to emphasize what, in their judgment, human groups they consigned to lower stages of development had not yet achieved (tone systems, for example). Furthermore, early conceptions of ethnomusicology as study of "the *traditional* music and musical instruments of all cultural strata of mankind" allowed for research on "the hybridizing influence of alien musical elements" while excluding "Western art- and popular (entertainment-) music" (Kunst 1959, 1). It was left "for scholars to decide what's alien and what's indigenous" (Blum 2011, 6), not for those subjected to "hybridizing influence." In the final third of the last century, ethnomusicologists learned to pay attention to varieties of theorizing and were increasingly prepared to rethink theories and methods that were not well grounded despite their prevalence in institutionalized scholarship. Current knowledge of human evolution and social history far surpasses that on which comparative musicology and studies of musical folklore were based.

An ethnomusicologist's assimilation of music theory often starts with early musical training and continues with research projects that may include intensive training in other musical practices with their own theories. Experience of multiple approaches to musicking and theorizing may inspire reflection on their similarities and differences, raising the prospect of more comprehensive theories that might clarify some of those similarities and differences. In an essay on "Integrating music: Personal and global transformations," Michael Tenzer (2011) offers a candid account of his own reflection and exploration along those lines. Ethnomusicologists are active in a world where many musicians and music scholars are engaged with more than one approach to music theory, and this is a good thing. We are blessed with continual reminders of what we do not know and can learn from multiple sources, assessing an approach's potential merits in specific projects and trying to remedy limitations as they make themselves known. The fact that ethnomusicology is developing at a time of considerable creativity in music theory increases the options available to those who do not find the conventional academic theory they have learned relevant to experience of other practices. Ethnomusicologists are now in a good position to ask how current theorizing in the discipline could facilitate a less parochial approach to research on the world's music theories than those of the comparative musicologists, folklorists, and early ethnomusicologists who relied too heavily on the conceptual apparatus of academic music theory.

The mandate for the concise books of the *Oxford Theory in Ethnomusicology* series is to survey past accomplishments and suggest extensions, alternatives, and new directions. Much existing research assumes that music theory must be formulated and communicated in words, an assumption that strikes me as unduly restrictive for reasons discussed in the first chapter. All the same, my review of what ethnomusicologists have learned about music theory does concentrate on studies of concepts communicated in words, though I suspect that a majority of ethnomusicologists working today would agree, as I do, with the premise that *musical concepts* are "not necessarily tied to language" (Zbikowski 2002, 60).

The agenda for comparative musicology that Carl Stumpf (1848–1936), E. M. von Hornbostel (1877–1935), and their colleagues outlined early in the past century called for research on music perception, and we can expect ethnomusicologists to be increasingly engaged in collaborative projects with specialists in music cognition and kinetics. An ICTM Study Group on Sound, Movement and the Sciences (SoMoS) held its first meeting in 2020 (https://doi.org/10.5281/zen odo.5514167), aiming "to bridge gaps between ethnography based research and methods applied in the sciences" with "conversations on the challenges and possibilities raised." Graduate programs in ethnomusicology should do more than most are now doing to familiarize students with research of cognitive scientists, especially those working in what is called *4E cognition*: Enactive, Extended, Embedded, and Embodied (see Newen, De Bruin, and Gallagher, eds., 2018).

Recent proposals for "a new comparative musicology" (Savage and Brown 2013) and "a 21st century comparative musicology" (Giannattasio and Giuriati, eds., 2017) are clearly relevant to a consideration of prospects for research on music theory. The most common

4 MUSIC THEORY IN ETHNOMUSICOLOGY

criticism of Stumpf and Hornbostel's comparative musicology was the lack of an adequate basis for comparison (see Hood 1963, 233–35). We can hope to do better by working toward a global perspective on human history and refusing to grant an unwarranted "scientific" status to the conceptual apparatus of "Western music theory" as commonly taught, or to analyses of staff notations made from recordings (as was done in the early decades of ethnomusicology).

Hugo Zemp (1979, 34–35) drew a sharp contrast between what he called the many existing "ethno-theories," including that of the West, and a "truly scientific theory of music." Related distinctions are those between *cultural theory* and *scientific theory* (Zbikowski 2002, 114–17), *ethno-theory* and *theory* proper or *meta-theory* (as in Nattiez 1987, 230–43 and 1990, 186–97), *local theory* and *global theory* (cf. Hijleh 2012). The second term in each of these juxtapositions (*theory*, unmarked or qualified as *scientific, meta-*, or *global*) implies a greater, though not necessarily total, independence from the cultural situations in which theory is produced and used. Cross-cultural research on sound, cognition, and movement, aimed at developing a "truly scientific theory of music," could provide music scholars with a solid basis on which to compare earlier modes of theorizing and their outcomes without removing people's needs for *local* and *cultural* theories (including those that rely on conventional staff notations).

The subtitle of Giannattasio and Giuriati's collection offers a choice of "ethnomusicology or transcultural musicology?"—with the latter term highlighting the challenges of intercultural communication. The late composer-scholar-educator Akin Euba (1935–2020) pointed out several advantages of the term *intercultural musicology*, one of which is dropping the problematic *ethno-* prefix (see Euba and Kimberlin, eds. 1995). Under whatever name, those who continue the work in which ethnomusicologists are now engaged will be obliged to confront the many transcultural and intercultural dimensions of that research and teaching. "It is the work of intercultural scholarship to translate between cultures and between modalities of representation," in David Locke's apt formulation (Locke 2019, 106). Each of this book's chapters addresses specific difficulties of such work.

1
Ethnomusicologists and Music Theory

Humans have long been interested in exploring the resources and actions that enable us to make music, and in reflecting on their origins, development, current state, and potential. This book surveys ethnomusicological research on those explorations and reflections, which can result in *music theory* even in societies that do not treat *music*, let alone *theory of music*, as discrete areas of practice and inquiry. Ethnomusicologists study production, communication, and uses of theories bearing on actions of music-makers, the knowledge enabling those actions, and experience of possible outcomes. Understood in this broad sense, music theory has assumed many forms, from a pan-human capacity for theorizing that leads us to pose and respond to such questions as: What moves are possible, even obligatory, in situations of this kind? Why is it better to make *this* move rather than some other move? Do the available options meet our present needs and desires? How can we recognize and evaluate our obligations and options?[1]

Responses to these questions entail reflection on and insight concerning possible moves, reasons for specific choices, prospects for discovering or creating different options, and the *process* of posing and responding to such questions. They are instances of what in this book I term *theorizing*, to cover some of the many processes that can also be understood as reflection, introspection, speculation, conceptualization, imagination, judgment, or argument. Ethnomusicologists use these and other terms in discussing how people think about music-making or *musicking* (following Small 1998 and the similar usage of French *musiquer* in Rouget 1980, 155, and 2004).

Theorizing has often been motivated by experience of differences among two or more musical practices. It is fundamental to the process Gregory Bateson termed *Learning II*, "a corrective change in the set of

Music Theory in Ethnomusicology. Stephen Blum, Oxford University Press.
© Oxford University Press 2023. DOI: 10.1093/oso/9780199303526.003.0002

6   MUSIC THEORY IN ETHNOMUSICOLOGY

alternatives from which choice is made" or "a change in how the sequence of experience is punctuated" (Bateson 1972, 293).[2] I agree with the Athabascan scholar Dian Million (2014, 32–33) that "theorizing is something that we do plainly every day, in any moment where we make a proposition about what is happening and why." Propositions that offer a clearer understanding of a given situation can be remembered as potentially useful lessons abstracted from experience. People may not remember or document results of theorizing, or communicate them to others, but when results have been recalled, reproduced, and perhaps combined in various ways, ethnomusicologists can pursue an interest in how people assemble and use music theory.

The premise that acquisition, retention, and modification of knowledge requires recognition and assessment of alternatives is consistent with Merlin Donald's outline of three transitions in human cognitive evolution: from episodic to mimetic, mimetic to mythic, and mythic to theoretic, with earlier adaptations retained and extended as new capacities were developed (Donald 1991, 274). Donald (256–58, 273) compares his distinction between mythic and theoretic with Jerome Bruner's discussion of two modes of thinking (Bruner 1986): narrative and analytic/paradigmatic, both of which are evident in much music theory. In Donald's view, development of the three "cognitive phenomena" he describes as "graphic invention, external memory, and theory construction" (272) made possible the emergence of "theoretic culture," which "was from its inception externally encoded" (274).

Sound-producing instruments should be numbered among Donald's *external memory devices* (308), since they have enabled humans to accumulate and call up memories of relationships among movements and sounds.[3] Jonathan Sterne (2011, 221) includes musical instruments in the "technologies prior to writing that served some of its functions." Instruments function as "extensions of the body" (Wachsmann 1970; Wachsmann and Kay 1971) in a specific sense: as "a type of transducer, converting patterns of body movement into patterns of sound" (Baily 1991, 152, and 1992, 149; see also Bielawski 1979 and De Souza 2017). When people who make or experiment with instruments remember results of directing appropriate motions toward specific locations, repeated interaction with those instruments can help in retaining knowledge, not least through muscle memory.[4] Instruments have facilitated creation, retention, and transmission of music theory for reasons articulated by George Herzog (see also Picken 1975, 537):

> terminology and technical theory may well develop where there is an object or instrument on which an otherwise abstract system can be observed in visible operation; the growth of musical theory and of scale-systems also is connected with observations on musical instruments, not on the singing voice or on acoustic phenomena in the abstract. (Herzog 1945, 232)

Still, if early records of tone systems resulted from observations on musical instruments,[5] much theorizing about musical performance has focused on vocal actions of humans, birds, animals, and spirits. Rowell (1992, 309) points to "the great attention devoted to the correct production of musical sound—especially vocal sound" in early music theory of India. Correct production of sounds has remained a major concern of music theory.

The Scope of Music Theory

Ethnomusicologists have given more attention to the question of *"what is or is not to be treated as music"* (Blacking 1981, 186, his italics) than to the question of what we might understand as music theory. Only in certain times and places has music been recognized as a discipline or a distinct art, though musicking is widely regarded as "a human core-capability" (Schulkin 2013, 1). It is often conjoined with other modes of action to produce a whole greater than the sum of its parts, and the relevant theory may relate to the larger whole (cf. Gourlay 1984). In addition, common activities such as singing, lamenting, drumming, marching, and dancing are not always gathered under one heading (cf. Rice 1980 on Bulgarian and Zemp 1971 on Dan categories). Activities many of us group together as musicking may well have had different origins (Nettl 2006, 10, and 2015, 42; Tomlinson 2015, 29).

8 MUSIC THEORY IN ETHNOMUSICOLOGY

Much theorizing about disciplines and arts currently recognized as musical has treated these within such larger configurations as ritual (in ancient China), drama and recitation of ritual texts (in ancient India), and mathematics (in ancient Greece, the Muslim world, and medieval Europe). A world history of music theory would need to consider many points of departure and intersections of itineraries originating at different points. In texts and conversations touching on music-theoretical topics, ethnomusicologists can discover assumptions, explicit or implicit, concerning relationships among several fields of inquiry and action. What distinctions do participants make among modes of engagement with sound and movement in performances and ceremonies where they move rhythmically to sequences of sounds? We overhear and participate in discussions of actions and energies that produce or respond to sequences of sounds deemed appropriate (or not). Documentation of such discussions resonates with early texts that theorize musical dimensions of ritual and drama, such as the *Li Ji* (Record of Rites) and other Chinese works on ritual,[6] Aristotle's *Poetics*,[7] and the Sanskrit *Nāṭyaśāstra* (ca. 200 CE).[8]

Cross-cultural studies of music, like those of such other topics as *religion* and *art*, take concepts developed in certain intellectual traditions as points of departure for exploring cultural practices that challenge us to reassess their broader applicability without just appropriating something and calling it whatever we like. Kofi Agawu suggests (2016a, 31) that "the act of designating a species of expressive behavior as 'music' represents a beginning, a first step in conceptual exploration, a point of departure; such an action does not describe a final state or outcome." Research on diverse practices of theorizing could enrich our understanding of the universality of musicking by identifying interests that both are and are not widely shared.

The entry on "Music theory" in the fifteenth edition of the *Encyclopaedia Britannica* (1974) by one of my mentors, the composer-theorist Ben Johnston (1926–2019), opens with a broad conception of the subject that was uncommon at the time:

A theory of music comprises acoustics, aesthetics, and stylistic practice. The musical theories of a culture reflect not only its attitude to the arts but also its religious, philosophic, and scientific biases. China, India, Greece, and Islam developed musical theories long before the modern era, and western Europe has since medieval times contributed extensively to this multiple heritage. (reprinted in Johnston 2006, 53)

Different relationships among these areas of knowledge are to be expected, and attempts at a cross-cultural distinction between, say, *music theory* and *music aesthetics* are likely to fail.[9] Ethnomusicologists cannot accept a definition like that in *Grove Music Online* where "Theory" is "An area of study that tends to focus on musical materials per se, in order to explain (and/or offer generalizations about) their various principles and processes" (Berry 2013, 169, and *OMO*).[10] That definition posits a separation between *musical object* and *human subject* which Jairo Moreno (2004, 1) attributes to "*Western* music theories" (my emphasis), understood in broad terms as "discourses that address the organization of musical objects" with descriptive or prescriptive aims. Moreno argues that understanding what is said about musical objects in those discourses requires attention to the underlying conceptions of subjectivity.

Separation of musical object and human subject is not the only possible starting point for music theory. In his book *Reason and resonance: A history of modern aurality*, Veit Erlmann emphasizes an important difference between his two key terms: "While reason implies the disjunction of subject and object, resonance implies their conjunction" (Erlmann 2010, 10; see also Erlmann 2015). A shift of focus from *theory* to the *theorizing* that generates and alters theory, like the shift from *music* to processes of *musicking*, can direct researchers' attention to the full range of interactions that concern musicians in their theorizing—those with instruments, spirits, fellow humans, and other living or deceased beings ("subject-subject relations" in Feld 2015, 19). In much theorizing, sounds are understood as results and sources of energy rather than as "material" to be organized.[11] Gavin Douglas (2019) has discussed ways that Burmese performing arts are consistent with "a Buddhist epistemology that highlights interconnections among all things" and recognizes "illusion in the concept of discrete identities or bounded selves" (see also Sykes 2018, 7–8). Music theories and social theories are interdependent, commonly linked by ethical concerns.[12] What understandings of responsibilities toward others constitute a musician's subjectivity? How are relationships with others transformed as one's musical development continues?

Viewed globally, music theory takes in actions that produce distinctions and relationships among sounds and among possible responses, along with plans and rationales for action. Holly Wissler, for example, describes a vocal technique of the Quechua Q'eros community in Andean Peru, *aysariykuy* "to pull," as an "active way to send the song out so that it will reach the spirit powers": "ends of phrases are sung in prolonged, held tones with a final, forced expulsion of air" (Wissler 2009, vii). Identifying *techniques* that can sustain vital relationships among humans, spirits, and other sources of energy is a common move in theorizing.

We can expect the conceptual foundations of any musical practice to be articulated in metaphors and analogies that link tactile, kinesthetic, auditory, or visual dimensions of musicking to multiple areas of experience. Writing on the *theoretical content* of African music, Meki Nzewi observes that "the philosophical foundations of the African musical environment and phonofacts are not always music-specific" and "the same principles and rationalisations of 'repetition,' syncopation, relational tension, complementarity and lineal circularity are given synaesthetic manifestations in music, dance, visual arts and dramatic theatre" (Nzewi 1997, 13–14). Hence, an interest in music's "theoretical content" requires attention to its "philosophical foundations" and to any "synaesthetic manifestations."

Though I use the terms somewhat interchangeably, one advantage of *musicking* over *music-making* is that the former readily takes in modes of engagement with other performing arts whereas the latter implies a primary focus on music. For much the same reason, Nzewi preferred *African musical arts* as a replacement for *African music*. Members of the Pan African Society for Musical Arts Education (PASMAE) agreed and acknowledged the vital links joining music, dance, and drama in 2001 when they adopted that name one year after establishing the Pan African Society for Music Education.[13]

Attention to *musicking* can also heighten a researcher's sensitivity to ways that listeners become actively engaged in the process.

ETHNOMUSICOLOGISTS AND MUSIC THEORY   11

Ethnomusicologists have good reasons not to assume "that whatever is analogous to music is separable from other things and that it should be studied as an entity in itself" (Diamond 2008, 25). Steven Friedson opens his monograph on ritual healing among the Tumbuka people of Malawi by noting that "Music, trance, and healing form a continuum that is often functionally irreducible into constituent parts" (Friedson 1996, xiii). Jean-Jacques Nattiez notes that moving from the noun *music* to "the adjective 'musical' . . . allows us to escape a totality wrongly conceived as unique, and to recognize the 'musical' aspects of a whole range of sound phenomena" (Nattiez 1990, 60; French original, 1987, 87). Like Nattiez, Marcello Sorce Keller also judges the word *music* to be "an obstacle rather than a tool in helping us acquire knowledge about how, and why, human beings so often organize sounds in the course of their social interactions" (2010, 25; see also Sorce Keller 2016). Much research on what Sorce Keller (2010, 24) terms "activities focused on, completed by, strengthened by sound" (*klangzentrierten, klangergänzten, klangverstärkten Tätigkeiten*) is now carried out under the rubric of *sound studies* (see further Novak and Sakakeeny eds. 2015; Kapchan ed. 2017). Motivations, instruments, and techniques for producing sounds have been subjects of theorizing in many languages, and research on the outcomes belongs on the overlapping agendas of sound studies and ethnomusicology.

Paja Faudree argues that "music and language are socially determined constructs that arbitrarily divide, in fundamentally cultural ways, a communicative whole" (Faudree 2012, 519), and many ethnomusicologists would include dance and other body movements (cf. Torp 2013). How such divisions have been articulated, maintained, and challenged has been a subject of controversy over the long history of speculation on origins of music and language.[14] In a comment on Steven Brown's hypothesis that both have developed out of a primal "musilanguage" (Brown 2000), Robert N. Bellah observes (2011, 129) that "even today, ritual is apt to be a kind of musilanguage: however sophisticated its verbal, musical, and gestural components have become, they are still deeply implicated with each other." Bellah's generalization, in a study of *Religion in human evolution*, is supported by much ethnomusicological work on ritual.

12 MUSIC THEORY IN ETHNOMUSICOLOGY

Distinctions between music and language have been based on *function* and on *the primary basis of sound categorization*. According to Aniruddh D. Patel (2008, 9), the latter is pitch in music, timbre (i.e., the distinctive features of consonants and vowels) in speech. His criterion is consistent with the widely held view that "musicking ramifies discrete pitch in ways that are consistent enough to suggest structural constraints built into the human auditory system" (Tomlinson 2015, 158). Experimental support for this view comes from research like that reported by Janata and others (2002) in which the use of functional magnetic resonance imaging (fMRI) enabled "identification of tonality-tracing brain areas." Yet, as Donald A. Hodges recognizes in reviewing work on "Music through the lens of cultural neuroscience" (2019, 32), only when studies based on neuroimaging are conducted with culturally diverse subjects will they allow for cross-cultural conclusions, and that has yet to happen on a sufficiently broad scale (see Jacoby, Margulis et al. 2020; Patel and Demorest 2013, 666–68, give a few examples).

Is a hierarchy of "primary" and "secondary" categories of sound appropriate in cross-cultural studies? Ethnomusicologists and composers may hesitate to assume that timbre is necessarily secondary rather than primary in human theorizing about what we regard as music, see: Levin and Süzükei (2006, 45–58) on *timbre-centered music*, Schneider (2001) on *sonological analysis*, Porcello (2004, 328) on "identifiable and significant principles that structure ways of speaking about timbre" in sound recording studios, proceedings of a 2008 conference on timbre (Schmidhofer and Jena, eds. 2011), and Lochhead's *Reconceiving structure in contemporary music* (2016). This issue links premises of ethnomusicology to developments in composition such as *musique concrète*, electronic music, electronica, techno, spectral music, the *musique concrète instrumentale* of Helmut Lachenmann, and much else. These, along with experience in recording studios (see Fink et al., eds., 2018) and recognition of the limitations of conventional Western notation, lead some ethnomusicologists to agree with Udo Will (1999, 24) that "we cannot simply assume that musically relevant sounds have fixed pitches." The categories developed in Alan Lomax's *cantometrics* project to compare singing styles (Lomax 1968, 38–74) avoid that assumption.

With respect to social function, Lawrence Zbikowski (2008, 519–20) maintains that music and language "comprise different domains of experience" and that "one of the primary functions of music is to manipulate the emotions of others" whereas a primary function of language is "to manipulate the attention of another person within a shared referential frame." This formulation does not rule out other functions, and inventories of those have shown that musicking serves highly diverse purposes.[15] Richard Wolf chose not to describe "the musical life" of the Kotas in the Nilgiri Hills of South India "because music-making is so diffuse"; instead, he adopted a "focus on the spatiotemporal processes by which actions are carried out" (Wolf 2005, 20).

Outcomes of Theorizing and Genres of Theory

Theorizing about music has long been more common among humans than most music scholars will admit. Consideration of alternatives can be activated by what musicians perceive as errors or shortcomings in rehearsals or performances, limitations of an instrument, missed opportunities, or overly restrictive norms. Discussion of alternatives may touch on criteria for evaluating the merits of a new or modified instrument, playing technique, model, ordering of events, classification of resources, pedagogical program, or doctrine designed to meet an individual's or group's needs or criteria. Motivation to assess alternatives may also come from encounters with musicians whose concepts and procedures suggest options well beyond time-honored conventions. If "common sense is but dead theory" (Gellner 1989, 11), musicians may enjoy dancing on its grave as they proceed with a revitalized theorizing.

Recognizing with Zbikowski (2002, 114) that "the process of theorizing is both various and omnipresent," ethnomusicologists can learn to recognize variables in both the processes and their outcomes, such as differences in scope, purpose, mode of expression, degree of reflexivity, and susceptibility to revision. Zbikowski draws attention to music theory's "alliances with everyday thought" (2002, 5). He understands a *musical concept* as "a product of the process of categorization" and "an essential part of the means through which

14   MUSIC THEORY IN ETHNOMUSICOLOGY

we guide present and future actions"; it is capable of being "related to other concepts" and is "not necessarily tied to language" (60–61). Compare Kubik's assumption (2010, 21) that "In any musical culture, concepts must exist which make it possible accurately to carry out the cooperative effort which music requires," some of which deal with "interaction of bodily parts—voice, breath control, coordination of striking actions, etc." Researchers should not expect people to verbalize all such concepts (see also Merriam 1964, 63). Blacking (1990, 214) recognized two varieties of music theory: one that "can be transmitted by demonstration and without words, though in most societies words are used" and also "a philosophical enterprise [that] must be transmitted in words." In learning to play the Afghan *rubāb*, Blacking's student John Baily came to understand how movement patterns relate to concepts of an underlying music theory (Baily 1985, 1991, 1992, 2008). Matt Rahaim appreciated the complementarity of "note-based and motion-based models of melody" in Hindustani music, given the "concurrence and nonredundancy of vocal and gestural improvisation" (Rahaim 2012, 48, 52). Researchers have also managed to "theorize through using movement in ethnographic encounters" and have found that "first-hand experiences of making physical movements may both support and problematize theories" (Väätäinen 2017, 208, 216).

Zbikowski defines a *conceptual model* as "concepts in specified relationships" and is interested in "how relatively low-level structures like conceptual models coordinate with relatively high-level structures like theories," recognizing "that the lines between entities such as concepts, models, domains, and theories are more often blurry than clear and that there are no simple neurobiological explanations for any of them" (2002, 108–9). For ethnomusicologists to replace those "blurry lines" with sharp ones would make it harder to recognize diverse outcomes of theorizing and their uses. Marc Perlman argues that musical knowledge is "distributed among disconnected or loosely connected cognitive islands of coherence": "the components of any cognitive system are only loosely integrated" and "can usually be brought into relation with one another in many different ways" (Perlman 2004, 17, 200). This makes a good point of departure for ethnomusicologists trying to notice and record connections among outcomes of theorizing, from the modest and provisional to decisive steps in ambitious projects.

Genres of speech, writing, and performance used in communicating outcomes of theorizing provide formats, topics, vocabularies, rhetorical figures, and movement patterns that ethnomusicologists can learn to associate with specific situations and intentions—for example, a speech genre through which teachers make explicit a principle or norm students may have begun to infer from experience, or musical passages teachers perform for the same purpose. A music lesson or a theoretical treatise will generally include several *speech genres* as defined by Mikhail Bakhtin (1986, 64): "relatively stable thematic, compositional, and stylistic types of utterances." Names of verbal genres with rough equivalents in many languages include *list, roster, proverb, maxim, Q&A, dialogue, summary, introduction, exposition, classification, typology, lesson, anecdote,* and *narrative,* among others. Formats and content of genres may overlap, as Margaret Kartomi observed (1990, 17) in comparing a classification of musical instruments with a proverb: each is "a highly compressed form of expression that may nevertheless be pregnant with cultural meaning." With experience, historians and ethnographers can identify the verbal genres pertinent to research on music theory in a given context. Amnon Shiloah's inventory of Arabic writings on music theory (1979 and 2003) covers what he termed (1979, 2–3) a "category of literary and anecdotal writings" known as the literature of *adab,*[16] along with efforts at systematic theory and debates over the legality of music. Writings concerned with the etiquette expected of participants in musicking, like those on *adab,* are highly relevant to music theory.

On the premise that "Complementarity is mind-expanding" (Wilczek 2021, 206–22), pedagogies often take advantage of complementarities among such diverse "modes of expression" (C. Taylor 1994, 32)[17] as speech, gesture, touch, writing, and music notation (see Fatone 2010 on "intermodal imagery," also Gritten and King, eds. 2011). Students may improve their understanding of theory through performance genres such as *varnam* in the pedagogy of Karnatak music (Wolf 2009b) and *qā'ida* as taught in the Lucknow tablā *gharānā* (Kippen 1988, 161–68). Compositions have been presented as demonstrations of specific skills.[18] Benjamin Brinner (1995, 27) quotes

16   MUSIC THEORY IN ETHNOMUSICOLOGY

two pieces of advice he was given "in one form or another" by Javanese musicians: "These pieces contain all you need to know," and "If you know how to play X then you must know how to play Y."[19] Countless jazz musicians have enhanced their command of music theory with the help of Lester Young's *Tickle Toe* and John Coltrane's *Giant Steps*.

Musicking depends on the *techniques of the body* associated with producing and responding to sound. Many of the relevant techniques are outcomes of theorizing, whether or not they are explicitly taught. In a pathbreaking 1934 lecture on that topic, the French ethnologist Marcel Mauss (1872–1950) developed a conception of *habitus*, "the techniques and work of collective and individual practical reason" cultivated in diverse "societies, educations, proprieties and fashions, prestiges" (Mauss 1973, 73; original in Mauss 1966, 369). Mauss emphasized an acquired "bodily *competence* at something, a sense which he named by the Latin *habilis*" (Asad 1997, 47, his italics), which relates well to training (and associated theorizing) on uses of the voice, making and playing instruments, postures and motions for preparing and carrying out performances. In principle such training, meant to instill a sense of how to act in performance situations, neither requires nor excludes the use of words. The same is true of *habitus* as "a system of dispositions" in Pierre Bourdieu's *theory of practice* (1977, 214n1; French original in Bourdieu 2000 [1972], 393n39) though Mauss used the term with reference to training. Nonetheless, Tom Turino's comment on Bourdieu's conception also holds for Mauss's emphasis on cultivation of *habitus*: "the often 'unspoken,' 'taken-for-granted' character of the *habitus* or *common sense* does not necessarily have to imply unconsciousness—especially if linguocentric attitudes can be set aside when viewing the problem—but rather may merely suggest a different kind of consciousness and articulation" (Turino 1990, 402), which an ethnographer could attempt to observe and experience.

Roles of Researchers in Knowledge Production

In preparing a comprehensive bibliography of the new field that was becoming known as *ethno-musicology* in the 1950s, Jaap Kunst (1891–1960) included writings of anthropologists, historians, philologists,

ETHNOMUSICOLOGISTS AND MUSIC THEORY 17

and scholars of myth and literature as well as work in comparative musicology, musical folklore, musical ethnography, organology, and music archaeology (Kunst 1959).[20] His own writings were among the few that drew on statements of indigenous musicians concerning music theory, taking advantage of his lengthy residence in Java (1920–35) (see Kunst 1973 [1949] and Sumarsam 1995, 145–46). Such prominent musical folklorists as Béla Bartók (1881–1945) thought of *peasant music* as "a spontaneous expression of the musical feeling of that class" (Bartók 1931 [1924], 1), a viewpoint that makes *peasant theory* an oxymoron. E. M. von Hornbostel and Otto Abraham assumed that Japanese musicians "usually lack theoretical knowledge" (Abraham and Hornbostel 1902–93 in Hornbostel 1975, 46) and based their account of "the Japanese tone system" on measurements of frequencies from recordings, instruments tuned by musicians prior to performance, and museum instruments with fixed tunings. Description of tone systems was a major aim of comparative musicology, though (as mentioned in the Introduction) many musical practices were thought not to have reached the stage of establishing tone systems.[21]

By the 1960s some ethnomusicologists, anthropologists, and folklorists were interested in thought processes of music-makers and ritual specialists, posing questions that needed to be explored through fieldwork, such as "How are performers thinking about this process or that structure?" In the early 1960s Gerhard Kubik learned much about that topic from Evaristo Muyinda (b. ca. 1914) and other Kiganda musicians (Kubik 1983 and 1991), and his monograph on "Polyphony and tone systems in Central and East Africa" (1968) set a new standard for work on music theory in Africa. Other pioneering works based on thorough field research include Hugo Zemp's study of concepts related to music making among the Dan people of Côte d'Ivoire (1971, 69–92, 304–9), Jan Stęszewski's delineation of conceptual schemes of Polish folk musicians (1972), Ankica Petrović's study of the vocal genre *ganga* in Herzegovina and parts of Bosnia (1977), Rafael José de Menenzes Bastos's analysis of the "acoustic-musicological system" of the Kamayurá in the Brazilian Amazon (1978; cf. Bastos 1986, 72), Zemp's research on music theory of the 'Are'are (1978, 1979), Carol Robertson's engagement with "Mapuche philosophies of time, thought, growth, and transformation" (1979),

18   MUSIC THEORY IN ETHNOMUSICOLOGY

and Steve Feld's monograph on Kaluli poetics (1982, 3rd edn. 2012). The dissertations of Paul Berliner (1974) and David Locke (1978) marked the beginnings of decades-long collaborations with expert musicians, who were rightly credited as co-authors of major publications (Locke with Agbeli 1992; Alorwoyie with Locke 2013; Berliner and Magaya 2020).

Music theory and musical knowledge are not like the material goods scholars can discover and acquire but are subject to continual reinterpretation and transformation. One consequence of reflection on the dialogical nature of ethnomusicological work (see Feld 1987; Ellis 1994; Impey 2002; Macchiarella 2011) was description of the conversations researchers instigate or join or happen to overhear (e.g., Mitchell ed. Frisbie and McAllester 1978, 2–10; and Fabian 1990). Among the obstacles to be overcome were an interest in locating spokespeople for a cultural consensus, sometimes called an *ethnotheory* (see Perlman 2004, 4–7 and Agawu 2017 for critiques of assumptions attached to that term). The *ethno-* prefix marks a theory as limited to an ethnicity's presumed consensus as judged by outsiders who pay little or no attention to discussions and intercultural communication of theory.[22] Researchers interested in links between what Nzewi termed philosophical foundations and theoretical content can note cultural continuities and areas of agreement without positing a consensus that precludes close attention to how individuals think and act in relation to continuities and commonalities. *Ethnotheory* should be replaced by *indigenous theory*, which can draw much needed attention to the complex histories of indigeneity (see Steeves 2018). In an introduction to the work of Mauss, Claude Lévi-Strauss (1966 [1950], xxxviii–ix) maintained that "indigenous theory bears a far more direct relation with indigenous reality than would a theory based on our categories and problems" as applied by specialists who remain susceptible (like all theorizers) to "misrecognition (*méconnaisance*) of the reality of the 'mechanism'" of such social interactions as gift exchange (Bourdieu 2000 [1972], 337).[23]

The interests of ethnomusicologists in music theory intersect with those of systematic musicologists, taking in such topics as musical thought (i.e., thought about music as in Rice 1980; Haefer 1981; Maceda 1981; Nettl 1989),[24] musical thinking (conducted through music as in Kresánek 1977 and Berliner 1994), music cognition (Dowling and Harwood 1986; Thaut and Hodges eds. 2019), music and emotion (Juslin and Sloboda eds. 2010), musical competence (Blacking 1971; Brinner 1995), poetics and aesthetics (Feld 1982), education for living (Ellis 1985; Music Educators National Conference 1985), classification and typology (Kartomi 1990), notations (Kaufmann 1967; Pian 1967; Picken 1977; Ellingson 1992), mathematics (Chemillier 1995 and 2007; Brenner 1997), and cosmology (Hornbostel 1929; Basso 1985). Work on all these topics deals with ways humans theorize about musical dimensions of our activities.

Musical thinking requires comment, given the powerful hold of the assumption that thinking requires the use of words. The great pianist Artur Schnabel (1882–1941) acknowledged that "I always hesitate to use the verb 'to think' for music (although all my life I have done practically nothing else than 'think' in music) because this word evokes an association with recognition, purpose or judgment" (Schnabel 1942, 21). He need not have hesitated, as *thinking musically* was a prominent concern in European musical culture from the 1780s onward.[25] In his 1802 biography of J. S. Bach, Johann Niklaus Forkel (1749–1818) wrote that Bach "no longer needed to expect his ideas from his fingers but could derive them from his own fancy" once his reworking of violin concertos for keyboard had "taught him to think musically" (Forkel 1968 [1802], 49, trans. David and Mendel, eds. 1966, 317). In the early twentieth century "pictorial" or "visual" thinking was the central focus of work such as Paul Klee's pedagogical writings of the 1920s, published as *Das bildnerische Denken* (Klee 1964 [1956]) and translated as *The thinking eye* (Klee 1961).[26] Some ethnomusicologists may choose to follow Kresánek and Berliner in describing musicians' creative processes as musical thinking, and some will prefer to speak of cognitive or semiotic processes. Bell Yung, writing on the Chinese *qin* (a seven-string zither), distinguished three *cognitive components* of musical experience: aural, visual, and kinesthetic (Yung 1984, 505). Berliner chose words that could elicit responses from musicians with whom he had spoken and circulated drafts of *Thinking in jazz* hoping to incorporate some of their suggestions (Berliner 1994, 14–15). More important than choice of terms is attention to ways that aural, visual, and kinesthetic dimensions of musicking complement and enrich one

20 MUSIC THEORY IN ETHNOMUSICOLOGY

another. Thinking and theorizing are actions of human bodies, which sometimes focus on bodily action.

Although products of ethnomusicological research result from interactions of ethnomusicologists with those from whom we learn, access to the products is far too often restricted. The composer and ethnomusicologist José Maceda (1917–2004) spoke of a *system* linking "universities, research institutions, museums, publishers, writers, and readers" which "has detached itself from the object of study, the native peoples, who . . . are not a part of the system, and . . . do not share its discussions" (Maceda 1979, 162). In the twenty-first century that system must be replaced by arrangements allowing for satisfactory answers to questions that Agawu (2003, 203) and others have posed: "whose is the resulting knowledge, where is it kept, who benefits from it?" Maceda outlined "a musical orientation for Southeast Asia . . . which would be based both on very old traditional concepts and practices of native peoples, and on those developed more recently in urban cultures," an orientation he adopted as a composer (Tenzer 2003). Agawu (2003, 70) advocates "work towards the direct empowerment of postcolonial African subjects so that they can eventually represent themselves," and he suspects that some ethnomusicologists are uncomfortable at "the prospect of non-Westerners becoming theorists in their own right, not just 'native informants'" (203). In my view failure to recognize all the theorizing currently underway is a major symptom of that discomfort. Southeast Asian musicians and scholars can now benefit from the project known as Decolonizing Southeast Asian Sound Archives, "a transnational research project focused on hearing and listening as dialogical modes of knowledge production in order to renegotiate established understandings of heritage curation" (decoseas.org).[27] It should become a model for similar projects in other regions.

Decolonization (including "internal decolonization" in the Americas and elsewhere)[28] has at long last become a major concern of those involved in ethnomusicology and transcultural music studies. The International Council for Traditional Music organized a series of *ICTM Dialogues 2021: Towards decolonization of music and dance studies*, and a statement circulated in August 2020 and signed by eleven past presidents of the Society for Ethnomusicology calls for "a strong and proactive response" to an unacceptable predicament: "Deep-seated

ETHNOMUSICOLOGISTS AND MUSIC THEORY 21

white supremacy and colonialism shape SEM, and SEM is a site in which these systems of power are produced and reproduced."[29] Future research on music theory will need to address the many questions raised through efforts at decolonization.

Western Music Theory in Ethnomusicology

The powerful presence in ethnomusicology of varied understandings of "Western music theory" is due above all to imperialism and colonialism (including "settler colonialism"). Key concepts (*music theory* among them) have undergone processes of "expansion and internationalization"[30] which ethnomusicologists must now study and discuss with musicians whose practices were affected by those processes. Ethnomusicologists can engage with concepts and procedures they associate with "Western music theory" while questioning underlying premises and dismissing specious representations of "Western civilization" or "Western culture" (trenchantly criticized in Davies 1996, 19–31; Appiah 2016; and Appiah 2018, 191–207).[31] In none of its diverse manifestations is Western music theory the only possible foundation for music-theoretical work by ethnomusicologists, and its concepts should not be made a standard against which to judge those of other ways of theorizing. Ethnomusicology's heritage embraces all of the world's music-theoretical practices, and a better book than this one on *Music theory in ethnomusicology* would explore lessons that music theories in languages not considered here can offer ethnomusicologists.

Introducing a collection of eleven *Analytical studies of world music*, Michael Tenzer noted that "All authors use indigenous terms and concepts, combining them in differing amounts with imported ones" (Tenzer, ed. 2006, 13). "Indigenous terms and concepts" do now turn up more frequently in ethnomusicological accounts of music-making than they once did, and the training of many musicians and scholars with whom ethnomusicologists converse has embraced both "imported" and "indigenous" terms. People engaged with music theory have long made good use (and sometimes bad use) of "non-indigenous" terminologies and will continue to do so.

22   MUSIC THEORY IN ETHNOMUSICOLOGY

Two recent histories of Western music theory, the multi-volume *Geschichte der Musiktheorie* (Zaminer, ed. 1985–2006) and single-volume *Cambridge history of Western music theory* (Christensen, ed. 2002), acknowledge that music theory "has been undertaken for a wide variety of aims and motivations," hence "is not one cultural practice but many, given a largely spurious unity by virtue of its singular appellation" (Cook in Christensen, ed. 2002, 79; compare Dahlhaus 1985, 11–19). Ethnomusicologists should bear that point in mind while assessing the aims, motivations, and outcomes of theorizing. Dahlhaus (1985, 11) observed that the history of music theory comprises theorizing *in* music alongside theorizing *about* music; ethnomusicologists might discuss theorizing *through* organizing rituals or making and exploring instruments alongside theorizing *about* these.[32]

The editors of the recent *Oxford handbook of critical concepts in music theory* (*CCMT*) speak of "the pluralism that characterizes music theory in the early twenty-first century," with the result that "foundational concepts that music theorists deploy every day have become exhilaratingly mobile—open once again to critical appraisal and (re-)definition" (Rehding and Rings, eds. 2019, xvi–vii). Most of the book's twenty-six contributors limit their appraisals to what the editors call "music theory as practiced in the Anglo-American world," though Scherzinger, Tenzer, Gelbart, and Iyer address their topics (temporalities, polyphony, scale, and improvisation) from interests that extend beyond that provincial world, and in "Pitch, Tone, and Note" Parkhurst and Hammel argue that current senses of all three terms relate to developments in the history of capitalism. Work by musicians and scholars trained in Western music theory and interested in "critical appraisal and (re)definition" of its concepts can be found in the online journal and biennial conferences of the *Analytical Approaches to World Music* project. Music scholars can benefit from work toward *Provincializing Europe* (Chakrabarty 2000) by reflecting on the potential of that province's achievements in music theory in relation to those of other provinces and outliers.[33] Histories of ethnomusicology should not promulgate unilinear narratives at the expense of multiple linear and nonlinear connections.

This Book's Agenda

Music theory is not *only* a discipline cultivated by specialists. By acknowledging a pan-human capacity for theorizing, as for musicking, ethnomusicologists can break with the practice of scholars who see themselves as capable of theorizing but not those from whom *data* is "taken" (rather than "given" as the term implies!). The best future for ethnomusicological engagement with music theory would expand the situations and media of communication along with the topics and viewpoints.

In describing existing work of ethnomusicologists and others, I highlight what I see as potentially productive insights that could inspire and guide future work. A section on *Issues* pertaining to orientations of researchers follows each of the first four chapters: (1) questions on how theory relates to practice; (2) distinctions between *explicit* and *implicit* theory, *oral* and *written* transmission; (3) processes and results of *systematization* and *assemblage*; and (4) variables among interrelated concepts.

The next two chapters are concerned with teaching and learning. Chapter Two looks first at studies of social relationships such as master/disciple or instructor/pupil before turning to efforts at transforming or replacing unsatisfactory pedagogies. Chapter Three considers research on production and uses of music theory in modern nations, with an emphasis on institutions. A *modern* theory is widely expected to be *scientific* and *systematic*—values that ought to imply a solid foundation in practical experience, though their connotations vary according to the aspirations and skills of those who invoke them. The conception of theory presented by Sindoesawarno (1905–64) in his *Ilmu karawitan* "Knowledge of Gamelan Music" (first published in 1955) is a good example:[34]

> Ilmu Karawitan is science, so its character is theoretical. But a man can compile knowledge of karawitan only if he has already examined and become sensitive to the practice of karawitan, so that he is familiar with the issues involved. The intention of this book is to inform, to explain all karawitan matters systematically. (Sindoesawarno, translated by Hatch 1987 [1955], 313)

24 MUSIC THEORY IN ETHNOMUSICOLOGY

The second half of the book concentrates on theorizing as carried out in speech and writing. Chapter Four addresses a major challenge of intercultural scholarship: using abstract concepts in ways that respect local realities and the metaphors that are key terms of many practices. One way to circumvent irrelevant associations attached to such concepts as *mode, composition,* and *improvisation* in modern European languages is to make explicit a *conceptual model* and judge how well it accommodates words and other actions of those engaged in a musical practice.

Chapters Five and Six discuss implications of the vocabularies used in theorizing concerned with musicking, with attention to names and terms for sounds, motions, roles of participants, and larger entities bringing together sounds, motions, and actors. Noting each term's unique implications is compatible with efforts to identify topics frequently addressed as people theorize, and Chapter Five opens with a provisional roster of "Common referents of metaphors and technical terms in theories of music."

Recommendations and Questions:

1. While researchers have tended to think of music theory as a body of shared concepts and procedures, understanding how people generate and live with theory calls for attention to processes of communication, debate, and transformation. Areas of controversy and topics of ongoing discussion are just as significant as relatively stable doctrines.
2. Ethnomusicologists should cultivate an interest in the interdependence of music theory and social theory, especially around the question of how concepts of action in musicking relate to understandings of participants' social responsibilities. A related question is what purposes theory is meant to serve and whether it comes to be used in other ways as well (or instead).
3. Research on music theory calls for attention to relations of reciprocity among different areas of practice. Changes in construction and playing techniques of instruments, for instance, result from theorizing and may also contribute to modification of theories, which are often shaped by capacities and limitations of instruments.

ETHNOMUSICOLOGISTS AND MUSIC THEORY 25

4. Increasing interest in musicians' techniques of the body should stimulate more research on theories that support or alter regimens of training and practice.

5. With respect to the social networks that facilitate exchange and discussion of ideas and doctrines, what are the relevant affordances, motivations, and constraints, including conceptions of the faculties and resources deemed necessary for an engagement with theory?

6. Studying ways that humans construct and use theories requires an openness to diverse uses of language through long-term contact with speech and, where relevant, writing, through which researchers can begin to recognize implications of the relevant vocabularies and formats.

7. Attention to relationships musicians perceive or probe among concepts requires close attention to philosophical foundations of their theorizing, critiques of those foundations, and stories about how humans have acquired and used musical knowledge. How do performers conceptualize the interrelationships in which they are engaged as actors?

8. As discourse is often qualified, enhanced, or contradicted by other modes of communication and expression including musical performance, it is important to assess the relative usefulness of various media in retaining and sharing outcomes of theorizing. Current interest in "alternative ways of doing and presenting ethnography" (Panopoulos, Scaldaferri, and Feld 2020, 427) promises to transform ethnomusicological exploration and communication of music theory through creative uses of film, recording, and music-making.

26   MUSIC THEORY IN ETHNOMUSICOLOGY

Issues, 1: Theory and Practice

Writing on "Music theory and philosophy," Judy Lochhead (2011, 506) sees *practical* and *speculative* modes of music theory as "a type of thought about music that permeates all aspects of musical activity"— a claim worth traking seriously. I see the relationships between thinking and musicking as a major topic for ethnomusicological inquiry. Many languages allow for distinguishing actions from thoughts, and researchers concerned with music theory should be interested in how people make and use that distinction. Does thinking focused on musicking presuppose a basis in concepts of *music* or *theory*? What type or types of thought should we equate with *theory*?

The Greek distinction between *theoretical* and *practical* knowledge, directed respectively toward truth and action in Aristotle's formulation (*Metaphysics* 993b, 20), was subsequently applied to concepts and classifications of musical knowledge in the Latin West, Byzantium, and the early Islamic empires.[35] Two philosophers well versed in Aristotle's books on logic applied that distinction and others to musical knowledge. The *Great Book on Music* of Abū Nasr al-Fārābī (d. 950 CE), Aristotle's true successor to his contemporaries, contains what a modern scholar has called "one of the most substantial passages of his entire oeuvre on his epistemological principles" (Germann 2020, 162). We acquire knowledge (*'ilm*) of music or whatever else by starting with the conviction that "the thing exists" and determining "the reason (*sabab*) for its existence and that it is entirely impossible for it to be other than what occurs in our [minds]" (Fārābī 1967, 82, trans. Germann). Al-Fārābī insisted that the theoretical (*nazarī*) branch of the art (*sinā'a*) of music must be grounded in experience accumulated over time in its practical (*'amalī*) branch (1967, 100–05 and Germann 173, French trans., Erlanger 1930, 30–36). He based a typology of "three levels of practical musical art" on the discussion of perception, imagination, and thought in Aristotle's *On the soul*: "for imagination [*phantasía*] is different from both perception and thought; imagination always implies perceptions and is itself implied by thought" (*De anima* 427b, 15, trans. W. S. Hett). Al-Fārābī recognized the imagination's power to take apart and recombine images retained from sense-perception, as well as the intellect's power to identify reasons for preferring, tolerating, or rejecting an actual or potential combination of elements. As musicians develop their imagination, they are no longer dependent on habits formed on an instrument or in a familiar social setting (Fārābī 1967, 54–55; Erlanger 1930, 9).[36]

The imagination is conspicuous by its absence in the chapter on "What a musician is" in the much earlier *De institutione musica* of Boethius (d. 524).[37] He distinguished "three classes of those who are engaged in the musical art": instrumentalists, makers of songs, and "those who judge instrumental performance and song" (Boethius 1966 [1867], 224–25, trans. 1989, 51). A true musician "exhibits the faculty of forming judgments according to speculation or reason relative and appropriate to music," a faculty that instrumentalists and those who make songs "by a certain natural instinct" lack. Many subsequent theorists writing in European languages have echoed his assertion that "rational speculation is not dependent on the act of making, whereas manual works are nothing unless they are guided by reason" (50). *De institutione musica* was a compendium of revealed truths about music as one of four mathematical disciplines "that lead the soul to its first encounter with incorporeal knowledge" (Bower 2002, 141). Al-Fārābī believed that a true science of music would be based on the Aristotelian epistemological principles leading ultimately to incorporeal knowledge, yet he understood the immense importance in human life of both the imagination (Arabic *takhayyul* or *wahm*) and the reasoning that can lead to certain knowledge.

If at times the distinction between theoretical and practical music has been equated with that between intellectual and manual labor (see Sohn-Rethel 1983 [1970]), it has also prompted reflection on how theory and practice implicate and complement each other. Some historians have attributed the development of European art music to a powerful reciprocity between theory and practice, arguing that practice becomes capable of generating theory once it is shaped by theory.[38] In contrast, representations of musicking as activity pursued without theorizing are common in writings of folklorists and ethnomusicologists. Luis Felipe Ramón y Rivera (1913–93), longtime director of the Venezuelan National Institute of Folklore, defined *etnomúsica* "ethnomusic" as "a branch of musical creation

28 MUSIC THEORY IN ETHNOMUSICOLOGY

characterized by a lack of interest in speculation" (1980, 7).[39] Times have changed, and ethnomusicologists can no longer presume to be theorizing about people who do not themselves theorize.

Current knowledge of the world's musical practices does not provide an adequate basis for cross-cultural comparison of how musicians relate theory to practice. We can trace uses of labels that mark one practice as more tightly regulated than others, such as the *śāstriyya sangit* of India (music based on doctrines laid out in *śāstras*, treatises), the *yayue* "refined music" of China, or the *art music* or *classical music* of many modern nations. An early European classification of practices by degree of regulation is the thirteenth-century Parisian writer Johannes de Grocheio's typology of music by "usage and sociality" among residents of the city (*ad usum vel convictum civium*). One type was "composite," "regulated," "canonical," and "mensural," in contrast to that which was "simple," "civic," and "popular"; a third type, the "ecclesiastical," drew on both with the aim of praising God (Rohloff 1972, 124–25).[40] In the *Muqaddimah* "Preface" to his *Kitāb al-'ibar* ("Book of Examples"), the Arab historian Ibn Khaldun (d. 1406) likewise contrasted those who needed only their natural aptitude (*midmār*) for harmonious proportion (*tanāsub*) among sounds to sing simple melodies, with those whose instruction (*ta'līm*) in "the craft of singing" (*sinā'at al-ghinā'*) made them capable of composition (*ta'līf*). This was "the last of the crafts attained in civilization," cultivated after more basic needs had been met (Ibn Khaldun 1961, 761–62, trans. 1967, 2, 399, 405).

Despite ample precedent for restricting a concept of *music theory* to doctrines publicly recognized as regulating the music-making of those versed in the theory, it is wrong to infer an absence of theorizing in music-making described as "unregulated" or "without instruction." A task for (ethno)musicologists is to study the *interests* that have motivated efforts at regulation and claims for their significance, along with evidence of resistance to such efforts and claims. In his "self-laudation," King Shulgi of Ur (twenty-second century BCE) boasted of his contribution to the regulation of music in such statements as "I formulated all the rules for both 'rising/raising' and 'overturning/throwing down' [the scale? pitch? interval?]" (Shaffer 1981, 82). Many more representations of success in formulating rules were to follow.

ETHNOMUSICOLOGISTS AND MUSIC THEORY   29

Notions of who is engaged with theory, in what formats and for what purposes, are major variables in the world's musical practices. Some answers to the question of purposes show an engagement with what Max Weber (1864–1920) described as processes of *rationalization* in a text on *The rational and sociological foundations of music*, drafted around 1911 and published a decade later (Weber 1921, trans, 1958). A concern with those processes has become widely shared in the century since Weber's death (among thousands who never heard of him), without displacing all other approaches to music theory. Weber's interest in comparative history led him to ask which spheres of life have been subject to rationalization at a given time and place through efforts to increase human control of the relevant tools and resources. He saw music as one of many spheres in the modern West marked by projects of rationalization with deep historical roots, evident in uses of notation, equal temperament, construction of instruments, formation of huge orchestras, and much else.[41] Faced with all this, it would be wrong, even with respect to the West, to equate theorizing with rationalization, since it can engage the human imagination in so many ways.

Michel de Certeau argued that, in sixteenth-century Europe, "the traditional binominal set of 'theory' and 'practice'" began to be replaced by a distinction between "two different *operations*, the one discursive (in and through language) and the other without discourse." The latter was "composed of multiple but untamed operativities," each some sort of *savoir-faire* that language might "colonize" through discourse unconstrained by the methods of science. In the music theories and practices of modern Europe, we can recognize what de Certeau described as "the fundamental schema of a *discourse* organizing the way of *thinking* as a way of operating, as a rational management of production and as a regulated operation on appropriate fields" (Certeau 1984, 65). Ethnomusicologists with whatever regional specialization are likely to encounter modes of theorizing committed to this use of discourse as well as theorizing that values the *savoir-faire* of more or less "untamed operativities." Results of those modes are sometimes distinguished as *explicit* and *implicit* theory, respectively (see *Issues, 2*).

2

Communication and Transformation of Music Theory

Questions addressed in studies of how music theory is created or assembled, communicated, employed, and transformed have long been concerns of theorizing in many languages, for example:

What must people know to make music well, to evaluate compositions and performances, or to construct and maintain instruments?

What norms and principles of a practice are learned without being taught?

How can verbalized theory complement what students learn as they imitate mentors and practice exercises?

How is access to musical knowledge controlled?

Do presentations of theory invite, discourage, or even prohibit consideration of other possibilities?

What are the strengths and weaknesses of procedures for assembling and using theories?

Table 2.1a lists six topics for consideration in research on the uses of theory. When procedures for communicating musical knowledge identify relationships between theory and practice as an issue to be addressed, theory generally comprises models, schemata, procedures, doctrines, admonitions, and so on, perhaps attaching these to a larger worldview. Novices can familiarize themselves with such constructs without an explicit concept of theory. Musicians who do identify theory as certain kinds of musical knowledge are often inclined to comment on attributes that enhance its value, six of which are listed in Table 2.1b.

Music Theory in Ethnomusicology. Stephen Blum, Oxford University Press.
© Oxford University Press 2023. DOI: 10.1093/oso/9780199303526.003.0003

Table 2.1a. Six topics for consideration in research on uses of music theory

1. social relationships between novices and experienced musicians
2. differences in media and formats of presentation as they relate to intended uses
3. criteria for assessing a musician's command and application of a theory
4. effectiveness of efforts to restrict or grant access to musical knowledge; strategies to gain access despite efforts to restrict it
5. situations in which musicians wish to display command of theory or contempt for its irrelevance
6. responses of musicians and others to music-theoretical projects of a state's institutions of education, broadcasting, and other areas of cultural policy

Table 2.1b. Six attributes that may enhance the value of a music theory

1. Identity as a body of doctrine, one "science" or branch of knowledge among others
2. Recognition as a prerequisite of competence in a specific role or set of roles
3. Effectiveness of its models or rules in lessons, rehearsals, and performances
4. Association with a prestigious style, practice, or center
5. Legitimacy gained through connections with a specific court, lineage, body of doctrine, or official delimitation of "cultural heritage"
6. Accessibility to all and sundry; *or*, the degree to which it is *not* widely available in a trustworthy form

Lawrence Gushee introduced his consideration of "Questions of genre in Medieval treatises on music" with the proposition that "The work of musical theory must be seen as a response to the goals and methods of certain institutions (university, monastic school, choirschool)" (Gushee 1973, 366).[1] State ministries of education, broadcasting, or culture and associated institutions are common sites for fieldwork by ethnomusicologists interested in production and uses

32   MUSIC THEORY IN ETHNOMUSICOLOGY

of theory. In most nations the histories of such ministries extend over no more than a few centuries, the great exception being China where the *yuefu* "Bureau of Music" of the Han empire, established in 113 BCE, was presumably modelled on the *yuefu* of the Qin dynasty (221–207 BCE) about which little is known (Gimm 1995, 712). Stability, even survival, of the empire was thought to require standardization of pitches, twelve of which within an octave are named in a dialogue between King Jing of the Eastern Zhou dynasty and his music official, Ling Zhoujiu, written down around 430 BCE (Gimm 1995, 704; Needham and Robinson 1962, 170, 204, 219).[2]

Ethnomusicologists have the advantage of being able to observe steps in assembling and using music theory in such institutions as the Rashidiyya Institute in Tunis (Davis 1986, and 2004, 51–70), the National Folklore Research Department of the Ministry of Culture and Tourism in Ankara (Markoff 1986), and the Institut de Recherche et de Coordination Acoustique/Musique (IRCAM) in Paris (Born 1995). Some of us encounter musicians who prefer "a mode of thinking with others separate from the thinking that the institution requires of you" (Halberstam 2013, 11).[3] Fieldwork in a modern institution inevitably includes perusal of written materials as well as conversations with people involved in its activities. Difficulties in gaining access can be considerable, as Sabine Trebinjac indicated in reporting on her efforts in the late 1980s to learn how Uyghur music was notated, further arranged, and corrected at specific locations (Beijing, Ürümchi, and Kashgar) in China's vast network of officials charged with transforming musics of "minority nationalities" into "national music" (Trebinjac 2000, 299–343). In the second decade of the twenty-first century, state policy toward Uyghur cultural practices shifted from transformation to eradication, with support for hollow stereotypes and nothing more (Zenz 2018; Byler 2021; Ha et al. eds. 2021).

Projects to develop a written theory have often entailed neglect of knowledge that students had assimilated by other means. Scheherazade Qassim Hassan notes that the written theory produced in the 1930s for schools offering instruction in the *Irāqi maqām* coexisted with an orally transmitted theory until "the weight and authority of the written theory . . . led to a certain neglect of the oral terminology and its underlying concepts" (S.Q. Hassan 2008, 101). Knowledge could first be

COMMUNICATION AND TRANSFORMATION OF THEORY   33

"taken" surreptitiously before it was "given" overtly: students often began by imitating one or more masters without "a formal, direct master-student relationship" until, possibly, at a later stage in their education (S.Q. Hassan 2002, 313–14). As they attended performances and heard broadcasts and recordings, students could begin to internalize norms and values on which musicians and listeners based their (often conflicting) evaluations of artists and performances.

In many nations, teachers and students who acknowledge written theory's "weight and authority" nonetheless find oral commentaries crucial supplements to the written doctrines. Conversely, those engaged in a master/disciple relationship may find written theory or musical notations useful supplements to oral instruction. Topics of great importance may receive little or no mention in a corpus of written theory. After confronting the information he found in more than fifty published works of Arabic theory with the oral theory he assimilated during lessons and conversations with Egyptian musicians, Scott Marcus (1992, 191) stressed the need for attention to "musicians' oral concepts and performance rules and strategies" on such topics as modulation, given the "virtual absence of comments on the subject in modern Arabic theoretical literature." Students can absorb "a special kind of musical knowledge, transmitted silently from body to body" without any discussion, as Rahaim (2012, 2–3) realized while learning to sing the Hindustani vocal genre *khayal* and internalizing the vital "knowledge of melody as motion." Few areas of an ethnomusicologist's education are more important than learning to recognize complementarities between what is written, spoken, and communicated through posture and movement. These become evident while learning how musicians theorize the right sequence of stages in a novice's education and each participant's responsibilities at each stage.[4]

This chapter looks first at research on master/disciple and master/apprentice relationships. Both are the subject of excellent work by ethnomusicologists and anthropologists who describe and interpret their experience as a disciple or apprentice, treating issues that are also relevant to research on other relationships and situations such as classroom instruction, formal and informal rehearsals (Koskoff 1988; Gay 1991; 63–187), and mentoring. Musicians often recall

34 MUSIC THEORY IN ETHNOMUSICOLOGY

music-theoretical concepts learned from mentors, such as the statement made to Duke Ellington by the composer and conductor Will Marion Cook (1869–1944) when Ellington asked for advice on how to connect musical ideas: "First you find the logical way, and when you find it, avoid it, and let your inner self break through and guide you. Don't try to be anybody else but yourself." Ellington (1973, 104) found this "one of the best lessons I ever received in music," and those who love his compositions can appreciate the many ways he applied that lesson.

We need more research on how musicians interact with sources of oral, written, and kinesthetic knowledge as they prepare to meet expectations that are no longer those faced by their teachers and mentors. The final section of the chapter starts to explore motivations and strategies for transforming existing theories and pedagogies.

Disciples and Apprentices

As well-established practices for training professionals, discipleship and apprenticeship have too much in common to be treated as mutually exclusive categories. The term *disciple* implies an aspiration to enter a way of life where specific competencies are associated with an ethic that masters attempt to inculcate. Successful apprentices achieve professional competence in a craft and may also become sensitive to its moral values without necessarily making them the very basis of their way of life. Neither disciples nor apprentices can rely entirely on verbalized theory to learn what they need to know, however helpful they may find words linked to actions. A remark of Trevor Marchand's in an essay on craft apprenticeship also applies to the master-disciple relationship: "learning is achieved primarily through observation, mimesis and repeated exercise" even if "words are regularly used to direct focus, coordinate activities and communicate conceptual ideas or values related to the enterprise" (Marchand 2008, 247). As a student of the Turkish *ney*, Banu Şenay (2020, 143) found that "with its rich texture of metaphors and analogies, [her instructor] Salih Hoca's verbal articulations always acted as vital aids in generating new insights about the potential meaning of an embodied action, facilitating new ways of approaching music, artistry, and skilled knowledge." Şenay (94–95) sees an analogy between an instrumentalist's improvised *taksim* and the discourse her instructor would generate spontaneously during events he called *sohbet* "conversation," a term adopted from Arabic via Persian for conversational exchanges between Sufi masters and their disciples.

Regula Qureshi and Amanda Weidman draw on their training in Hindustani and Karnatak music, respectively, in reflecting on "discipleship as a site of ethnography" (Qureshi 2009) and apprenticeship as "a mode of ethnography" (Weidman 2012; see also Woolner 2021). In either of these roles, researchers are apt to form relationships with other students, colleagues, or rivals of their master (see Neuman 1980; Baily 1988a; Kippen 1988 and 2008; Slawek 1994 and 2000; Bakan 1999, 281–315; Qureshi 2007 and 2009; Gill 2017; Şenay 2020), enhancing their relationships with one or more masters (see also Yung 2009; M. G. Katz 2017; Amoozegar-Fassaie 2018; Pocorobba 2019). When the network of a master's students is limited to family members (perhaps broadly defined), foreign researchers can attempt to develop mutually beneficial exchanges with prospective instructors. Charry (2000, 337–41) lists a few benefits ("advantages") he successfully offered to his Mande teachers, and Niranjana (2020, 137) notes "kinds of assistance" given to teachers of Hindustani music by students who do not act as disciples.

Discipleship

Daniel Neuman was one of the first ethnomusicologists to attempt a description of "the social organization of specialist knowledge" in his book on *The life of music in North India* (1980, 85–144). The relationship of master and disciple (Hindi *guru* and *shishya*, Urdu *ustād*, and *shāgird* from Persian) is initiated with a ceremonial commitment and sustained through mutual devotion so long as the master finds a disciple worthy of receiving instruction in what Neuman (50–58) summarizes as "things and ways": "a body of knowledge which is both secret and esoteric, and the way a musician must lead his life." The phrase "things and ways" applies well to the many practices in which transmission is theorized as a fund of knowledge plus guidance in how to act in relation to it.

36   MUSIC THEORY IN ETHNOMUSICOLOGY

In his fieldwork of the early 1970s on Muslim musicians in Delhi, Neuman (98) found a strong preference for marriage within a patrilineal descent group (*khāndān*) on the assumption that only from father to son can musical knowledge be fully transmitted. Marriage with women from other groups could increase a khāndān's store of knowledge, and descent groups with a history of intermarriage might become a *gharānā*, "family tradition" or "stylistic school" (99). Without mentioning Bourdieu, Neuman showed how music theory can become "symbolic capital in the form of collectively recognized *credit*" (Bourdieu 1977, 41): musicians assigned to the social category of *soloist* were more readily credited with knowledge of theory than were those regarded as *accompanists*, such as players of the *sarangi* (a short-necked waisted fiddle). The latter were "not usually recognized by others as being authorities on musical theory, although they themselves claim to be so" (Neuman, 122).

Looking at "Indian music as a cultural system," Neuman (1985, 102–3) contrasted the reliance of Hindustani musicians on oral instruction within professional lineages with the coexistence of oral instruction and written theory in South India, where the treatise (*śāstra*) was long seen as a source of authoritative doctrine, even if "the degree to which [written] theory acted on performance in the South is arguable." As Harold Powers noted (1980a, 72), the Sanskrit term *śāstra* may refer either to a treatise or to the doctrine it contains. In contrast, Arabic *'ilm* "science, body of knowledge," used in several languages spoken by Muslims (including Urdu and Bahasa Indonesia), neither implies nor excludes existence of an authoritative redaction of a given body of knowledge in writing. It sometimes designates techniques of the body associated with a specialized role (see Ewing 1997, 135–42, for an example). The totality of a master's teaching, which generally includes techniques of the body, is their *ta'līm*, from the same root as *'ilm*.

The conversations presented in Qureshi's *Master musicians of India: Hereditary sarangi players speak* (2007) support the claims of sarangi players to be "authorities on musical theory." Her translations of conversations conducted in Urdu or Hindi show how sarangi players acquire and maintain musical knowledge through "orally transmitted words that are being generated not declaratively but interactively" (2007, 3). The distinction is important for ethnomusicologists'

COMMUNICATION AND TRANSFORMATION OF THEORY 37

reporting strategies. Qureshi's roles in the conversations were those of "personal discipleship, informal studentship, and research inquiry" (5). Like Neuman she worked with Sabri Khān (1926–2015), who told her that he learned "the technique of teaching" from his grandfather: "No one gives his knowledge easily. First he has to know how to teach; only then can he teach someone" (36). Sabri Khān once insisted that Qureshi ask him the question, "What is this process of developing the notes?" (94–95). She records concise statements of fundamental assumptions of theory and pedagogy, such as "It is amazing how a person can shape one thing in so many different ways. . . . [he plays a phrase] You should get at least fifty ideas from this" (Qureshi 2009, 175). Although "few specifics of musical and technical content are verbalized," "theory operates more vigorously" in the model of transmission from "heart to heart" (*sīna ba sīna*, adopted from Persian) and a "theory of imitation, . . . where the disciple copies the master" (2009, 177).

Stephen M. Slawek (1987, 33–91) and James Kippen (1988, 112–202) have published detailed accounts of the *ta'līm* they received from masters of *sitār* and *tablā*, respectively: in Slawek's case Dr. Lalmani Misra (1924–79) and Pandit Ravi Shankar (1920–2012), in Kippen's Ustad Afaq Husain Khan of Lucknow (1930–90). Kippen (119) makes explicit the "underlying theory" for his master's attention to posture, arm and hand positions, and finger placements: "tension in the musician's body will result in tension in the sound produced." Slawek (33–35) prefaces his description of how basic *sitar* techniques are combined on three levels with the doctrine that "the resultant tension of poor posture" will be audible in the music unless the instrument is held properly and correct posture maintained; he is most concerned with teaching on the third level. Like Qureshi, both Kippen and Slawek highlight the importance of what Kippen calls "instruction in creative thinking," as vital a component of *ta'līm* as training in technique and repertory: "the giving of a musical intelligence to the disciple . . . will help him to think creatively and to make his own musical decisions in . . . 'the light of the *ta'līm*'" (Kippen, 115). Kippen offers examples of common speech genres: formulas like "the light of the *ta'līm*," statements of certain "rules of composition and improvisation" (126), and "moral advice" conveyed through stories or verses (132).

38   MUSIC THEORY IN ETHNOMUSICOLOGY

Kippen (1988, 136–42) compared the experience of his ustad's *ta'līm* with observations of the training offered in a few music colleges, which in his judgment did not prepare students for careers as professionals unless they went on to study under a master. Andrew Alter (1994) offered more positive reports on two institutions (the Sangeet Research Academy of Calcutta and the Sri Ram Bharatiya Kala Kendra of New Delhi) that managed to make room for master-disciple relationships, though he did not discuss students' subsequent careers. A master's *ta'līm* may demand several years of instruction for students to assimilate explicit and implicit theory while developing as performers; the theory taught in most institutions is more easily isolated from performance and tends to be dependent on written communication, as mentioned with respect to the *Irāqi maqām*. How instruction in music colleges differs from what Qureshi termed "the culture of discipleship" is a major concern in scholarship on Hindustani and Karnatak music (e.g., Weidman 2006; Jairazbhoy 2008; M. G. Katz 2012 and 2017; Niranjana 2020, 128–61). Jairazbhoy (2008, 355–56) saw the cultivation of an "unquestioning attitude" among disciples as having had a "detrimental impact on the cultivation of music theory" since no loyal disciple would ask "Why?" Max Katz (2012) finds institutionalized instruction in Hindustani music responsible for fostering an ideology of Hindu "communalism." Robert Garfias delivered a keynote address on "The demise of the gurukula system in Asia and the condition of music tradition in the post-industrial era" at the 2014 meeting of the Society for Asian Music, though further research might reveal some signs of life.

Farzad Amoozegar treats the relationship of a Sufi elder (*pīr*) or guide (*morshed*) with a disciple (*murīd*) as a model for that of master and disciple (*ostād* and *shāgerd*) in a dissertation on *Ethical dimensions of music-making in Iran* based on his studies of Persian "traditional music" (*mūsīqī-ye sonnatī*, also called *mūsīqī-ye kelāsīk* "classical music") with Ata-Allāh Jankouk (1936–2007) and Mohammad-Rezā Lotfi (1947–2014). The *ta'līm* he experienced drew upon ideas of Islamic philosophers, notably Abū Hāmid al-Ghazālī (1058–1111), as articulated and reworked in classical Persian poetry. What Amoozegar (2018, ii) terms ethical principles that "form the attitudes and actions relevant to the process of music-making" include an engagement with the structure and content of Persian poetry through which students can begin to comprehend and reproduce small-scale and larger-scale rhythms of Persian traditional music, extending to experiences of a spiritual journey. It is now rare for an Iranian student to work for several years with a single master in order to fully assimilate a *ta'līm*.[5]

Apprenticeship

The anthropological literature on apprenticeship is more extensive than that on discipleship, though ethnomusicologists may have produced more studies of the latter. Apprentices are commonly expected to pick up much of what they must learn with little overt instruction. In an excellent study of apprenticeship in the *huju* opera troupes of Shanghai during the first half of the twentieth century, Jonathan Stock (2002, 1) stresses the importance of "unstructured imitation and experimentation by the pupil in the hope that his master might sometimes react with guidance or corrections." That is a familiar predicament of apprentices to artisans in various fields: the anthropological literature offers numerous examples of artisans neglecting apprentices and even concealing crucial procedures (see the endnotes in Herzfeld 2004). Apprentices in a *huju* troupe were to learn "elements of opera and ways of fitting these elements together" (Stock 2002, 15), topics addressed with highly explicit theories in some practices but not in those like *huju* that are "not so much taught to new apprentices as learned by them" (22). Faced with the need to learn *how* to memorize and recall information gleaned by observing and imitating practitioners, apprentices might evaluate ways of organizing information.[6] Comparing the relatively short apprenticeships of *huju* performers with those of performers in more elite operatic genres, Stock found that the best of the former acquired "truly exceptional learning skills" (23) that served them well in their subsequent careers.

As described by Tsao Pen-yeh (1986, 224–26, and 1988, 16–18), the four stages in the education of a boy or girl apprenticed to a master of *t'an-tz'u*, a genre of sung narrative in the Chinese dialect of Su-chou, had much in common with *huju* apprenticeship. After the requisite formalities, an apprentice lived in the master's household, carrying out various duties while trying to surreptitiously observe performances.

40 MUSIC THEORY IN ETHNOMUSICOLOGY

The second stage, imitating every detail of the master's rendition, began the instruction in basic techniques. In the third stage the apprentice could go beyond strict imitation and take on minor roles in the master's performances. Even after a public performance concluding the apprenticeship, performers were expected to continue learning through reading and observation of other performers and of human interactions more generally. While "the basic oral-aural methods of *t'an-tz'u* training" had evidently remained intact at the time of Tsao's research in the early 1980s, he noted such changes as a shorter period of training, less ceremonial interaction of master and apprentice, and the option to seek private instruction rather than joining a troupe (Tsao 1988, 18).

John Baily's study of Persian-speaking professional musicians active in the 1970s in Herat, the main city of western Afghanistan, discusses "musical training (in the broad sense)" in a chapter on "the science of music" (*'ilm-e mūsīqī*) (Baily 1988a, 37–59). Although Herati professionals found it advantageous to present themselves as pupils of a master, their training did not match the comprehensive *ta'līm* of Hindustani musicians.[7]

"The science of music" was an Afghan adaptation of the Hindustani theory imported to Herat in the 1930s by way of Kabul, where court musicians from India arrived in the late nineteenth century and taught barber-musicians, some of whose descendants were recognized as *ustād* "master" or *honarmand* "artist" (162). The theory was closely associated with a style born of encounters between Indian and Afghan musicians that became the basis of an Afghan national music. It provided Herati musicians with terms used in conversation and perhaps in training novices, though for Baily (56) "it was not clear to what extent technical terms were used as a teaching tool." Musicians who heard an Afghan vocalist's weekly demonstrations on radio of differences between Hindustani rāgs and Afghan analogues tended to accept the Hindustani versions as correct (44). A few were literate enough to write melodic patterns in notebooks, and one owned an Urdu treatise with descriptions of 157 *rāgs* (40). For most the science of music was an assemblage of what Baily terms *representational models*—those with "little or no direct role in performance"—as opposed to *operational models* with "a dynamic role in the control of ongoing musical performance" like the sequences of *sargam* syllables for scale degrees that are fundamental to Hindustani theory and performance (Baily 1988b, 114).[8]

Only one of the musicians Baily encountered had benefitted significantly from a relationship with a master, Ustād Nabi Gol of Kabul. Amir Jān Khushnawāz still owned the notebook in which Nabi Gol had written out the lessons, and he was the only Herati musician Baily met who could sing *sargam* syllables (1988a, 56). Members of the Khushnawāz family saw their knowledge of music theory as a means of gaining advantage over their rivals, and recognition of his family's competence in the national style and its *'ilm* did help Amir Jān maintain a dominant position in the musical life of Herat for several decades.

What can be taught, and when?

Assertions that a given topic "cannot be taught" have long been a staple of music pedagogy in many cultures. For instance, Takahashi Chikuzan, a master of the *Tsugaru-jamisen* music of northern Japan, contended that how "to produce the right tone quality on the shamisen" is "not something that can be taught. You have to discover it on your own by thinking and experimenting a lot." Like many others, he contrasted what cannot be taught with what can be: "the only thing [a teacher] can teach you is the logic of the music" (Takahashi 1991, 79).

Also common are restrictions on what students are permitted to concern themselves with in the early stages of training. Students starting to learn to sing verses of Japanese *Noh* dramas in the *hiranori* style must refrain from counting or marking with movements the eight beats of the metric cycle that guides the actions of drummers, nor can they take lessons in drumming, and the libretti from which they read the verses do not show how verses fit with metric cycles (Fujita 2019, 214–15). The pedagogy's underlying premise, expressed in such admonitions as "If you study the underlying rhythm in the first stage of your training you will not make further progress," is a conception of verse unit and metric cycle as separate strata that are coordinated in complex ways during performance.

42 MUSIC THEORY IN ETHNOMUSICOLOGY

Some pedagogies based on imitating a master leave no room for verbal explanation, so that students will develop an embodied, intuitive understanding of how to act musically. That was the premise of the instruction in the Japanese *shakuhachi* that Andreas Gutzwiller received from masters of the Kinko school in the 1970s, as described in a dissertation (1974, 147–67) and monograph (1983, 64–89). Students would learn the Kinko school's repertory by playing pieces from notation in unison with the master (1983, 71), trying to emulate his control of momentary changes within the meaningful units that Gutzwiller terms "tone-cells" (Gutzwiller and Bennett 1991), a slow process. Ultimately, imitation "has to go beyond mere copying and to become . . . an emulation of the teacher not only in his specific art but also in his way of life, of which his art is a reflection" (Gutzwiller 1983, 244).

Hugh de Ferranti's account of his training in the Japanese narrative genre *Satsuma biwa* (1985–89) under the master Fumon Yoshinori suggests that the pedagogy of the Seiha school gave a prominent role to verbal theory, which de Ferranti deploys in outlining four stages in the "sequence of procedures, types of modeling and variation techniques involved in making and performing a *Seiha Satsuma biwa* recitation" (1991, 107). Performers of this genre intersperse preludes and interludes on the *biwa* (a short-necked lute with four strings) with sections of sung verse, which they write out after choosing a text from an anthology. The second stage, *fushizuke*, is the process of coordinating melodic patterns with the text, long a major topic of the music theory taught to performers of sung poetry in other cultures as well.[9] De Ferranti pursued that topic in a doctoral dissertation (1996) on two other genres of *biwa* narrative; its importance in so many practices offers ample material for comparative studies of how performers have theorized and transmitted ways to coordinate melodies with words.

Transformation of Theories and Pedagogies

Ethnomusicologists are engaged with music theory as musicians, researchers, and educators. Weaknesses in theories and pedagogies become painfully apparent through all these engagements, making development of alternatives an important thrust of ethnomusicology

COMMUNICATION AND TRANSFORMATION OF THEORY   43

and a potential contribution to the larger field of music studies. The laudable aim articulated in the titles of Catherine Ellis's *Aboriginal music, education for living: Cross-cultural experiences from South Australia* and a collection of essays from a symposium of the Music Educators National Conference on *Becoming human through music*, both published in 1985, requires educators to continually assess the adequacy of teaching techniques and learning strategies, including uses of music theory.

Prominent among Patricia Shehan Campbell's *Lessons from the world: A cross-cultural guide to music teaching and learning* (1991) is "the suggestion that aural learning plays a significant role in the making of a young musician in many of the world's cultures, and that creativity as demonstrated through improvisation follows naturally from the emphasis given by certain traditions to ear-training and the development of aural perception" (Campbell 1991, 114).[10] Ethnomusicologists will quickly agree, finding it bizarre that any music educator would need the "suggestion" that aural learning is crucial, though some clearly do, alas! Campbell discusses jazz pedagogy in the part of her book on "the world," not in that on "the West," and, indeed, many jazz musicians have understood their engagement with "development of aural perception" more in a global than a Western framework.

This chapter concludes with a brief consideration of problems faced by ethnomusicologists concerned with cross-cultural approaches to music teaching and learning. Ellis in South Australia and Nzewi in South Africa created new institutions where they were able to put results of their ethnographic research to good use, and their publications (e.g., Nzewi 2007a) offer invaluable guidance to teachers of whatever music, wherever. Research on modes of theorizing among musicians engaged in various ways with *jazz* is complicated by that word's complex history over more than a century of creative music making that continually challenged social and musical constraints imposed on those involved. While many musicians have not seen the word itself as limiting or demeaning, others have understood themselves as *musicians*, not as a separate species of "jazz musicians." Their pedagogical publications bear titles like *Exercises for creative musicians* (Anderson and Steinbeck 2002) rather than *Jazz improvisation: A comprehensive method of study for all players* (Baker 1969).

44 MUSIC THEORY IN ETHNOMUSICOLOGY

They also publish broader theories (e.g., Braxton 1985), histories of organizations they have participated in (e.g., Lewis 2008), and video statements on websites. Other literature pertinent to this large topic includes ethnographies (Fraser 1983; Such 1985, 1993; Berliner 1994; Wilf 2014), biographies of musicians that draw on interviews with their students (e.g., Shim 2007, 123–68, on Lennie Tristano's teaching), transcripts of conversations among musicians (A. Taylor 1993; Parker 2011), discourse analysis of classes (Duranti 2009), recordings and transcripts of interviews in archives, published interviews, and numerous "as told to" autobiographies.

The Centre for Aboriginal Studies in Music

When she initiated a Programme of Training in Music for South Australian Aboriginal People at the University of Adelaide in 1971 (renamed The Centre for Aboriginal Studies in Music in 1975),[11] Ellis took on the challenge of creating environments where tribal teachers could offer instruction in their traditions to anyone interested and non-tribal Aboriginal students could receive "training in selected areas of Western music (those most closely related to non-tribal folk traditions but adaptable to professional training)" (Ellis 1985, 161, 166). This was only a few years after the 1967 Referendum that removed from the Australian Constitution an article headed "Aborigines not to be counted in reckoning population." There was a clear need for an institution that could both instruct non-Aboriginals in Aboriginal traditions and "provide a more culturally-meaningful educational experience for non-tribal Aboriginal people" (161) through training oriented toward professional competence in urban popular idioms such as country and rock. At the end of 1977, when Ellis left the Centre, Aboriginal students could choose between Section A, centered on participation in the Adelaide Aboriginal Orchestra (open to students of all ages), or Section B, in which students were "encouraged to verbalize more about their experiences and . . . expected to develop professional kinds of skills and a theoretical knowledge of music" (Ellis 1985, 180). In Section C, any university student could study with tribal teachers, and because many non-Aboriginal students felt confused

COMMUNICATION AND TRANSFORMATION OF THEORY   45

and disoriented by a pedagogy based on imitation and repetition, Ellis added analytical sessions taught by herself to alternate with singing lessons taught by tribal masters. Learning terms for specific features helped non-Aboriginal students "to hear the feature being named and subsequently to imitate it more reliably" (1985, 114).

Ellis has written about the first seven years of the Programme and Centre (1985, 112–33, 161–85, and in Barwick et al. 1995); her student Guy Tunstill has described his participation in lessons that afforded "insights into how the Pitjantjatjara order the elements that constitute their musical heritage and how this ordering compares with the needs and interests of their students" (Tunstill 1995, 60). Ellis had found that song texts were always presented in the correct rhythm (1985, 115), but by the time Tunstill participated teachers had modified their traditional practice by presenting texts "out of musical context" and allowing them to be written down for future use (1995, 61). Apparently, the principle of starting with the text was retained at the cost of separating it from rhythmic performance.

From her experience as a performer, Ellis (in Barwick et al. 1995, 202–3) drew up a set of instructions detailing the "specific knowledge of the musical system" that enables individuals to perform with groups:

maintain accurate intonation
maintain accurate durational and accentual communication
understand and communicate the extra-musical meaning of the
    performance
understand and communicate the spiritual essence of the
    performance
be touched by the spiritual force of the performance
experience empowerment through the act of performing

This roster results from Ellis's interest in Bateson's three levels of learning, mentioned in Chapter One. *Learning II*, "a corrective change in the set of alternatives from which choice is made" or "a change in how the sequence of experience is punctuated," might suffice for knowledge in the first three areas; knowledge in the others becomes accessible through *Learning III*, with "a corrective change in the system of *sets* of alternatives from which choice is made" where "The concept

46 MUSIC THEORY IN ETHNOMUSICOLOGY

of 'self' will no longer function as a nodal argument in the punctuation of experience" (Bateson 1972, 293, 304). Ellis believed that "all tribal students are well aware of this higher goal, whether or not they have the capacity to attain it"; in contrast, the aims of non-Aboriginal students who studied under Aboriginal teachers at CASM were "more technical in nature" (1985, 112).

African musical arts

In 2004, with support from the Norwegian Foreign Office that ended in 2011, Meki Nzewi founded a Centre for Indigenous Instrumental Music and Dance Practices of Africa (CIIMDA) in Pretoria, South Africa, aiming "to promote and advance the learning of the philosophy, theory and human meaning of African instrumental music and dance practices in classroom settings in SADC countries" (www.cii mda.org, consulted July 8, 2016; no longer online).[12] Nzewi connects the words *philosophy* and *human meaning* with *theory*, differentiates his concern with *musical arts* from Western discourse on *music*, and prefers *play-shop* to *workshop* (Nzewi 2007b, iv). His innovative theoretical and pedagogical work emphasizes "the unique features of African musical arts thinking and theoretical context" while aiming as well to "incorporate knowledge of conventional European classical music" (Nzewi 2007a, vii). His approach to music theory and pedagogy is laid out in the five volumes of *A contemporary study of musical arts informed by African indigenous knowledge systems* (Nzewi and Nzewi 2007). The first three levels of his pedagogy have eight modules each on such topics as "Music and society" and "Musical arts theatre" as well as "Musical structure and form" (with sections on both "indigenous" and "European tonal" practices). At the advanced level, "The structure of an indigenous festival" is the subject of a unit in "Music and society," and the module on "Technique for school songs" starts with "the sound system of the music-making mouth." Exercises in performance, transcription, and analysis develop proficiency in reading conventional Western notation along with aural skills and prepare students for the three books of volume 5, *Theory and practice of modern African classical drum music* (Nzewi and Nzewi 2007).

Nzewi became the first president of the Pan African Society for Musical Arts Education in 2001 as *musical arts* replaced *music* in its name. Three papers presented at PASMAE's 2003 conference and subsequently published (Herbst, Agawu, and Nzewi 2003) are titled "Improvisation," "Oral composition," and "Written composition." The authors of "Oral composition" see that topic as "referring specifically to most music making by the people of Africa" (Strumpf et al. 2003, 118)—as it does, we may add, to most music making elsewhere over humanity's long history.

"Jazz musicians" and music theory

The term *jazz theory* gained currency as universities and conservatories began to offer instruction in jazz performance and some music theorists became interested in analysis of recorded jazz. Surveying the short history of jazz theory in published form, Henry Martin (1997) distinguished *analytical* theory, based on a listener's perspective, from two varieties of "musician-based" theory, *pedagogical* and *speculative*, the latter exemplified by George Russell's *The Lydian chromatic concept of tonal* organization (1959 [1953]).[13] In Martin's view, analytical theory at its best would aim "to show how the music works in and of itself" (10), rising to the standards of sophisticated work on Western concert music (1997, 13–14). I consider musicians to be engaged in analytical theory when they discuss live or recorded performances or make transcriptions, even without focusing on "how the music works in and of itself." Martin acknowledged that "players who play 'by ear' are not without theory . . . though it may be unarticulated" (5).

In an evaluation of pedagogical materials on jazz issued between the early 1950s and mid-1980s, the ethnomusicologists Robert Witmer and James Robbins urge writers of new texts to pay "much closer attention to the ways in which jazz musicians have traditionally learned" (25). They point to common misuses of print: notating exercises in all keys rather than requiring students to transpose on their own; paying lip service to the benefits of eartraining without integrating it into the text; isolating "components," "elements," or "parameters" without discussing their interrelations right from the start; and insufficient attention to "the less-easily objectifiable but no less teachable aspects of the music" (Witmer

48   MUSIC THEORY IN ETHNOMUSICOLOGY

and Robbins 1988, 25). A text that urges students to transcribe recorded solos ought to show them "*how* to absorb, apply (and transform) the aural and visual stimuli of recordings and transcriptions" (26).

How jazz musicians have traditionally learned is the subject of Al Fraser's 1983 dissertation, *Jazzology: A study of the tradition in which jazz musicians learn to improvise*, which uses his training in folklore studies to describe social interactions involved in becoming a musician. The second of his five stages of learning—ear training (broadly defined) and observation—might include gaining proficiency with names of chords, other sets of symbols, and what the alto saxophonist Sonny Fortune (1939–2018) termed "the logistics of notes, tones, sound with reason," which he "came to . . . from just singing" (63). Fraser stressed the importance of "listening to or discussing jazz records or personal appearances" with others in a learning process he saw as "folkloric in character" (67). Alongside Fortune, his well-chosen roster of fourteen interview subjects included musicians who were also creative teachers of theory; Robert Lowery (1914–96) of Wilmington, Delaware, for example, developed a distinction between *active* and *inactive* notes with numerous analogues in other pedagogies (Fraser, 109–11).[14] Fraser had previously worked for five years with Dizzy Gillespie on To be, or not . . . to bop. Memoirs (1979), which has more discussion of music-theoretical topics than most jazz autobiographies (e.g., 134–37 on "the minor-sixth chord with a sixth in the bass"). Like Gillespie, Fraser (1983, 155–57) was attentive to kinesthetic modes of learning.

Paul Berliner's discussion of learning processes (1994, 63–119 and *passim*) is based on interviews with more than fifty musicians, several of whom mentioned benefits of their engagement with music theory: learning "to distinguish the functions of different chords and their harmonic activity within progressions" and "to enter the world of musical forms" (74) by analyzing tunes in order "to grasp the building blocks of form on different hierarchical levels" (79). Berliner notes that some musicians find "notational and theoretical symbols" to be "helpful initially when studying a piece's form, but unnecessary afterwards" (92). In these comments, *theory* refers above all to notes, intervals, chords, and formal schemes that can be identified with symbols and notated, even as aural learning remains primary.

David Sudnow's account of how he learned to play jazz as an amateur pianist, *Ways of the hand: The organization of improvised conduct* (1978, revised 2001), can be compared with the experiences that professionals reported to Berliner. The revision describes more clearly how Sudnow went about "practical theorizing, searching for instructions that would work" (2001, 78) and abandoning images and terms that were holding him back as his skills developed. Hubert L. Dreyfus, in his preface to the revision (2001, ix), sees Sudnow's topic as "the ways embodied beings acquire the skills of giving order to, or, better, finding order in, our temporally unfolding experience."

Experience of institutionalized jazz pedagogy has led numerous young musicians to explore alternative modes of theorizing as they continue an involvement in jazz or, more broadly, in *improvised music* or *creative music*. Several of the eighteen musicians interviewed by Daniel Blake for his dissertation on "Performed identities: Theorizing in New York City's improvised music scene" commented on limitations of their university training (Blake 2013, 34–42, and 2016). The bassist and vocalist Esperanza Spaulding remarked to Blake that "the version of jazz being taught in schools is really just one version. So it's really up to each individual person to find out what their internal music is" (38). Musicians who stand entirely apart from (or maintain a critical attitude toward) the institutions that support the jazz theory described by Henry Martin engage in theorizing that either ignores or relates in innovative ways to work that was marketed as "jazz" (at times against the musicians' wishes). Eric Porter devotes a chapter of *What is this thing called jazz? African American musicians as artists, critics, and activists* (2002, 240–86) to "Theorizing the art and politics of improvisation" in writing. He interprets writings of Yusef Lateef (1920–2013), Marion Brown (1931–2010), Wadada Leo Smith (b. 1941), and Anthony Braxton (b. 1945) as these relate to recordings and notations of their music.

Models of how people interact in musicking are prominent topics in the world's music theories. Through a "metaphorical and richly associative way of thinking about music, one which hardly lends itself to the conceptual framework of academic theory" (Wilson 1999, 73), the theorizing of Ornette Coleman (1930–2015) offered musicians and listeners options "to use a multiplicity of elements to express more than one direction at a time" (ibid., 69, quoting Coleman). The African

50 MUSIC THEORY IN ETHNOMUSICOLOGY

American musicians who formed the Association for the Advancement of Creative Musicians (AACM) in 1965 valued "performances in which the predominance of personal virtuosity as the measure of musicality is removed, and where individual style is radically devalued in favor of a collective conception that foregrounds form, space and sonic multiplicity," requiring engineers to rethink techniques developed for the familiar jazz model of "leader and sidemen" (Lewis 2008, 155).

The approaches to theory and theorizing sketched here exemplify the diversity generated by intercultural contacts in much of the world following the Second World War. While the history of what the percussionist and composer Max Roach (1924–2007) called "[t]he new music, loosely called 'Jazz' and born out of communalism" (Roach 1979) may be a particularly rich and complex one, there are many histories of musicians who were not intimidated by any loosely applied labels, were interested in music and theory "generated not declaratively but interactively" (Qureshi 2007, 3), and opted for "a mode of thinking with others separate from the thinking that the institution requires of you" (Halberstam 2013, 11).

Continuing Issues

Ethnomusicologists have learned much about circumstances in which people acquire knowledge of how to act musically and about theories that guide musical action.

Questions on how to relate musical technique to ways of living have occasioned much theorizing, from reflection on the viability of practices to consideration of optimal conditions for rehearsing, performing, and recording. As people become musicians, they may well hear or read presentations of explicit theory, and they can hardly avoid picking up ideas with the potential to stimulate theorizing.

Questions relevant to the situations in which theory is generated, communicated, and transformed include:

1. What do participants typically hope to accomplish in those situations? How are social relationships that foster learning and teaching modeled?
2. To what extent does a program or practice of instruction include explicit theory? Is an existing body of theory or doctrine, such

COMMUNICATION AND TRANSFORMATION OF THEORY 51

as "the science of music" or theoretical portions of a master's *ta'līm*, the main or a lesser focus of attention? Do students experience what they have learned as an assemblage of "disarticulated knowledge" (Perlman 2004, 17) drawn from disparate sources?

3. To what extent are teachers concerned to transmit a fund of knowledge along with norms on how to act in relation to that knowledge (the "things and ways" of the Hindustani pedagogies Neuman analyzes)?

4. Do teachers find effective ways to activate theorizing? How do they prepare students for the socioeconomic networks in which they will work?

5. What situations do students typically find most conducive to learning?

6. How do the structure and content of music pedagogies relate to those of other pedagogies? What changes do pedagogies undergo when detached from ethical norms and ways of life they were designed to support and enhance?

We can hope to learn more about how bits and pieces of theory have been appropriated for new purposes from conversations and writings in which musicians and educators discuss what they remember learning from diverse sources, how they have used and perhaps extended that knowledge. Research on this topic and others will require soliciting more first-person accounts of learning processes to supplement and extend the insights gleaned from published and archived interviews. More narratives of learning processes will assist in distinguishing between norms and exceptions in a given practice with respect to

1. the order in which topics and exercises were introduced and the rationale for that order,

2. how interrelationships among topics were theorized at various stages of instruction,

3. imagery that students found (or did not find) effective at one or another stage, and

4. what experiences made students aware of progress (or lack thereof).

52 MUSIC THEORY IN ETHNOMUSICOLOGY

Issues, 2: Explicit and Implicit Theory

Several accounts of learning in Chapter Two mention complementarities between oral, manual, and written articulation or transmission of theory. Much face-to-face instruction depends on oral theory, which may remain *implicit* until it is made *explicit*, at least in part, through speech, demonstrations, performances, or writings. The philosopher Robert Brandom's treatise on *Making it explicit* (1994) could prevent a theorist or pedagogue from underestimating the difficulties of that process, and as it happens many musicians find it best that much be left implicit.

José Maceda outlined "a theory of scale formation in Southeast Asia which in essence is abstract" (Maceda 1990, 207) and was developed and used in making bamboo instruments. He reconstructed what he called an *oral theory* while studying a large collection of bamboo flutes, ethnographic data, and recordings at the University of the Philippines. Maceda's use of the term is consistent with the common extension of *oral tradition* and *oral transmission* to cover modes of communication that do not involve writing but may involve gesture and touch as well as (or even without) vocalizing.[15] Since Maceda was more concerned with actions of making and playing instruments, I would describe the "abstract" theory he discerned as implicit until communicated in part through demonstrations of how to construct and play bamboo flutes. Instrument makers can leave many details unspoken in presenting theories of the type that "can be transmitted by demonstration and without words" (Blacking 1990, 214, quoted in Chapter One).

The term *acoustemology*, coined by Steve Feld (1996 and 2015) to denote ways of knowing through hearing, lacks the baggage attached to the term *orality*, which is often construed as a condition opposed to *literacy*. Scholars who identify "characteristics" of "the world of orality" (e.g., Lord 1991, 32, 36, 98) tend to repeat what Jonathan Sterne terms an "audiovisual litany" in which differences between hearing and seeing become "a necessary starting point for the cultural analysis of sound" (Sterne 2003, 15; see Sterne 2011 for "a critique of orality"). Haun Saussy's statement (2016, 59) that "the oral and the literate are mixed, interrelated, or overlaid" in "the great majority of cases as they stand"[16] is confirmed in the experience of many ethnomusicologists.

COMMUNICATION AND TRANSFORMATION OF THEORY   53

I agree with Feld (1986b, 18) that "'orality' does not determine, fix, or cause differences in world view, or consciousness."

As Ruth Finnegan concluded in a lecture titled "What is orality, if anything?" (1990, 148), "there is nothing clear, definite or agreed to which that abstract noun can refer." She acknowledged it has prompted scholarly attention to neglected topics, including creation and communication of *oral literature*, or *orature* as it has been called to avoid the awkwardness of "unwritten literature."[17] Ngũgĩ wa Thiong'o remarks (Ngũgĩ 2012, 72) that both Kiswahili and Gĩkũyũ are among the African languages with a single term (*fasihi* and *kĩrĩra*, respectively) that covers both orature and literature with no "preconceived ranking of art forms." Pio Zirimu (d. 1977) coined the term *orature* for "the use of utterance as an aesthetic means of expression" (Ngũgĩ 2012, 73)—clearly a human universal, like oral communication itself. That universality is belied when orality designates absence of literacy.

The techniques of the body used in oral communication, as in hearing, remembering, and performing vocal genres, will vary and may allow for recourse to written texts.[18] Walter Ong (1982) coined the term *secondary orality*, which he used in ways that emphasize dependence on literacy and fail to recognize the multiple *types* of orality in the daily lives of most humans. The term pairs well with *aurality* in highlighting differences between vocalizing and listening. In *Aurality: Listening and knowledge in nineteenth-century Colombia*, Ana María Ochoa Gautier (2014, 140) examines "a particular history of comparativism and of difference, articulated by the relation between aurality (what is heard or references the ear) and orality (what is pronounced or references the mouth)." Negative consequences of "the contrasting perception of those who produced the sounds and those who listened to them, as mediated by potentially radically different interpretations of the same sounds" (33) are too often overlooked: categorizations of sound and movement in nineteenth-century Colombia (and not only there) enabled listeners to identify certain sounds as those of their alleged "inferiors."

Nineteenth-century intellectuals who sought to hear what was voiced or played without interpreting what they heard by standards foreign to those who made the sounds were important figures in the history of what became ethnomusicology. Speaking at the opening of the Moscow Conservatory in 1866, Prince V. F. Odoyevsky (1804–69) saw interpreting folk melodies according to an *a priori* theory, along with "empty philosophizing," as obstacles to hearing them "as they are"; such hearing was necessary if transcriptions were to respect "local variants and nuances." Theory "must be extracted (*izvlechenya*) from the folk melodies as they are, in the voice and in the hearing of the people (*v golose i slyxe naroda*)" (Odoyevsky 1956, 306). Izaly Zemtsovsky kindly pointed out to me that James Campbell's translation of this passage is misleading: Odoyevsky called for extracting theory by hearing melodies "with virgin ears" as the people hear them, whereas in Campbell's version, *after* "writing down folksong as it is heard in the voice and ear of the people . . . then one must try to extract their theory from the tunes themselves as they really are" (Campbell 1994, 92). Ethnomusicologists have devoted considerable attention to the questions of how hearing shapes interpretations of transcriptions as well as methods of transcription, and how to improve our hearing.

Hornbostel argued that notation is "the most powerful means for intellectualizing music, for acquiring a theoretical outlook. Notation keeps alive the theory that it embodies" (1913, 14).[19] We have learned that it can import the theory it once embodied (to some extent implicitly) into situations where that theory should not be "kept alive," imposing an inappropriate "theoretical outlook" on music transcribed in a notation foreign to those who made it. Hornbostel and Abraham proposed use of a modified notation alongside instructions on how to read it. Transcribers using a modified Western notation could carefully evaluate each symbol's relationship to the sounds they heard, avoiding irrelevant time-signatures and bar-lines, marking pitches located slightly above or below the values associated with a given position on a staff, and so on (Abraham and Hornbostel 1909). Transcribers and readers of transcriptions could begin to imagine premises of theories other than those they associated with the unmodified notation. Ethnomusicologists experience limitations of the theory in which we were socialized as we hear, perform, notate, or otherwise interpret music to which that theory's premises are alien. Notations supplemented by explanatory prose are prominent in two long-term collaborative projects of American ethnomusicologists with African musicians (Alorwoyie with Locke 2013; Berliner and Magaya 2020).

COMMUNICATION AND TRANSFORMATION OF THEORY 55

In the final quarter of the twentieth century, music theorists, music historians, and ethnomusicologists were increasingly concerned with *tacit knowledge*, including implicit or "unvoiced" (Charry 2000, 328) theories. A major text in those discussions, Michael Polanyi's *Personal knowledge: Towards a post-critical philosophy* (1958), is still consulted by music educators and others.[20] Carl Dahlhaus (1984, 1) recommended that historians of music theory attempt "not only to take into consideration whatever has been said about music, but in addition to reconstruct the unspoken, 'implicit' theory integral to the history of composition but lacking in literary documents (for reasons that themselves would be thematized in a comprehensive history of music theory)."[21] Whereas for Dahlhaus implicit theory was "the quintessence (*Inbegriff*) of the overt or latent premises of a compositional technique or a style" (1984, 38), the ethnomusicologist David Coplan was concerned in his history of Black city music and theater in South Africa with actions that "performers accomplish . . . by applying an implicit theory of composition and expression" (Coplan 1985, 242, paraphrasing Blum 1975, 214).

Other ethnomusicologists and music theorists speak more readily of implicit or tacit *knowledge*. Leonard B. Meyer (1989, 10) cited Polanyi in maintaining that "knowledge of style is usually 'tacit': that is, a matter of habits properly acquired (internalized) and appropriately brought into play." Marc Perlman (2004, 21) likewise sees "knowledge of musical style" as "one of the many kinds of musical knowledge that . . . is usually acquired and exercised without explicit formulation." Humans often lack the desire or capability to articulate the underlying premises of kinds of knowledge we have learned to use successfully.[22]

In a study of "Interaction and improvisation between dancers and drummers in Martinican *bèlè*," Julian Gerstin (1998) distinguished between "major aspects of dancer-drummer interaction that bèlè performers articulate fairly readily" and others "of which performers are marginally aware and which they partly articulate." This seems consistent with the difference between the explicit and implicit systems of *long-term memory*. According to Jäncke (2019, 238), the two systems "do not overlap": the implicit system "contains information that is not easy to verbalize but can be used without consciously thinking about

56 MUSIC THEORY IN ETHNOMUSICOLOGY

it," and the explicit system is "a mechanism constructing the past on the basis of stored and new information using specific strategies."

Participants in a round table at the 1987 Bologna congress of the International Musicological Society on "The relation of theory and practice in non-Western musical traditions" voiced different attitudes toward implicit theory. The chair, Simha Arom, acknowledged the existence of theories that are implicit "to varying degrees" and of explicit theories that can be "exclusively oral." He saw "tangible proof of the existence of a theory" in recognition and correction of performers' errors (Arom 1990, 189; see also Arom 1985, 224; 1991, 140; and 1994, 148). Tilman Seebass (1990, 200) preferred to restrict *theory* to "its traditional area of meaning, viz. objectivating reflection which is verbalized and put in writing" without extending the term to "non-verbalized and unwritten conceptual systems." He distinguished (201) between "vocabulary of the practitioner and terminology of the theorist," although "the two phenomena . . . do not have to be completely separated from each other."[23] Francesco Giannattasio also posed the question "Theory or concepts?" and warned against "an indiscriminate overestimation of autochthonous metamusical statements and concepts" (1990, 225; see also Giannattasio 1992, 133–34).

Implicit theory is a more controversial concept than *oral theory* and *oral* (or *non-graphic*) *notation*. I find it useful, but there are other terms for knowledge of models, schemes, norms, options, restrictions, and the like that musicians have not yet made explicit in the presence of someone willing and able to remember or document those formulations or demonstrations. Philosophers, social scientists, and ethnomusicologists alike have found it necessary to distinguish ways of knowing, modes of consciousness, models, taxonomies, or parameters that facilitate practical action from the more explicit and abstract formulations of knowledge, usually from a linguocentric perspective. Distinctions like those listed in Table 2.2 are pervasive in scholarly discourse. If our everyday lives are more dependent on *knowing how* than on *knowing that*, some of what we know how to do results from theorizing and experimenting.

Benjamin Brinner (1995, 34–39) reviews implications of four distinctions between ways of knowing—active/passive, intuitive/explicit, conscious/automatic, procedural/declarative—without

COMMUNICATION AND TRANSFORMATION OF THEORY 57

Table 2.2. Some distinctions in ways of knowing, modes of consciousness, models, taxonomies, parameters, and the like

living acquaintance / theoretic knowledge	William James (1909 [1987b, 742])
knowledge by acquaintance / *knowledge by description*	Bertrand Russell (1912)
knowing how / knowing that	Gilbert Ryle (1949, 25–61)
practical and *discursive* consciousness	Anthony Giddens (1984, 374–75)
operational and *representational* models	John Baily (1988b, citing Caws 1974)
practical and *abstract* taxonomies	James Robbins (1989)
latent and *manifest* knowledge of music making	Gilbert Rouget (1996, 13)
latent and *overt* parameters	Dalia Cohen and Ruth Katz (2006, 325)
ways of knowing that are	
active or *passive*	
intuitive or *explicit*	
conscious or *automatic*	
procedural or *declarative*	Benjamin Brinner (1995, 34–39)

worrying about which implications are compatible with conceptions of music theory. The word *theory* in the subtitle of his *Knowing music, making music: The theory of musical competence and interaction* stands for an ethnomusicological project, not for theories of non-ethnomusicologists who reflect on performance genres or on knowing and making music.[24]

In glossing *rāg* as "a complex of latent possibilities" whose "ethos . . . becomes manifest through recognisable melodic patterns," Nazir Jairazbhoy (1971, 32) noted that the technical terms of Hindustani theory can only "convey some idea" of the relationship between latent and manifest. Harold Powers might well have agreed, notwithstanding his judgment that "North Indian raga theory is much

58   MUSIC THEORY IN ETHNOMUSICOLOGY

more explicit than South Indian raga theory" (Powers 1977, 313). Judgments that one formulation or pedagogy is more explicit than another are not uncommon. Needs that motivate fuller elaboration and rationalization are often associated with specific social roles or institutions, and musicians may also have good reasons to avoid overly explicit formulations of what they sense are important truths. We need more studies of processes through which outcomes of theorizing that had been latent or implicit are articulated in words or other actions, creating new possibilities for critique—and also for recognizing additional implications. The explicit becomes implicit when musicians transform detailed instructions into habits.

Making music theory explicit by oral, written, or tactile means is normally a question of degree, in response to the dynamics of situations where it is remembered or communicated. Ethnomusicologists may need to ask "Implicit? Explicit?" (as in Rouget 2006, 22) and should regard explicit theory as work in progress that under favorable conditions may articulate insights in appropriate media, formats, and situations even while leaving major premises implicit. Few if any have access to all that a master teacher has confided to his or her most trusted students. We can attempt to discern implicit premises of the models of interaction we experience in one or more performances.

If *theory* is to be limited to explicit verbalizations, there are terms for other types of musical knowledge that are either implicit or communicated through such non-verbal actions as performance of conventional patterns or models. The ability of musicians to articulate and manipulate patterns composed of a discrete series of attacks is sometimes attributed to "unnamed experiences of numbers" (Dauer 1983[1966], 41), "natural mathematics" (Chemillier 2007, 111–30), "non-conceptual mathematics" (Brenner 1997), or "arithmetic . . . that takes place in the heads of drummers" and other musicians (Agawu 2016a, 187). The numbers are real and are made explicit in performance, whether or not they are named or counted out. Those who agree with Zbikowski that musical concepts are "not necessarily tied to language" (2002, 60, quoted earlier) may hesitate to speak here of "non-conceptual mathematics." Brinner (1995, 37) observes that "The ability to simplify a complex musical pattern for the sake of demonstration depends on an awareness of the workings of such patterns that is as explicit as notation or verbal explanation." Does that awareness become *explicit theory* once it is communicated in a demonstration? The question strikes me as much less important than recognizing the process of simplifying complex musical patterns as an act of theorizing with several possible outcomes.

While *orality* remains a problematic term when opposed to *literacy* in ways that obscure the universality of oral communication, concepts of *oral transmission* and *oral tradition* proved indispensable in the work of musical folklorists and ethnomusicologists, and only a few ethnomusicologists object to the concept of *oral theory*.[25] Results of a process of *transmission* depend on participants' techniques of the body: how they move, control specific muscles, produce and interpret sounds or written symbols, remember, use, and perhaps modify earlier experience of relevant interactions. The term itself might suggest a process of transporting a package of information from one location to another, which is not what usually happens in the learning processes ethnomusicologists observe and participate in (see the critique of *transmission* in Ingold 2011, 159–63).

3

Making Music Theory
for Modern Nations

Development of a modern music theory came to be seen as an essential undertaking of nation-states and of "nationalities" within or split among them like the Uyghurs of the PRC and USSR or "non-state nations" like the Kurds. Motivation for that work in Asia and Africa came through movements seeking liberation from foreign rule, as in British India (1857–1947) and the Dutch East Indies (1800–1942, 1945–49); through programs of reform such as those in the Ottoman Empire with the *Tanzimat* period (1839–71) and in Japan with the Meiji Era (1868–1912); and alongside efforts to impose uniform cultural policies throughout the multinational USSR (1922–91) or upon the many nationalities of the People's Republic of China (est. 1949). The imperialism of France in North and West Africa, of Britain in Egypt and Southeast Asia, of Japan in China, and of the United States in the Philippines left fertile ground in "the ruins of empire" (Mishra 2012) for eventual work in music theory.

One key question for ethnomusicologists is how representations of a nation's (or a nationality's) past and present have shaped the production and use of music theory. Several studies concentrate on music theory in one nation (e.g., Markoff 1986; Marcus 1989; Perlman 1994 and 2004; Greve 2005; Allen 2008; Ayangil 2008 and 2010; Peiris 2018). It also comes up in work on several overlapping topics: construction of national culture (Lee 1998 and 2009), discourses and policies of modernization (Heimarck 1999 and 2003; Miller 2004; Thomas 2006), music education (Khoshzamir 1979; Eppstein 1985; Alter 1994; O'Connell 2000 and 2010; Ogawa 2000; Miller 2004), state control or patronage of traditional music (Trebinjac 2000; Douglas 2001), classicization (Roongruang 1999; Moro 2004; Bakhle 2005; Kippen 2006; Weidman 2006; Schofield 2010), canonization (Davis 1986 and

Music Theory in Ethnomusicology. Stephen Blum, Oxford University Press.
© Oxford University Press 2023. DOI: 10.1093/oso/9780199303526.003.0004

MAKING MUSIC THEORY FOR MODERN NATIONS 61

2004; Harris 2008; Fossum 2015), issues of representation (Capwell 2010; M. G. Katz 2010), revitalization and reform (Rosse 1995 and 2010; Kobayashi 2003; Thomas 2006), genres with problematic relationships to a state's cultural policies (Stokes 1992; Trebinjac 2000), and cultural interaction from the period of colonial rule to the late twentieth century (Sumarsam 1995). Most studies focus on projects in one nation or in several that share a language (e.g., S. Q. Hassan 2004 on the Arab world) or were obliged to implement the USSR's policies (e.g., Frolova-Walker 1998 on the Caucasian and Central Asian republics).

Table 3.1 lists eleven modernization projects requiring or supporting work in music theory. Undertaken in whatever sequence or combination, they typically generate controversy over what practices of the past (including those of colonizers) to abandon, retain, revive,

Table 3.1. Projects of modernization calling for work in music theory

---

Establishment of military bands, initially with non-native instructors

Training of choirs and congregations to sing hymns and other music in Christian worship services, often through use of Curwen's tonic sol-fa method

Publication of instruction manuals in the national language

Formation of ensembles, clubs, or informal circles dedicated to revitalization of a music or propagation of a national dance

Creation of conservatories and institutes devoted to Western music, or to a national repertory, or treating both in separate streams

Institution of formalized procedures for certifying music professionals

Discussion of controversial topics at conferences and in music journals

Introduction of music education in public schools, supervised by government agencies

Recording and/or notation of substantial parts of the nation's cultural heritage or classical music, most often in Western notation, perhaps with additional symbols

Editing and arranging those notations or recordings for broadcasting or live performance by newly formed ensembles

Formation of archives, usually connected to the national radio

---

62 MUSIC THEORY IN ETHNOMUSICOLOGY

modify, or assimilate in processes of "continual constitution and re-constitution of *multiple* institutional and ideological patterns" (Eisenstadt 2003, 536, emphasis added). Ethnomusicologists are obliged to come to terms with the existence of what S. M. Eisenstadt termed *multiple modernities*, even if many might agree with the historian Carol Gluck that "[w]hile not unitary or universal, the modern possesses commonalities across time and space, however differently it is experienced in different places" (Gluck 2011, 676). Among those commonalities are interests in recovering or creating *authentic* musical *traditions* and efforts to canonize a *musical heritage* or *classical music* by creation of institutions and publication of music theory, often with notation of a *canon*.

Pamela Moro (2004) has compared the histories of classicization and canonization of music in India, Indonesia, and Thailand, outlining a "noticeably consistent" process with differences owing, perhaps, to "the nature and timing of the appearance of a sizeable middle class and its relation to nationalism" and "the position of colonial power-holders and/or old elites *vis-à-vis* emerging nationalism and twentieth-century national culture" (210). Writing on "Processes of canonisation across the Islamic world," Rachel Harris (2008, 12) makes the valuable point that such processes "are not solely the product of 20th-century nationalism" and can be understood "more broadly as part of the political process of centralisation and consolidation." Likewise, Katherine Butler Schofield (2010) has examined "classicization processes before European colonialism" in India. Historians and ethnographers of music theory can examine how the earlier processes and the programs of modernization alike have served the interests of certain social groups (see further Niranjana 2020).

Commonalities are also evident in aims and methods of music education in public and private institutions, and in the debates over problems and possible solutions at conferences and in ministries. When smaller ensembles that had functioned well without notation gave way to larger ones, difficulties with intonation and coordination were frequently addressed by adopting Western notation and teaching musicians to interpret it in appropriate ways (see Tsui 2002 on "The modern Chinese orchestra").

MAKING MUSIC THEORY FOR MODERN NATIONS   63

Music theory has been prepared for use in what are now familiar situations, hence common venues of an ethnomusicologist's fieldwork: rehearsals of bands and choirs; lessons in conservatories, private studios, and "houses of culture"; social gatherings of music lovers; conferences on music; meetings of committees on curricular or editorial policy; and residencies or visits of external consultants. Intercultural encounters in these situations have fostered what Greve (2005), with reference to Turkey, terms "hybrid musical thinking." He judges the Turkish Republic's *cultural hybridity* to be "extensive, dynamic, and by no means free of contradictions" (2005, 149). Sumarsam (2013, 139) agrees that "Heterogeneity, contestation, and ambivalence define the hybridization process." Marcel Mauss's argument that civilizations "define themselves (*se circonscrivent*)" through "resistances of the societies that constitute them" is relevant here: he emphasized the need for attention to "what is not borrowed, the refusal to adopt even something useful" (Mauss 1974, 471–72).[1]

Ethnomusicologists have tried to develop strategies of research and presentation that respect the heterogeneity, contestation, and ambivalence we learn to recognize through fieldwork and examination of documents. What documents can we locate or create to assist in understanding theories communicated at specific moments in a musical practice's history when presented in ways that invite multiple interpretations? Examples of intelligent and imaginative ways to deal with these challenges are readily available. Sumarsam's writings are enriched with excerpts from Javanese poetry that illuminate music-theoretical issues. The subtitle of Brita Heimarck's *Balinese discourses on music and modernization: Village voices and urban views* (2003) registers her concern to juxtapose speech of residents of Sukawati, a village known for expertise in the shadow play, with materials written by personnel of the Indonesian College of the Arts (STSI) in Denpasar; her book includes extensive passages of speech and writing in the original. Eshantha Peiris (2018) carefully describes texts of three Sri Lankan musicologists in which they responded to diverse ideological currents in their postcolonial nation-state as they constructed a theory of rhythm in "up-country" percussion music. Though meant to bring out the uniqueness of up-country dance as a symbol of national culture, the theories of all three adopted the principle of isochronous counting

64   MUSIC THEORY IN ETHNOMUSICOLOGY

from Indian music theory: "metrically flexible rhythm categories were rationalized according to measurable time-units."

Looking at approaches to research on just a few of the projects listed in Table 3.1, the three remaining sections of this chapter attempt to highlight issues requiring further investigation and critique. Study of early twentieth-century *conferences* centers on analysis of published proceedings and other documents, looking at constraints on social interaction among participants as well as topics and styles of discourse. Research on *notations, scales, and solfège* extends from analysis of published notations and manuals to accounts of how notations and treatises have been produced and used. Studies of modernization projects generally rely heavily on fieldwork carried out in and around the relevant *institutions*.

Conferences

Arab music

Rarely, if ever, has a music conference been as well documented or attracted as much interpretation as the 1932 Congress of Arab Music, an unprecedented gathering of scholars and musicians from Europe and the Arab world convened in Cairo with the support of King Fu'ād. The proceedings were published in Arabic (Wizārat al-Ma'ārif al-'umūmiyya 1933) and French (Ministère de l'Instruction Publique 1934), and the available documentation provides ample evidence of social barriers to effective communication among the participants and of ideological constraints on production of music theory.[2]

The Congress itself became the subject of a 1989 colloquium convened in Cairo by the Centre d'Études et de Documentation Économique, Juridique et Sociale (CEDEJ) at which Jean-Claude Vatin spoke of a "Colonial symphony and national variations," noting that all ensembles invited to perform were from nations colonized by France or Great Britain with at most "limited sovereignty"; none came from the Arabian Peninsula or the Gulf (Vigreux ed. 1992, 16).[3] S. Q. Hassan, organizer of the colloquium, pointed to serious flaws in two major aims of the Congress (ibid., 23–28): to establish laws that would endow Arab music with a scientific foundation and protect it from the

MAKING MUSIC THEORY FOR MODERN NATIONS 65

vagaries of oral transmission, and to foster its development by adopting European scientific and technical concepts. Musicians deemed willing and able to help in establishing a stable theoretical system were more highly valued than performers engaged in the evolving art. Failure to acknowledge the scientific status of earlier attempts to systematize and codify music theory in Arabic writing may have led participants to devote excessive attention to the recent conception of an octave divided into twenty-four equal intervals.

Europeans chaired five of the seven commissions: General Issues (Baron Carra de Vaux), the Musical Scale (X. M. Collangettes), Musical Instruments (Curt Sachs), Recording (Robert Lachmann), and Music History and Manuscripts (Henry George Farmer). The other chairs had been educated in Europe: Mahmud Ahmad al-Hifnī (Music Education) and Rauf Yekta Bey (Modes, Rhythms and Composition).[4] Reviewing the evidence of interactions among participants, Anne Elise Thomas (2006, 87–93) echoes S. Q. Hassan's point that performers were not treated as potentially valuable contributors to the deliberations. She finds that the Recording and Music Education committees accomplished the most (2006, 99–109), with the latter contributing to development of what Marcus (1989, 35) terms "a new type of music theory, a pedagogical theory which explained the existing music in a simplified, systematized, and standardized fashion." Thomas calls the Congress "a defining moment in the discourse of modern Arab music" (2006, 52) but rightly treats it as one episode in a movement of musical reform with "four related priorities": revival, preservation, systematization, and development. S. Q. Hassan likewise sees the Egyptian project of musical renewal as internally generated, to the point that "the opinions and recommendations of the scholars invited to offer advice . . . were not in a single instance a determining factor" (Vigreux ed. 1992, 29).

"Arab music" as one variety of "Oriental music" was a relatively new topic in 1932 (S. Q. Hassan in Vigreux ed. 1992, 24; Thomas 2006, 75; Lambert 2007, 2), evident in such titles as Farmer's *A history of Arabian music to the XIIIth century* (1929) and the first volume of Baron Rodolphe d'Erlanger's *La musique arabe* (1930).[5] "The Arab scale" was a topic with a longer history, which Farmer summarized for the commission he chaired in a "Short history of the Arabian musical scale" (printed in I. J. Katz 2015, 339–51).[6] Egyptian participants wished to distinguish

66 MUSIC THEORY IN ETHNOMUSICOLOGY

Arab music from that of the Ottoman Empire and proposed that the first degree of the general scale should be represented as C rather than G as in Ottoman theory. S. Q. Hassan (Vigreux ed. 1992, 24) speaks appropriately of a shift from "Ottoman pan-Islamism" to "pan-Arabism."

Hindu music

Research on an event like the 1932 Congress of Arab Music leads easily to critique of underlying assumptions as they relate to the participants' other interests. This is also true of the scholarly literature on the five All-India Music Conferences organized in various cities by V. N. Bhatkhande (1860–1936) and others in the decade between 1916 and 1926, and the five annual conferences convened between 1918 and 1922 by V. D. Paluskar (1872–1931) to celebrate the educational institution he had founded in 1901, the Gandharva Mahavidyalaya with schools in Lahore and Bombay.[7] In a study of the two men's roles in "the making of an Indian classical tradition," Janaki Bakhle (2005, 180–210) compares the aims and social dynamics of the two sets of conferences, contrasting the prominence of debate at the All-India Music Conferences with its absence at Paluskar's, which emphasized carrying forward his work in music instruction. David Trasoff (2010) examines the debates at Bhatkhande's first four conferences as reported in the proceedings, looking at ideological currents evident in the discussions, organization and rhetoric of the conferences in relation to "the reality of musical life and patronage," and the organizers' ideals with respect to musical culture and social organization of music—good topics for research on other conferences.

At the time of their first conferences Bhatkhande and Paluskar could both look back on impressive records of accomplishment as they sought to realize their respective visions of a modern musical culture, Bhatkhande's secular and scientific, Paluskar's centered on Hindu devotionalism. Their conferences contributed to a culture of *classical music* resulting from "the advent of music schools with their structured pedagogical apparatus, detailed notations, instruction manuals and a national—even nationalist—vision of music's power to galvanize the middle classes and steer them toward a more progressive, modern, Hinduized future with strong roots in a glorious, though

MAKING MUSIC THEORY FOR MODERN NATIONS 67

imagined, Hindu past" (Kippen 2006, 6). Bhatkhande had published the first three volumes of *Hindustānī-sangīta-paddhati* "The system of Hindustani music" (1909–14 in colloquial Marathi as a dialogue between master and pupil). Max Katz observes (2017, 148) that he "was motivated to systematize the theory of Hindustani music such that it could be easily taught, and such that professional performers would not have a monopoly on determining the correct rules and regulations for the music's many rāga-s." Bhatkhande's program, like Paluskar's for "the re-Hinduization of North Indian music in the twentieth-century" (Slawek 2007, 507), was meant to reduce the prominence of Muslim ustāds in music pedagogy. Bhatkhande classified *rāgas* by what he took to be their relationships to the ten abstract scale-types he termed *thāṭs* (Jairazbhoy 1971, 46–64; Powers 1992b, 12–15). One of Paluskar's disciples, Omkarnath Thakur (1897–1967), became a severe critic of Bhatkhande's theories and eventually produced pedagogical publications based on the premise that affinities of melodic shape were more important than scale-type in musicians' experience of relationships among *rāgas*. Widdess (1995, 35) finds both approaches, as continued in the work of Jairazbhoy and Powers respectively, to be useful in "comparison of early and later systems."

Kurdish music

The idea of a "Kurdish music" with its own theory was still somewhat novel in 2006, when the first conference on that subject was convened in Diyarbakır, Turkey. Neighbors of the Kurds had long since developed theories of "Arab music," "Turkish music," "Armenian music," and "Persian music." Excluding or marginalizing musicians was out of the question: the musician Dilşad Saîd (b. 1958) envisioned "one theory for all regions, preserving the characteristic style of each" and "finding a common ground" for the "huge variety of styles" (my notes from his presentation). That aim recalls arguments concerning languages regarded as "Kurdish" by their speakers but classified differently by non-Kurdish philologists (Hassanpour 2020, 113). The conference had to provide simultaneous translation for speakers of Kurmanji and Sorani Kurdish, which are not mutually intelligible.

68   MUSIC THEORY IN ETHNOMUSICOLOGY

Beginning in the 1960s ethnomusicologists became active participants in international conferences on "Preservation and Presentation of Traditional Music" (see Trân 1977), which was typically demarcated by national boundaries. The history of such conferences now extends for well over half a century and calls for critical examination as ethnomusicologists seek to recognize and remedy some of the field's shortcomings. An international seminar on "The 'discovery' of the musics of the world in Europe after WWII (cold war, Unesco, and the ethnomusicological debate)" was convened in May 2020 by the Intercultural Institute for Comparative Music Studies at the Fondazione Cini in Venice. More are likely to follow.

Notations, Scales, and Solfège

Japan

The foreign instructors who taught solfège and note-reading to members of newly formed military bands made a lasting impact on musical life in nations where those skills became fundamental in educational programs. Music education based on solfège and note-reading was energetically pursued in Meiji Japan during the 1870s and 1880s, a well-studied period of Japanese music history (May 1963; Malm 1971; Eppstein 1985 and 1994; Ogawa 2000; Miller 2004). The term *solfège* came to be "used loosely to encompass training in sight-singing, dictation, and sometimes harmony and even composition," as Bonnie Wade found on visiting Japanese classrooms in the early 2000s (Wade 2014, 24).

By focusing on activities of a Music Investigation Committee (MIC) established in 1879, Richard C. Miller's dissertation brings out relationships among projects undertaken by its members and associates under the direction of Isawa Shūji (1851–1917). Uses of Western notation were crucial to the MIC's main aims: developing a music curriculum for public schools, conducting research on Japanese music with a view toward reform, and "creating a new music hybridizing East and West" (Miller 2004, 2). Japanese national music (*kokugaku*) was to be "a compromise between European and oriental music" (Eppstein 1994, 56–57).

MAKING MUSIC THEORY FOR MODERN NATIONS   69

Isawa was the key protagonist in planning for vocal instruction in schools and preparing six songbooks published in the 1880s and revised after the MIC became the Tokyo School of Music in 1887. He traveled to the United States to study Luther Whiting Mason's music pedagogy and arranged for Mason to teach music-reading in Japan between 1880 and 1882. In conferences with court musicians, Mason advocated replacing five-tone scales with the "more natural" Western diatonic scale and, as reported in a *Scientific American Supplement* of 1905 (quoted in May 1963, 59), "restrung and altered Japanese musical instruments so that they could be used on the new musical scale."

Debate continued for several decades on what Isawa termed the "question as to the tonality of Japanese music, whether it is similar to, or dissimilar from, European music" (Eppstein 1985, 26). Isawa himself considered Japanese music, like that of Europe, "a regional variety of a universal music" (Miller 2004, 120, 157). Miller sees these debates as a key moment in "the beginnings of comparative musicology." Two topics covered in the MIC's 1884 report on its activities (see Miller, 134 for the table of contents) were "Greek temperaments" and "differences between foreign and domestic tuning," and the report's English version reached Alexander J. Ellis and Hornbostel (Abraham and Hornbostel 1902–3 [1975, 27–28]). Miller finds "a much closer relationship in the Meiji period between the study and performance of western music and that of Japanese music than we might at first expect" (259).

North Africa and West Asia

Four nineteenth-century rulers relied on instructors from Europe for their new military bands: Muhammad 'Ali (r. 1805–43) in Cairo, who began in 1824 to establish five schools that trained musicians for army and navy bands (El-Shawan 1981, 80); Sultan Mahmud II (r.1808–39) in Istanbul, where Giuseppe Donizetti (1788–1856) arrived in 1828 and until his death directed the School of the Imperial Military Band founded in 1834; Ahmad Bey (r. 1837–55) in the Ottoman *eyalet* of Tunis; and Nasruddin Shāh (r. 1848–98) in Tehran, where Alfred-Jean-Baptiste Lemaire (1842–1909), the

70   MUSIC THEORY IN ETHNOMUSICOLOGY

third director of the department of military music, taught at the Polytechnic College for four decades and developed an eight-year curriculum (Advielle 1885, 8).[8]

Donizetti's "life, contribution and legacy" were the theme of a 2007 symposium in Bergamo (papers in Spinetti ed. 2010). He learned the notation developed around 1813 by Hamparsum Limociyan (1768–1839), which had symbols for thirty-nine scale degrees over three octaves (displayed in Jäger 1997, 393–94), then devised equivalents in Western notation and solfège, relying on the French terms for sharp and flat (e.g., both *fa-dièse* and *sol-bémol* came between *fa* and *sol*, as shown in Ayangil 2010, 43). Mehmet Hacı Emin Efendi attempted a transnotation of Hamparsum scale degrees to Western equivalents in his *Nota muallimi* "Notation instructor" (1884) and tried to show how band members could adapt the notation used in playing "Western" (*alafranga*) pieces for performance of "Turkish" (*alaturka*) pieces (see Ayangil 2008, 416–24, on the project and ensuing debates).

For Arabic-speakers the French or Italian solfège syllables taught to members of military bands provided an alternative to the Arabic-Persian names for the forty-nine degrees of the double-octave *general scale* described by two Syrian theorists in the first half of the nineteenth century and later adopted by others writing in Arabic (Marcus 1989, 78–99). Theorists found different ways of correlating both sets of names, which are hierarchically organized with seven primary degrees in each octave and two further categories (*'arabāt*, then *nīmāt* and *tīkāt*) in the modern Arabic system but only the five chromatic degrees in solfège.[9] The idea of a general scale of twenty-four quarter-tones to the octave became the dominant model in Arabic theory whatever adjustments musicians made in practice, with *demi-dièse* "half-sharp" and *demi-bémol* "half-flat" coined from French *dièse* and *bémol* (see Davis 1986, viii, for a table of equivalent Arabic and French names used by Tunisian musicians for twenty-one scale degrees covering an octave and major sixth). Ruth Davis found Tunisian musicians using the French syllables more often than their Arabic equivalents in the 1980s, and Marcus (1989, 146–51) tried to learn from Egyptian musicians how many of the Arabic-Persian names were still used in that decade and in what contexts.

MAKING MUSIC THEORY FOR MODERN NATIONS   71

The quarter-tone model was never widely accepted by Turkish and Persian musicians as a basis for practice. Yet, even if most Persian musicians reject the conception of a quarter-tone scale proposed by Alinaqi Vaziri (1887–1979), they have adopted his additions to the solfège syllables (outlined in Khāleqi 1967, 93): *koron* and *sori* for "half-flat" and "half-sharp," respectively. Students can learn that scale degrees qualified with those modifiers are variable and can make appropriate adjustments as they play or sing from notations using *koron* and *sori*.[10]

More generally, with or without additional symbols Western notation and solfège syllables are not inescapably bound to a norm of equal temperament. Participants in the Thai Music Manuscript Project of the 1930s notated 475 classical compositions with the understanding that the notations could be read in two ways: "The transcriptions would sound in major or minor scales when performed on Western instruments but the same music, when performed on Thai instruments, would be played in Thai tuning" (Roongruang 1999, 207). The Azerbaijani composer, theorist, and educator Üzeyir Hacıbäyli (1885–1948) allowed for the possibility that musicians could learn to perform the intervals he represented in Western notation without imposing a grid of equal temperament.[11] With that ploy, he could reject claims "that the international musical alphabet is not sufficient for the representation of the characteristics of Azerbaijani music" (quoted in Frolova-Walker 1998, 356) without denying that polyphonic music incorporating those characteristics (as mandated by the USSR's cultural policy) made an increasing reliance on equal temperament inevitable. He welcomed signs that players of the Azerbaijani *tar* (a long-necked lute played with a plectrum) "had begun to adjust their movable frets to conform more or less to equal temperament" (ibid.). After the breakup of the USSR, prominent *tar* players restored some intervals of pre-Soviet practice (e.g., the minor semitone of 64 cents) and increased the number of frets within an octave (During 2006).

John Morgan O'Connell (2010, 21–28) reported at length on how Turkish conservatory students are taught to read and supplement notations. He argued that "the conservatory lesson is both a symbol of modernity and a bastion of tradition" and regarded his

72 MUSIC THEORY IN ETHNOMUSICOLOGY

own instruction in vocal performance at the State Conservatory for Turkish Music in the early 1990s "as a precondition for the interpretation of musical practice in the past" (21–22). O'Connell compared the older method of instruction known as *meşk* "lesson, model" with Dr. Alâeddin Yavaşça's procedure in teaching a *şarkı* to conservatory students, noting differences and retentions. An earlier focus on the poem was replaced by one on music, as training of amateurs who might perform in religious contexts yielded to training of professionals more likely to perform in secular contexts. Chief among the retentions are ways to supplement the notation (perhaps the teacher's own) with demonstrations of appropriate intonation, ornamentation, and phrasing[12].

Institutions and Projects

Other ethnomusicologists have also used experience of an institution's operations during their fieldwork as a basis for inquiry into its past through study of written and recorded documents as well as interviews, sometimes with musicians who were excluded from or declined to participate in an institution's projects. For her 1986 dissertation on *Modern trends in the ma'lūf of Tunisia, 1934–1984*, Ruth Davis necessarily devoted considerable attention to the Rashidiyya Institute in Tunis (est. 1934), where canonization of *The Tunisian musical heritage* (*al-turāth al-mūsīqī al-tūnīsī*) originated. She interviewed participants in that project, notably Salah el-Mahdi (1925–2014), who led the Rashidiyya's ensemble from 1949 to 1972 and headed both the National Conservatory and the Ministry of Culture's Department of Music and Popular Arts from 1961 to 1979. Notations in the nine published volumes are presented as the authoritative redaction of the suites (*nūbāt*, sing. *nūba*) known collectively as the *ma'lūf* (literally "familiar," "customary"); some volumes include el-Mahdi's expositions of music-theoretical topics (in Arabic, French, and English; portions summarized in Davis 1986, 55–76). In her dissertation and a later monograph Davis analyzed performances of the *ma'lūf* in Testour, a town whose residents "insist that they possess a distinctive *ma'lūf* tradition, which they have made a conscious effort to preserve" (Davis

MAKING MUSIC THEORY FOR MODERN NATIONS   73

2004, viii). She also compares prescriptive notations made by successive leaders of the Rashidiyya ensemble (2004, 57–67). Her well-designed research agenda undercut claims that el-Mahdi's edition had rendered all other versions of the *ma'lūf* superfluous.[13]

Irene Markoff (1986, 4–14) provides a detailed account of her itinerary over a period of twenty months in the early 1980s as she studied the music theory developed for the Turkish long-necked lute *bağlama*: three universities, two conservatories, two radio stations, the Department of National Folklore Research at the Ministry of Culture, the Turkish Folklore Society, and "private music schools, instruments shops, recording studios, concert halls, nightclubs and entertainment halls, and homes of musicians." She saw the project underway in all these venues as "legitimization of a rural folk musical tradition" (19–43, 364–70), in part through codification of a "Turkish folk musical theory" based on a standardized fretting of the long-necked lute *bağlama* (44–140). She outlined the curriculum for folk music majors at the State Conservatory for Turkish Music in Istanbul (39–41) and found the same reliance on Western notation and solfège in other institutions teaching folk music.

A researcher's experience in an institution may include intensive contact with major figures and their views of priorities and constraints in development and usage of music theory. In preparation for his dissertation on *The music and tradition of the Bukharan shashmaqam in Soviet Uzbekistan* (1984), Theodore Levin spent ten months at the Department of Oriental Music of the Tashkent Conservatory in 1977–78 under the supervision of Faizullah M. Karomatov (b. 1925), with a follow-up visit in 1981. He recalled that Karomatov's "aim was clearly to keep me on a short tether. I was to enroll in classes at the Conservatory, learn to play an Uzbek instrument, the *dutar* (a two-stringed lute), . . . read scholarly articles, and study musical transcriptions" (Levin 1996, 11–12).[14] Fieldwork was not on the agenda. Before defending his dissertation Levin published an annotated English translation of Karomatov and Ishaq Radjabov's introduction (in Russian and Uzbek) to an edition of the six suites known as *shashmaqom* (Karomatov and Radjabov 1981).[15]

To exemplify the ideological underpinnings of the musicology he encountered in Uzbekistan, Levin zeroed in on a theory expounded

74   MUSIC THEORY IN ETHNOMUSICOLOGY

in a study of Uzbek instruments by Karomatov's mentor, Viktor M. Beliayev (1888–1968): the "feudal basis of neutral thirds" (Levin 1984, 61–71, and 2002, 192–94).[16] It was not only in nations of the former USSR that concepts from history and ideology turned up in music theory: work at making a modern music theory for one's nation tended to call up representations of the nation's past with ample room for mythologized accounts of "racial" origins. The Turkish theorist Hüseyin Sâdeddin Arel (1880–1955) superposed the vision of a Turkish "race" with Central Asian and "old Anatolian" roots on music theory, claiming that Ottoman art music and Anatolian folk music were based on the same principles (Greve 2005, 158).

Projects of canonization and notation that required attention to questions of music theory include the Thai Music Manuscript Project of the 1930s (described in Roongruang 1999) and the first publication of the *radif* of Persian music (Barkeshli and Ma'rufi 1963), a repertory of melodic and rhythmic models arranged in twelve systems (seven *dastgāh* and five *āvāz*).[17] Canonization and notation of the Uyghur *on iki muqam* "twelve muqams" (suites comparable to the Tajik-Uzbek *shashmaqom*) resulted from work carried out in both the People's Republic of China and the USSR over the half century between 1952 and 2002. Rachel Harris's concise history of those efforts (2008, 29–43) starts with recordings and subsequent notations made in Ürümchi, capital of Xinjiang in the PRC, and continues with further recordings and notations made in the late 1960s in Tashkent under the direction of a Soviet Uyghur musician-scholar, Abdulaziz Khashimov. Sabine Trebinjac (2000), Wong Chuen-fung (2006), and Nathan Light (2008) also discuss relationships of Han Chinese scholars and officials with Uyghur musicians, scholars, and officials as the *on iki muqam* and other Uyghur repertories were assembled and edited. Wan Tongshu was largely responsible for the first notations of the *on iki muqam* from recordings of Turdi Akhun (1881–1956), published anonymously in 1960 with a theoretical introduction in Chinese and Uyghur (summarized in During and Trebinjac 1991, 45–47), which associated the three sections of each *muqam* with nobility, populace, and bards, respectively. Freshly minted music theory provided templates for composition of whatever pieces were needed to make each

MAKING MUSIC THEORY FOR MODERN NATIONS 75

muqam a full sequence following what the canonizers considered the proper ordering of genres. The performer Ömär Akhun (b. ca. 1912) considered the second and third sections extraneous to the authentic *muqam*. Light's extensive conversations with him (2008, 179–213), like Harris's with Abdulla Mäjnun (Harris 2008, 45–65), show how much can be learned from individuals involved for decades in a musical practice as it becomes *heritage*.

Continuing Issues

The history of music theory is a history of intercultural exchanges, and an attempt at a global history of music theory that treated developments discussed in this chapter in greater depth might also yield insights into such exchanges during earlier episodes of theory construction. Ideologies of progress, together with nationalist aims, placed severe constraints on participants in "the work of musical theory" (Gushee 1973, 366) as they responded to what were often formidable pressures from many directions. Sponsors, supporters, and critics of the projects have deployed narratives of social and cultural history with much in common, including claims to a unique cultural identity formed of both "indigenous" and "progressive" features.[18] For better and worse, projects to modernize music theory are shaped by conceptions of intercultural contact both within and among nations. A common result, and too often an aim, of these projects has been marginalization of groups and individuals not amenable to guidance from the modernizers who limit their concept of *theory* to work they can regard as modern.

Music theory and equivalents in other languages (often loan words) are now major topics of discussion among musicians, educators, and scholars concerned with the state of musical life in their homelands, which they do not always understand as nation-states. Consider the titles of two collections of conference papers: *Musical arts in Africa: Theory, practice, and education* (Herbst, Nzewi, and Agawu eds. 2003) from the Third Conference of the Pan African Society for Musical Arts Education, and *A search in Asia for a new theory of music* (Buenconsejo, ed. 2003) from the Seventh International Conference of the Asia Pacific Society for Ethnomusicology. Many participants in the conference and readers of the book would recall Maceda's classic article "A search for an old and a new music in Southeast Asia" (1979) and his vision of how renewed attention to the "village thinking" that nurtured "an old music" could contribute to creation of a new music in nations of Southeast Asia. The ubiquitous narratives of cultural history in which theories and practices based on scientific principles are destined to replace those of a pre-scientific past can prompt reappraisal of the supposedly "unscientific" thinking. Such reappraisals can lead to greater respect for traditional indigenous knowledge and its potential, and can motivate "work of musical theory" that transcends narrow conceptions of *authenticity* or *modernity* and recognizes cultural interactions and intersections within and across national (and continental) boundaries (see Lee 2021).

Ethnomusicologists are privileged to meet with musicians and scholars who have thought deeply about actual and potential relationships among older and newer theories and practices. To realize time and again how little we know is one of the continuing pleasures of an ethnomusicologist's life, spurring closer listening to voices of individuals while questioning conventional terms and formats of academic discourse—in favorable circumstances that can make our work relevant to participants in modernization projects by highlighting alternatives. More research on how subsequent generations have lived with the music theory produced in early phases of those projects would be helpful.

A comparative study of how people engaged in modernization projects have formulated issues might start with Isawa's question, whether "the tonality of Japanese music . . . is similar to, or dissimilar from, European music" (Eppstein 1985, 26), and his answer: both are "regional varieties" of "a universal music" (Miller 2004, 120, 157). More than a century after Isawa's death, ethnomusicologists interested in "a universal music" or a pan-human musicality might favor efforts to develop "a universal music theory," which could examine how common topics posited by researchers have been handled in well-documented theories. Ethnomusicologists and musicians who question whether the world needs "a universal music theory" can ask "Who would use it, and to what ends?" Interests in universality have stimulated impressive

MAKING MUSIC THEORY FOR MODERN NATIONS   77

work in music theory (e.g., Mâche 2001 on "Music in the singular") and above all in composition, at best inviting voluntary participation on a basis of social equality. Theories imposed under the banner of "inescapable progress" have no legitimate claim to universality. The American bassist and composer William Parker (b. 1952) speaks of a *universal tonality* that can be experienced as musicians of diverse backgrounds are musicking together (as on the recordings of Parker 2020). Mark Hijleh's book *Towards a global music theory* is addressed to musicians interested in developing a "global musicianship"; it "does not purport to constitute a theory for all music" (2012, 1; compare Rahn 1983, which does present a theory under that heading). Those engaged in a "new comparative musicology" and even a "global history of music theory" might choose to follow Hijleh in that respect. Participants in the Analytical Approaches to World Music project mentioned in Chapter One might or might not think of their work as directed toward developing "a theory for all music."[19]

Notes to Chapter Three

78   MUSIC THEORY IN ETHNOMUSICOLOGY

Issues, 3: Systematization and Assemblage

Discourse on systems and systematization is ubiquitous in the modernization projects discussed in Chapter Three, where those terms take on meanings that fit specific projects. Feld's definition of *theory* (1981, 23) as "a social articulation of systematic knowledge organized in such a way that it is applicable to a wide variety of circumstances" calls for attention to *processes* of social articulation. As a generalization allowing for many such processes, "social articulation of systematic knowledge" is compatible with Perlman's premise, mentioned in Chapter One, that "the components of any cognitive system are only loosely integrated" and "can usually be brought into relation with one another in many different ways" (2004, 200). Some components of a "loosely integrated" system might be tightly integrated subsystems like the phonemic systems of languages. How efforts to organize and apply knowledge relate to operations of memory and habit depends on such factors as the size of social formations and the available technologies. Musicians can recall and reassemble the pieces of theory relevant to a particular situation without worrying about how those pieces might otherwise fit together; theorizing directed at systematization of knowledge can yield more widely applicable outcomes by exploring relationships among the components.

The philosopher and mathematician Alfred North Whitehead (1861–1947) contrasted *systematization* with *assemblage*, terming the latter the "primary stage" of philosophy with "emphasis on a few large-scale notions, together with attention to the variety of other ideas which arise in the display of those chosen for emphasis" (Whitehead 1938, 2–3). In music studies *assemblage* has become an English equivalent for French *agencement*, a key term in *Mille plateaux* by Gilles Deleuze and Félix Guattari (1980, translated as *A thousand plateaus*, 1987). Nick Nesbitt, co-editor of a collection of essays on *Gilles Deleuze and the theory and philosophy of music* (Hulse and Nesbitt, eds. 2010), registers a "sense of ongoing, active construction [in the French term] that is lost in the more passive English 'assemblage'" (Nesbitt 2010, 161n9; see also Phillips 2006).[20] But in Whitehead's discussion *assemblage* does refer to processes, such as attending to ideas that "arise" while dealing with other ideas; it can designate both a process and its

MAKING MUSIC THEORY FOR MODERN NATIONS 79

result. Music theorists intent on systematization have emulated other systematic disciplines, notably cosmology and mathematics, spelling out relationships among parts in a comprehensive presentation.[21]

Ancient Greek *systēma* and its derivatives have long been central terms of music theory, one of several disciplines in which they acquired new meanings emphasizing the interdependence of a system's constituents and procedures.[22] As defined in the harmonics of Aristoxenus (fourth century BCE) a *systēma* was "something put together from more than one interval [*diastēma*]" (*Harmonic Elements* i.16; trans. Barker 1989, 136). A much later theorist, Aristides Quintilianus (third or fourth century CE), defined rhythm (*rhythmos*) as "a *systēma* of durations [*chronoi*] put together in some kind of order" (i.13, ed. Winnington-Ingram 1963, 31; Eng. trans. in Barker 1989, 433). Description of *tone systems* is a longstanding interest of music theorists in several cultures and of comparative musicologists.[23] By the eighteenth century, European dictionaries of musical terms listed additional types of system,[24] and innovative works of music theory bore such titles as Jean-Philippe Rameau's *Nouveau système de musique théorique et pratique* (1726).

Although references to musical systems are common in ethnomusicological texts and the field has even been defined as analysis of systems (Molino 1988), overviews of a musical system as a whole are relatively rare, as is advice on how to relate them to other relevant systems.[25] In the "traditional system" of the Venda over the decade 1956–66, according to Blacking (1990, 216–17), "the symbolic actions of dance, music and ritual were systematically interrelated as elements of an aesthetic (cultural) system."[26] Turino maintained that in the 1970s and 1980s ethnomusicologists had used the term without "arriving at a clear conceptualization of musical or cultural systems" (Turino 2015, 387). The term has designated constructs presented by teachers to students or, more often, drawn up by researchers to describe some *portion* of the knowledge deemed responsible for regularities in musicians' actions (or in traces of those actions). It takes on different meanings in Ellis's chapter on "The Pitjantjatjara musical system" (1985, 82–111) and Michel Guignard's account of the "systematic instruction" in instrumental technique and a repertory of modes and sub-modes offered to male lutenists in Mauritania but not to female harpists (1975, 103–10).

Table 3.2. Some systems described or mentioned as relevant to musicking

---

systems of music theory (Wellesz 1954)

acoustic-musicological system (Menenzes Bastos 1978)

systems of difference (Iyer 2019)

pitch systems (Thrasher 2008, 83)

musical memory systems (Jäncke 2019, 245)

pitch memory system and other memory subsystems (Deutsch 2013, 284–95)

scale systems (Kunst 1973: i, 11–104; Arom 1991, 23–25)

tuning systems (Hood 1963, 268–69 and 1971, 322–24)

tone systems (Kubik 1968)

tonal systems (Everett 2004)

solmization systems (e.g., "acoustic-iconic-mnemonic systems," Hughes 2000)

notational systems (Kaufmann 1967)

system of modes (Wright 1978, Baily 1981)

system of melodic models (Thrasher, ed. 2016)

melody systems (Lachmann 1929, Kuckertz 1970)

timing system (Kubik, 2010, 21–52)

cuing system (Gourlay 1972)

metrorhythmic system (Bielawski 1959, Estreicher 1964)

rhythmic system and metric system

system of performance roles (Marcu 1967)

system of performance genres (Ramanujan 1986)

system of an instrument (A. Tracey 1989)

song-producing system (Titon 1977, 169–77)

reference system (Wolf 2019)

system of stylistic reference (Estreicher 1974, 134)

response systems in expectation cycle (Huron 2006)
system of instruction

MAKING MUSIC THEORY FOR MODERN NATIONS   81

Ellis's description of the Pitjantjatjara system emphasizes "interlocking of structures" on larger as well as smaller scales, whereby "technical musical features are interlocked with extramusical events (such as dance) and information (such as the songtext) which occur simultaneously" (92). Guignard describes a modal system in which *invariant elements* "are more numerous at the level of the sub-mode" (108) and include subtle differences in attack (119, 126).

Table 3.2 (which could easily be twice as long) lists ethnomusicological writings that treat some portion of musical knowledge as a system thought to maintain relatively stable relationships among its constituents. The areas of a musical practice that appear to require assimilation of a system, and those (if any) said to have been systematized at some moment in the past, are major variables among practices.

In his "Reflections on collective musical creation," Constantin Brăiloiu (1893–1958) saw description of "all the original systems that govern melody, rhythm, form, not to forget polyphony" as a major aim of the field that was becoming known as ethnomusicology (Brăiloiu 1959, 93; 1973, 147).[27] In the final decade of his life Brăiloiu published overviews of three rhythmic systems: *aksak* rhythms (Turkish for "limping") with durations in the ratio 3:2 (1951); "children's rhythm" in a great many cultures (1954a); and the "syllabic *giusto*" as developed in Romanian folksong (1952, extended in 1954b to other types of sung verse among Romanian-speaking peasants). He considered them autonomous, with laws not yet formulated in words, unlike those of "classical rhythmics" (1954a [1973, 267]). Brăiloiu wished to demonstrate the "methodical exploitation" of resources in societies that continued to cultivate inherited procedures, a "certain type of civilization" he thought was disintegrating. He understood the "building blocks" (*pierres à bâtir*) of scales, rhythms, and structures in the music of European peasants to have been "determined by an intelligible principle that yields a more or less extensive set of procedures, or if one prefers, a *system*" (1959 [1973, 144–45]).[28] His procedure was consistent with Odoyevsky's desire "to extract their theory from the tunes themselves" (quoted in Issues, 2, from Odoyevsky 1956, 306): Brăiloiu identified a system's components ("building blocks") and underlying principles (five in the system of children's rhythm), then enumerated potential applications and combinations.[29] His emphasis in 1959 on

82 MUSIC THEORY IN ETHNOMUSICOLOGY

"methodical exploitation" of systems overlaps with the conception of "undomesticated thinking" presented three years later by Lévi-Strauss in *La pensée sauvage* ("Wild thought" in a recent translation): "Mythic thought thought expresses itself using a heteroclite repertory which, while extensive, *remains limited* all the same" (Lévi-Strauss 1962, 26, my italics).[30] Lévi-Strauss saw the "heteroclite repertory" as a product of what he called *bricolage*, assembled in the course of diverse undertakings and available for multiple new projects rather than designed to "govern" the timing of sung syllables and other demands of music-making.

Ethnomusicologists are now more likely to understand constituents of a system, not as "building blocks," but as "options that are differentiated in specific respects—as the tones in a tone system differ in pitch and perhaps in timbre or as the roles assumed by performers in one or more genres of performance carry different responsibilities and privileges" (Blum 2015b, 201). Often we do not know to what extent musicians internalize sets of distinctions among sounds (and movements that produce or respond to sounds) of the type linguists term *phonemic* as opposed to *phonetic*. While internalizing the phonemic system of one's mother tongue does not normally require recognizing it as a system, instrumentalists who learn sets of distinctions among sounds and movements are often well aware of what they have learned to do and can name the system's constituents, such as those of a tone system or the syllables learned by players of the North Indian *tablā* and South Indian *mrdangam*.

The linguist Kenneth Pike understood what he termed "etic and emic standpoints for the description of behavior" as, respectively, "external" and "internal" to a given system, insisting that "The emic structure of a particular system must . . . be discovered" (Pike 1967, 38). His "external" and "internal" standpoints contrast different situations of "outsiders" and "insiders," not different systems. In ethnomusicological discourse, the expression "emic statements" is too often a synonym for "statements of insiders," quoted apart from any reference to a system. Benamou (2010, 89) correctly observes that "emic analysis, as Pike conceived it, does not simply consist in reporting insiders' speech" and "does not . . . preclude interpreting what these insiders say."[31] Indeed, it requires identifying at least some of the distinctions

MAKING MUSIC THEORY FOR MODERN NATIONS   83

that matter to insiders. That criterion is met by the "'emic' oral theory" with which Slawek (1987, xvii, 33–91) describes techniques and performance practice he learned from two masters of the Hindustani *sitār*.

Pike's extension of the phonetic/phonemic distinction from linguistics to human behavior led Marvin Harris (1968, 570) to ask a pertinent question: "Why should we not also assume that there are sociocultural systems whose structure can be exposed independently of procedures modeled after phonemic analysis?" His perspective includes but is not limited to that model (571): "Emic statements refer to logico-empirical systems whose phenomenal distinctions or 'things' are built up out of contrasts and discriminations significant, meaningful, real, accurate, or in some other fashion regarded as appropriate by the actors themselves" (cf. M. Harris 1976). Harris's formulation allows for tests to learn whether actors judge specific "contrasts and discriminations" to be meaningful; it does not assume that each actor has internalized all discriminations made available by a system supposedly shared by multiple actors.

Must the contrasts and discriminations that are meaningful to social actors constitute a system?[32] Terms that might allow for less formality and stability than *system* include *ensemble, grouping, set, repertory, constellation, configuration*, and *network* as well as *assemblage*. Efforts to analyze a system or systematize an area of practice can consider the potential for transformation as circumstances change. Tone systems may be the least problematic area of practice where musicians and music theorists have identified consistent regularities in interrelationships among sounds.[33] Kubik finds *system* an essential concept in studying processes of intercultural contact, speculating for example that some blues musicians in the USA became proficient in more than one system (1999, 17–18). He regards the so-called *blue notes* "as *intrasystemic units* and not as deviations from another tonal system," noting that "blues musicians do not normally talk about 'blue notes' or any other intervals supposed to be special unless they have adopted the jargon from music critics or musicologists" (Kubik 1999, 15–17).

Explicit articulation of a music theoretical system often inspires resistance, as do codified lists of rules. Those who resist may prefer different rules, a different understanding of *system*, or musicking

84   MUSIC THEORY IN ETHNOMUSICOLOGY

unconstrained by systems and rules. Interests that motivate efforts to formulate and propagate constraints, and resistance to such efforts, are crucial topics for historians and ethnographers concerned with music theory. The title of Agawu's pioneering study of "Tonality as a colonizing force in Africa" (2016b) identifies one such interest: colonizers and imperialists have drawn upon techniques of regulation and control practiced in their homelands, with modifications deemed appropriate. The importance of Curwen's *tonic solfa* system of notation in Africa and elsewhere supports Hornbostel's thesis (1913, 14, discussed in Issues, 2) that "Notation is always the most powerful means . . . for acquiring a theoretical outlook"—and for promulgating it, supplementing the notations with written and oral presentations of theory.

One reason for humans to theorize is to confront limits and decide whether to respect them. That question has often been raised with respect to projects of systematization, which are easily pushed too far. *System* is not an indispensable term in ethnomusicological work on all music theoretical topics. Gary Tomlinson's thesis that "Musicking in the world today is the extended, spectacularly formalized, and *complexly perceived* systematization of ancient, indexical gesture-calls" (2015, 205, emphasis added) allows for multiple approaches to describing results of those processes as we learn more about the complexities of perception. Advances in research on music cognition should help ethnomusicologists refine current terms and procedures for recognizing and describing systems, which might make the resulting work relevant in turn to research on music cognition.

4

Concepts, Models, and Metaphors

Music scholarship in institutions and networks dominated by anglophone scholars remains *Imprisoned in English*, the title of Anna Wierzbicka's critique of *The hazards of English as a default language* (Wierzbicka 2014). Working to circumvent those hazards could make the increasing use of English in communication among scholars a more positive development than it is now. Best not to assume that other languages have words for concepts denoted by terms used in English, as when the chapter on *mode* in *The Oxford handbook of critical concepts in music theory* (*CCMT*) refers to "the concept of mode in other cultures, including the music of India and elsewhere" and even to "what he [Plato!] calls mode" (McClary 2019, 61–62), at least when he's quoted in anglophone classrooms beyond the classics department. Can we justify the assumption that specific words in ancient Greek and other languages refer to a general "concept of mode"?

Treating English as the default language for development and critique of ethnomusicological theory marginalizes the work of those who theorize in other languages. Formulations and presentations of theory are indebted to specific languages, rhetorical styles, institutional settings, and interpersonal relationships, and scholarly translations of music theory often include commentary on such topics.[1] Fortunately, musicians with whom ethnomusicologists converse often articulate bits of theory in humble, everyday expressions. Paired concepts such as *departure and return* often turn up in records of musicians' speech and writing, as do verbs that designate actions performed in musicking and other activities. With a nod toward Leibniz's "alphabet of human thoughts," Wierzbicka explores prospects for identifying a "core of simple words and concepts where all languages meet" (2014, xl).[2] Two of "the mini-languages hidden within all the languages of the world" she calls "Minimal English" and the even more severely reduced "Basic Human" (194–95). *Way* and *manner* are simpler words than *mode*,

Music Theory in Ethnomusicology. Stephen Blum, Oxford University Press.
© Oxford University Press 2023. DOI: 10.1093/oso/9780199303526.003.0005

86   MUSIC THEORY IN ETHNOMUSICOLOGY

for example, and a roster of "simple words and concepts" might prove useful in registering and comparing specific features of prominent words in musicians' vocabularies.

Developing "a way for linguistic expressions to be related to concepts" is crucial to "an integrated theory of language and thought" according to Ray Jackendoff in his essay "What is a concept?" (1992, 192). The earliest documents of efforts to identify or create equivalents or analogues of one language's musical terms in a second language are bilingual Sumerian-Akkadian tablets of the first millennium BCE (Kilmer 1997, 135–36, and 2001, 484–85). Many modern languages have adopted terms developed in earlier music theory (such as Greek *rhythmos* and Latin *modus*), often with substantial changes in meaning as terms are attached to concepts with different functions. Lexicographic work on musical terminology in western European languages is far more advanced than comparable work on other language groups, as evidenced in the *Handwörterbuch der musikalischen Terminologie* (*HmT*) which began publication in 1972 and is now described as "completed."[3] Musicology cannot become an international discipline without comprehensive lexicographic studies of pertinent terminology in all major language groups, such as the Bantu languages; Arabic and languages that have assimilated some of its musical terminology; and Sanskrit and Chinese, which have also contributed musical terms to many languages. Terminologies in less prominent languages and non-standard dialects are equally deserving of lexicographic research, as are terms for musical concepts shared by speakers of multiple languages in one region.[4] Such projects will need to modify the policies of *HmT* by compiling examples of usage from recorded sources as well as from printed and manuscript materials while retaining *HmT*'s historical approach.

Expansion and Internationalization
of Musicological Concepts

Only a small proportion of the terms humans have used in thinking and talking about musicking have histories of cross-cultural applications across much of the world. They are terms in modern European languages, generally with Greek or Latin antecedents, used by musicians,

CONCEPTS, MODELS, AND METAPHORS   87

scholars, educators, and others as they encountered what to them were exotic practices, then adopted by participants in intercultural discussions. Some identify major divisions of music theory such as the ancient Greek distinction of *harmonics* and *rhythmics*. Others designate *resources* used in making music, forty of which that are current in English, with cognates in other languages, are listed in Table 4.1.

In "Mode as a musicological concept," the final section of his article on "Mode" for the 1980 edition of the *New Grove dictionary of music and musicians*, Harold Powers interrogated the processes he called "expansion and internationalization of the concept" (Powers 1980b, 422–23; revised as Powers and Widdess 2001, 829–31 and "Mode, V.1" in *OMO*).[5] They resulted from the global expansion of European—and subsequently North American—power through projects of colonization and empire-building whose consequences are still with us. Musicians in the regions affected have adopted many of the "imported" terms as they formulate new theories, rework old ones, and engage in transregional communication. Research on music cognition is enriching the vocabulary

Table 4.1. Forty terms for musical resources (each column best read vertically)

system	scale	canon	genre	contour
repertory	interval	criterion	species	pattern
style	cycle	aesthetic	model	formula
idiom	progression	ethic	scenario	figure
	mode	rule	schema	gesture
		principle	template	motif
		norm	type	theme
		code	archetype	subject
			paradigm	topic
			matrix	idea
			texture	element
				cadence

88 MUSIC THEORY IN ETHNOMUSICOLOGY

available for international use, adding to the challenges but also the opportunities confronting ethnomusicologists and the musicians with whom we reflect on histories, limitations, and possible uses of terms.

Musicians and researchers may identify more than two *contexts for theory*, as Tenzer does in his monograph on Balinese *gamelan gong keybar* (2000, 115–41) where the relevant contexts are the existing work on Balinese music, the much larger body of scholarship on Javanese *gamelan*, and the semiotic theory developed in studies of eighteenth-century European music. Relevant contexts often relate to different epochs and areas of inquiry. Alan R. Thrasher (2008, ix–x) identifies "two theoretical domains of musical relevance" to his study of the *sizhu* "silk and bamboo" instrumental music of South China: "first, Confucian theory, the ancient corpus of written and practiced behavioral doctrine (ethos) which promoted music as a means to achieve social harmony and which, in turn, exercised unusually strong influence over common-practice musical style and aesthetics; and second, music theory, an overlapping combination of imperial court pitch theory and more recent Chinese modal and structural theory, much of which is related to (even derived from) Confucian theory."

Mode

Powers argued that no coherent concept of *mode* will accommodate the meanings assumed in diverse situations by such terms as Javanese *patet*, Japanese *chōshi*, Chinese *diao*, *rāga* in South Asian languages, or *maqām* and its cognates in several languages of the Muslim world.[6] While Mantle Hood (1971, 324) was willing to "hazard the guess that most musical traditions in the world are modal,"[7] Powers echoed the skepticism of his contemporary, the philosopher Hilary Putnam, "that whenever we have diverse phenomena gathered together under a single name, There Must Be Something They All Have in Common" (Putnam 1988, 2). Apparent commonalities may vanish on closer inspection: "The strikingly different semantic fields of the musical terms *rāga* and *maqām* suggest that their musical senses may have less in common than at first appears" (Powers 1980b, 429; Powers and Widdess 2001, 837; "Mode, V.1" in *OMO*).[8]

CONCEPTS, MODELS, AND METAPHORS   89

In a paper on "Modality as a European Cultural Construct," Powers (1992a, 207) expressed a desire "to subvert the notion of 'modality' altogether, first as an inherent musical property in the medieval chant and Renaissance polyphony of Europe, and second as a cross-cultural category for international musicological scholarship." Powers's critique has not stopped music scholars from applying the terms *mode* and *modal* cross-culturally or, more problematically, imagining them to be derived from a "property" of *modality*.[9] Widdess, in a monograph on *The rāgas of early Indian music: Modes, melodies, and musical notations from the Gupta period to c. 1250*, sees *mode* as a convenient term for "a set of pitches associated with a wide range of other melodic features, such as emphasized pitches or characteristic motifs, and various extra-musical characteristics." That "wide range of features" obligates scholars who use the term to specify which features come into play in each practice and *how*, including any rhythmic constraints.

In the first extensive study of Vietnamese music in a European language, Trân Văn Khê (1962, 213–16) posed the question "Can one speak of 'mode' in Vietnamese music?" Asian musicians and scholars may have been more inclined than their European and American colleagues to pose that question about Asian practices. Trân qualified his affirmative answer by acknowledging that Vietnamese *diêu* (derived from Chinese *diao*) lacks certain characteristics ascribed to *mode* by his teacher, Jacques Chailley (1960). Because *diêu* is "more than a system" (here meaning "more than an octave species"), Trân adopted the term *système modal* for the two *diêu* used by musicians throughout Vietnam, *Bac* (literally "North") and *Nam* (literally "South"), and he provided detailed accounts of each system's usage in diverse contexts (216–58). Writing on *mode* in eight musical practices of Asia, Trân argued that a mode is "not only a characteristic scale but also an ensemble of conventions that vary from one music to another" (Trân 1966, 208).[10] Here *modal* as a qualifier of *system* serves as a placeholder, awaiting precise description of conventions associated with each of two or more "characteristic scales." Hood's understanding of mode is closer to Trân's than to discussions of mode in Western art music and jazz.

Powers introduced a round table on "Eastern and Western Concepts of Mode" at the 1977 Congress of the IMS by asserting that efforts "to

90 MUSIC THEORY IN ETHNOMUSICOLOGY

reach reasonably clear understandings of individual 'concepts' as applied to individual repertories" should take priority over cross-cultural comparisons (1981, 501). Rulan Chao Pian's contribution made *mode* (as an ordered list of notes, with one specified as the finalis) one of four interrelated concepts in the history of Chinese music theory, along with *transposed scale*, *melody-type*, and *tune-type* (with a more stable identity, hence "usually identified by a proper name").[11] Pian noted that Chinese *diao* "has been employed for many meanings" (1981, 536n2) without attempting in a mere conference paper to outline the history of Chinese terminology in relation to her conceptual model.

Mode serves as a rubric covering terms in multiple languages that designate different ways to act musically. It can provide a point of departure for inquiries into differences among specific gatherings of pitches (or of attacks in so-called rhythmic modes[12]) in practices that do not mark such differences with abstract terms or proper names. Those using it as an imported term with reference to one practice, such as Javanese gamelan music, tend to agree on how it relates to indigenous terms though groups and individuals in certain situations may avoid terms that are common in other situations (see Weintraub 1993 for an example).[13] I agree with Powers that interpretation of terms for musical resources in ancient Greek, Arabic, Sanskrit, Chinese, and other languages does not require an internationalized "concept of mode," developed over the past century to designate resources serving quite different functions. Use of the term is sometimes justified with reference to "family resemblances," which are not always evident.

Composition, performance, improvisation

As a concept applied cross-culturally, *composition* has the advantage over *mode* of denoting creative processes or some of their outcomes rather than ways to generate or classify music. Musicologists, folklorists, and others have seen it as a topic inviting attention to the relevant social interactions, which often result in performances or models rather than "pieces" or "compositions." Cross-cultural application of the concept generated marked terms for processes lacking features commonly taken for granted in discourse on Western art

CONCEPTS, MODELS, AND METAPHORS   91

music such as "carried out by one individual in advance of performance and transmitted in writing." These terms include *collective composition, composition in performance, composition in real time, oral composition, mental composition, recomposition, composing for improvisers,* and *formulaic rhythmic improvisation among oral composers.*

Ethnomusicologists are latecomers to the arguments among scholars of literature concerning *oral composition* and *composition in performance.* In 1908–10 Jean Paulhan observed exchanges of *hain-teny* poems in Madagascar, and his analytic account (Paulhan 1913 [1939]) is an early formulation of what Saussy (2016, 27) terms a *generative model* based on "prefabricated verses known to all, and waiting to be called out for a use on a particular occasion." The discussion of "formulaic rhythmic improvisation among oral composers" in Marcel Jousse's pioneering monograph on *Le style oral* (1924, translated 1990 as *The oral style*) was an important precursor of the research on Bosnian and Albanian epic verse by Milman Parry (1902–35) and Albert Bates Lord (1912–91), which produced what came to be labeled *oral-formulaic theory* or *the theory of oral composition* (Foley 1988).[14] Lord argued (1991, 76) that the creative process of Balkan singers of epic verse could be considered *composition by formula and theme, composition in performance,* or *recomposition in performance,* but not *improvisation.*

Oral composition takes in much of what the composer-scholar Akin Euba termed *pre-performance composition* as well as composition in performance and musicking that requires or allows for both. Euba's student Kwasi Ampene complains (2005, 13) that oral composition "has received only marginal and cursory treatment in ethnomusicological studies." In his study of *nnwonkorɔ,* a vocal genre of Akan women in Ghana, Ampene recommends attention to "a continuum that is evident in pre-performance composition and in composition during performance." He emphasizes knowledge of "fixed and authentic texts which exist prior to performance" and use of "certain learned formulas" in recomposition (9), and he avoids speaking of improvisation in *nnwonkorɔ* so as not to imply "composition without forethought."[15]

Processes of oral composition often lack features widely associated with improvisation, such as unpredictability and appreciation of spontaneity, a lack of self-consciousness and willingness to take risks. In the final chapter of *CCMT,* "Beneath Improvisation," the

92 MUSIC THEORY IN ETHNOMUSICOLOGY

pianist-composer-scholar-educator Vijay Iyer writes (2019, 761) that "We cannot 'know' whether an action is improvised just by observing it in a vacuum. What we seem to be doing, instead of precisely identifying improvisation according to some intrinsic attribute, is allowing cultural and contextual factors to regulate its presence or absence. That is, we 'perceive' improvisation through systems of difference." His point applies equally well to perceptions of any activities identified with terms for musicological concepts, and music scholars need to recognize the *systems of difference* relevant to each of our projects.

Ethnomusicologists studying the musical terminology of a language generally find more words referring to composition (as process, product, or both) than to improvisation, which—as spontaneous invention or variation—is often taken for granted as the norm in singing or playing, with different ways of singing and playing designated by names of performance genres (though a comparative study of ways that improvisation is differentiated from 'non-improvisational" modes of performance could be illuminating).

In early phases of a creative process, acts of composition may anticipate future acts that will take up earlier results as remembered, notated, or recorded. The repertory of compositions for the Shona *mbira* exists to enable musicians to develop "practices of re-creating compositions in performance" in what is appropriately regarded as "an improvisation-based tradition" (Berliner 2020, 11, 15). The *radif* of Persian traditional music is generally understood to be "a set of pieces" that, in a musician's experience, "evolve from the fixed form of a memorized composition in which they are first encountered to a more fluid state, ending in certain cases as a template for improvisation" (Wright 2009, 26).

Adjustments made at the right time are often mentioned in accounts of composition as sociomusical action. George Dor describes *havɔlu* as "an institutionalized process among the Anlo Ewe that brings newly composed pieces before a select group of artists for scrutiny and subsequent refinement" (275). Rouget summarized the actions of Sèdémèkpon when King Gbèfa of Porto Novo in Benin commissioned her to compose a new "long song" (*han ga*) for his court music and provided the requisite offerings. She would invite the singers among his wives to her home to invoke the presence of Aziza, spirit of the

CONCEPTS, MODELS, AND METAPHORS 93

brush and forest who inspires a composer (called *aziza*).[16] They would leave her alone to make (*bayi*) the song, drawing on a stock of formulas, proverbs, and maxims for words that will fit the periodic structure of melodies appropriate to *han ga*. Having memorized the song she would summon the best palace singer to fine-tune the relation between the "throwing out" (*dó*) and the "taking up" (*yí*). Once all the palace singers had rehearsed the song and could perform it well, Sèdémèkpon would request an audience to seek the king's approval (Rouget 1996, 233–36 and 344).

Models and Conceptual Models

It is difficult to imagine a music theory lacking a concept of *model*. Like *system*, in ethnomusicology the term designates constructs presented by teachers and others with specialized knowledge, or that researchers attribute to participants in a practice or find useful in their own efforts at description and analysis. Certain uses of *model* overlap with those of *type* (as in *ideal type*, *melody-type*, *archetype*), *schema*, and *pattern*. Ethnomusicological usage extends to models of the discipline itself, as in Tim Rice's book *Modeling ethnomusicology* (2017).

Terms glossed as *model* often function as objects of verbs for actions taken prior to or during performance. In a study of Fulfulde terminology associated with the Ful'be praise song genre *mantoore* in northern Cameroon, Veit Erlmann (1985, 91, and 1987) offered "a model of different Ful'be models of sound organization centered around core concepts concerning performers, genres, performance, model, and variation." With respect to *mantoore*, Erlmann discerned "a certain overlap in the semantic fields of Ful'be concepts" and those of the *model/performance* dichotomy in European languages (94). Three verbs used in discussing a *taakiyaare* "model" were "*art-* (to begin first, to be first), *wa'd-* (to make, to do) and *wurtod-* (to bring out, to come up with)"; the verb *wadd-* (to bring) was used in discussing *fijirde*, its realization in performance, in which *sanja* "variation" is expected. Terms for variation are natural allies of the model/performance dichotomy.

Wright (2009, 22) remarked that analytic techniques devised for what he terms "the western score-to-performance relationship" may

94 MUSIC THEORY IN ETHNOMUSICOLOGY

not be relevant to analysis of music making based on a "model-to-performance relationship." Yet, how should we distinguish "score" from "model"? Performers can experience scores as highly detailed models, instructions to which they can respond on multiple occasions (see K. Berger 2000, 53–55), and when versions of a model exist in notation those who made them may have selected a few options from many that were just as compatible with their understanding of the model.[17] In a monograph on Shona *mbira* music, Gerd Grupe (2004, 243) mentions Oskár Elschek's suggestion that we think of a large class of *model-to-performance* or *model-to-realization* relationships as embracing much that "we otherwise subsume under concepts like composition, improvisation, performance practice, etc."[18]

Bruno Nettl had suggested as much in his widely cited "Thoughts on improvisation," where he maintained that "The improviser . . . always has something given to work from—certain things that are at the base of the performance," namely a *model* of "a series of obligatory musical events which must be observed either absolutely or with some sort of frequency, in order that the model remain intact" (1974, 11–12). In a later publication, Nettl (1998, 15) offered a different generalization: "improvisers always have a point of departure, something which they use to improvise upon. There are many types." Neither *point of departure* nor *referent* (as used by Pressing 1984, 346 and others) need be limited to "a series of obligatory events." *Model* is a serviceable term for diverse sets of expectations, as Leslie A. Tilley shows in a useful discussion of "variety in model specificity and flexibility," illustrated with a "continuum of overlapping terms for improvisation" extending from "formulaic variation" to "exploratory creativity" (Tilley 2019, 27–34).

Lortat-Jacob (1987, 46–49) outlined four types of model for improvisers, each composed of a finite number of elements that are more or less formalized and committed to memory, allowing in principle for an infinite number of realizations. Models whose formalization is precise and well established are best suited to that role in his view. Giannattasio, in the same collection of papers (1987, 243–44), described the "musical imaginary" of improvising musicians as "an ambiguous and complex gathering of perceptions, ideas, and behavioral schemas . . . which, if on one side it is realized as rules and formal models, on the other retains its dynamic in the modes of

CONCEPTS, MODELS, AND METAPHORS   95

treatment."[19] Tullia Magrini preferred a concept of *group plan* or *project* to Lortat-Jacob's conception of model, in order to focus on "a range of possibilities that constitute the very foundation of the activity of musical production, that is, the elements of a system of music which is open to various configurations" (Magrini 1993, 171–72, and 1998, 173). Even the briefest description of a plan or project will say or imply something about performers' intentions, which might involve avoiding or transcending models, as Giannattasio's remark on the "musical imaginary" suggests.

To what extent and in what ways are components of a model or group plan "formalized" or "open to various configurations" in specific situations? Expectations and desires of participants in a musical event, and the requisite competencies, are key factors. Ethnomusicologists have identified models that satisfy Lortat-Jacob's criteria of a finite number of elements, precisely formalized, by asking musicians to play or sing the simplest possible versions. In his study of polyrhythm and polyphony in Central Africa, Arom defines the *model* of a "musical entity" as "the pattern underlying each of its realisations, the 'skeleton' consisting of all the relevant features of the object to which its substance can be reduced" (Arom 1991, 168–69, 223). The Banda-Linda term àkɔ.nə (literally "husband, male"), used above all in teaching, designates the "simplest realisation of *each of the constituent parts of any musical entity.*" Arom has described in detail how he persuaded members of the *āngɔ̃* horn ensemble to play minimal versions of their parts, using one stereophonic tape recorder for playback of the whole and another to record each part as the performer listened to the playback through earphones (Arom 1974; 1976; 1985, 571–75; 1991, 370–73). He believed that musicians, in these abnormal circumstances of performance, would be "less likely to give free course to their creativity and improvisatory skills," hence more likely to concentrate on the "relevant features" (1976, 484). When he played recordings that reduced pieces in the *āngɔ̃* repertoire to each part's minimal formulas, listeners had no difficulty identifying each piece by name.

In a study of funeral music performed by men of the Fodonon group of the Senufo in Côte d'Ivoire, Michel de Lannoy (1987) was concerned with improvisation in realizing a *schema*, a *sequence* of seven modules rather than minimal formulas for each part in an

96 MUSIC THEORY IN ETHNOMUSICOLOGY

ensemble. He learned the schema by asking one performer to "sing the song" that had formed the basis of a twenty-minute performance by a *bolonyè* ensemble (literally "calabash people") of ten men who played single-string bow harps as pairs of men acted in turn as lead singer and second. Lannoy compared successive treatments of the schema in a performance by eight vocal duos, noting which modules each duo omitted, how many times they repeated each module, when they inserted an element foreign to the solo vocalist's version, and whether they sang in unison or in alternation. He tried to attribute some variants to "intentional musical behavior" (105), hence to "improvisation" rather than to chance. Lannoy's interest in identifying results of improvisation by comparing treatments of a Fodonon schema contrasts with Arom's assumption that improvisation would tend to obscure relevant features of a Banda-Linda model—a reminder of the tight relationship between interpretations of social action and choice of analytic terms and procedures. Both Arom and Lannoy explain their procedures in representing a model and schema, respectively, making the terms meaningful by connecting them to actions of musicians.

Regula Burckhardt Qureshi's monograph on the Sufi performance genre *qawwāli* describes "a process of interaction between the audience with its needs, and the performer, with the task of satisfying them" (1986, 75). Process and task, in her account, depend on "a model for sequencing the music which is broadly based on the textual structure" (73) and on "a common denominator which can act to generate some form of equivalence between musical and contextual variables" (135). What Qureshi termed the *code* of qawwāli offers "only a limited number of features with a limited degree of complexity [that] can be invested with contextual meaning" as the performer, the *qawwāl*, chooses from a few alternatives for each feature (229–30). More numerous and more complex alternatives would make it more difficult for qawwāls to satisfy needs and desires of specific audience members in turn. Qureshi's conception of *code* is indebted to the idea of *value* developed in the linguistics of Ferdinand de Saussure (1857–1913): each musical feature's value is determined by its differences from one or more alternatives as perceived by performers who must match musical features with contextual variables.

CONCEPTS, MODELS, AND METAPHORS   97

As a musicological concept, *model* works well enough in these and many other descriptions of musicking. It is the least problematic of the terms discussed in this chapter. A question like "What are the different types of model?" (posed by Lortat-Jacob and Tilley with respect to improvisation) probably allows for more useful answers than would the same question posed about *mode*.[20] Of terms commonly glossed as *melodic model*, Chinese *qupai* designates each unit of a "system of melodic models" that "is the very foundation upon which most Chinese music is based" (Thrasher, ed. 2016, viii). Other types of model include *conceptual model*, *generative model* (or *process model* as in Rovsing Olsen 2019), and *schema* as used by Lannoy in his account of Fodonon funeral music.

One conceptual model with a long history is the set of terms and topics treated in the *Nāṭyaśāstra* of Bharata, which "stands as a model even today for Indian musicologists" (Durga 1992, 156). Another is the sequence of seven major categories in the *Harmonics* of Aristoxenus (fourth century BCE), beginning with smaller units and proceeding to larger categories. It was retained in several subsequent Greek treatises (Mathiesen 2002, 120–29) and found its way into Arabic music theory (see the table of Greek and Arabic terms in Blum 2013, 115).

Ethnomusicologists often quote David Huron's definition of *schema* (2006, 419): "mental preconception of the habitual course of events." Qureshi's "model for sequencing the music" and Magrini's "group plan" might be regarded as process models or as schemas in Huron's sense. *Schema* is widely used in research on music cognition and in accounts of compositional process (see, further, Mavromatis 2005 and 2006; Widdess 2011; Gjerdingen and Bourne 2015). In Widdess's usage (2011, 192–94), *cognitive schema* covers "expectations based on the conventional patterns and structures" of a practice, including temporal schemas such as contours as well as pitch schemas with "hierarchical relationships among a group of defined pitches."

In his work on vernacular music of the United States, Nicholas Stoia has developed a conception of *scheme* as "a musical framework with certain constraints and allowances concerning the interaction of text, rhythm, harmony, and melody," which "generates discrete sections of musical form that correspond on a one-to-one basis with the verses of a song" (Stoia 2021, 18). In folk and popular music from the 1920s to

98   MUSIC THEORY IN ETHNOMUSICOLOGY

the end of World War II, he identified fifteen schemes in which "pre-existing harmonic grounds and melodic structures [were] common resources for the creation of songs" (Stoia 2013, 194), some of which allowed for greater variation in melody, others for greater variation in the rhythmic-harmonic cycle. Stoia's detailed study (2021) of a scheme he called *Sweet thing* after three versions of a "great song" printed by John and Alan Lomax (1947) required attention to a more complex "intertwining of the various musical components of many different sources, some with very deep roots in the past" (Stoia 2021, 2). A *scheme* allowing for changing relationships among multiple variables might draw upon more than one *cognitive schema* as defined by Widdess. Identifying variables among interrelated concepts, the topic of "Issues, 4" is one of the first problems to be faced in studying how musicians learn, remember, and alter such schemes.

Metaphors and Conceptual Metaphors

Aristotle's observation that metaphors bring things "before our eyes" by signifying them as "engaged in an activity" (*Rhetoric* 1411b) is consistent with an understanding of musicking as action that is capable of representing action,[21] which might suggest that metaphors would be prominent in discussions of musicking, as indeed they are. The flexibility of technical terms originating in metaphor can make them useful to musicians. The ambiguity and pliability of a metaphor like *the language of music* challenge efforts to specify just how musical "languages" resemble and differ from the spoken and written ones.[22] In contrast, *musical vocabulary*, *musical grammar*, and *musical rhetoric* commonly refer to specific procedures in performance, analysis, or pedagogy (as in Hughes 1991; Zbikowski 2017; Harnoncourt 1982; translated 1988).

The transformation of metaphors into technical terms was a major concern of the *metaphorology* developed by the philosopher Hans Blumenberg (1920–96).[23] In arguing that metaphors, especially those he termed *absolute metaphors* (such as "Probability"), have long served to designate totalities that resist a fully rational explication, at least for a time, Blumenberg (1998 [1960], 10–11], trans. 2010, 3–4) contrasted René Descartes' advocacy of clear concepts (in his *Discours de la méthode* of 1637) with the "poetic logic" of Giambattista Vico's "new science" (*Scienza nuova*, 3rd edn. 1744).[24] The philosopher Max Black (1909–88) similarly argued that "We need the metaphors in just the cases when there can be no question as yet of the precision of a scientific statement" (Black 1962 [1954]). Eve Feder Kittay (1987, 7) describes the models of scientists as "extended metaphors—not literally true, but useful representations of the phenomena which often led to fruitful theoretic conceptions and new empirical discoveries." Ethnomusicologists should not assume that musicians with whom we converse would prefer clear, scientifically precise concepts to the evocative metaphors of their theorizing and teaching.

In *Metaphors we live by* (1980), George Lakoff and Mark Johnson began to explore a relation between concept and metaphor that has attracted considerable attention from music theorists. Lakoff and Johnson argue that "most of our normal conceptual system is metaphorically structured" (1980, 58), in large part through "metaphors based on simple physical concepts" (61) such as up or down, hot or cold, light or heavy, active or at rest. Grounding of metaphors in physical experience generates affinities among multiple metaphors, and those associated with musicking are often linked by relations of analogy. When words used in speaking about music might suggest correlations or analogies with other actions or their outcomes, the speakers and listeners may ignore any such suggestions.

Lakoff and Johnson defined *conceptual metaphors* as "cross-domain mappings" whose *source domains* usually lie closer to our immediate physical experience than their *target domains*.[25] Music theorists interested in conceptual metaphor theory (e.g., Saslaw 1996; Cox 1999 and 2016; Zbikowski 2002; Johnson and Larson 2003; Perlman 2004; Spitzer 2004; Larson 2012) tend to treat music as a target domain, but without necessarily assuming that the source is closer to immediate physical experience.[26] From her ethnographic work among Berber farmers in the Anti-Atlas of Morocco, Miriam Rovsing Olsen (2004 and 2019) identified terms associated with growth processes of barley and date palms as the source domain for the terminology of the performance genre *aḥwaš*—a good example of terms that users would associate with physical experience in both domains. Music-theoretical metaphors such as *swing* and *groove* in American English refer directly

100   MUSIC THEORY IN ETHNOMUSICOLOGY

to physical experience, and "metaphors of technology" in the discourse of rock musicians refer to their interactions with electronic "gear" as well as with one another (Gay 1998). Hornbostel regarded "melodic movement" (*Melodiebewegung*) as "a case of physiological correlation and not a mere play of associations," hence "not a metaphor" (1904 in Hornbostel 1975, 208). The nature of that "physiological correlation" continues to attract the attention of researchers (see Clarke 2005, 63–76), and Hornbostel's premise that "melodic movement dominates a much larger sphere than the purely musical" (1975, 210) is consistent with much current work in ethnomusicology.

Mark Johnson and Steve Larson (2003, 66–76) see "two basic spatialization metaphors for time"—*moving time* and *moving observer*—as sources of three metaphors of musical motion: *moving music, musical landscape,* and *moving force.* Terms in many languages for a *path* followed or forged in performance connect all three. Such concept pairs as *movings force/landscape, activating/stabilizing, departure/return, foreground/background,* and *initiator/respondent* are hard to avoid in theorizing about music, given the emphasis in so many practices on coordinating energies and situations.

The source/target model applies well to processes of transferring portions of one field of activity's vocabulary to another field—as when Chinese writers on poetry and painting adopted musical terminology (DeWoskin 1983) and when European rhetorical terminology was applied to painting at the time of Giotto (Baxandall 1971) and later on to music (Wilson 1995; Zbikowski 2002, 291–99). Terms with clear definitions in a source domain, such as *point* and *line* in mathematics or *energy* in physics, generally lose that clarity when applied to music.[27] *Progress,* such a major concern of projects discussed in Chapter Three, was often more clearly defined in some other areas of social life than in music.

Some metaphors and analogies current among musicians (e.g., musical *material* and musical *progress*) have numerous potential sources.[28] Nicholas Cook (2014, 262) observes that "thinking of music in terms of quasi-material structure is more characteristic of the twentieth century than the eighteenth or even nineteenth," when metaphors relating to social interaction were more common. The familiar textbook definition of *rhythm* as "the organization of time" may not be appropriate to musicking in societies where "organizing time" is not the issue it became in those marked by efforts to control productivity following the time studies of Frederick W. Taylor (1856–1915). Without reflecting on implications of one's everyday language, it is impossible to understand experiences of people whose actions have been subject to very different sets of constraints.[29]

The formation of a music-theoretical discourse tends to foster a shared conception of the sources or analogues most pertinent to its key metaphors. Western European readers of the treatise on linear counterpoint (1917) by Ernst Kurth (1886–1946) could recognize *musical energy* as a metaphor drawn from physics, whereas Boris Asaf'yev (1884–1949), a prominent Russian admirer of Kurth's work, insisted that social theory was the source of the concept of musical *dynamics* or *kinetics* developed in his *Musical form as process* (1930, translated in Tull 1977, 183–564). Musical energy and musical dynamics in the work of these theorists and their followers exemplify what Rice (2003, 165) calls "the two sides of the coin of metaphor: its capacity to frame our understanding when taken as true, near, and obvious and its capacity to alter and reconfigure our understanding when taken as surprising, far, and insightful."

Continuing Issues

Ethnomusicologists inevitably become involved in translation, even if only with respect to one language's social or regional dialects, and the work of translation can direct attention to subtle differences as well as commonalities. Efforts to identify abstractions for which there are multiple terms (as well as the questions humans have addressed with those terms) requires close attention to each term's specific implications and to circumstances in which it has been used. As researchers attempt to judge how well multiple terms used in discourse about music refer to a single abstract concept, readiness to recognize discrepancies is crucial. Recognition of discrepancies was the function to be served by an *ideal type* in the sociology of Max Weber, each of which was to be "a purely ideal *limiting* concept against which reality is *measured*—with which it is *compared*—in

102   MUSIC THEORY IN ETHNOMUSICOLOGY

order to bring out certain significant component parts of the empirical substance of [that reality]" (Weber 2012, 127).[30]

Terms and concepts acquire new relationships to others, hence new meanings, as they pass from one discourse or conceptual model to another. This chapter looked at usage of two terms for musical resources, *mode* and *model*, and three for musicking—*composition*, *performance*, and *improvisation*. Of the five, *model* is the most likely to have close analogues in multiple languages and the least likely to carry usages in one musical practice into discourse about others. It is free of associations with such dichotomies as *orality/literacy* or lists of features purporting to define *mode* or *improvisation*. Both *composition* and *improvisation*, with their analogues in other languages, can refer to processes with successive phases involving different participants; they do not always designate a pair of alternatives. *Mode* is firmly established in musicological discourse as a component of diverse conceptual models in which its meanings vary and need to be specified. Its history in the twentieth century should be enough to convince music scholars that a musical term, like any other, will "change in meaning according to the power that appropriates it" (Deleuze 1962, 4, with reference to Nietzsche on genealogy).

There are times when theorizing about music requires precisely defined terms, and times when metaphors and analogies are more helpful in developing or communicating ideas about what musicians are doing or could do. Those deriving from immediate physical experience can prove especially useful in theorizing from a cluster of associations. Benamou (2010, 58n1) cites a linguist's observation that "scientific terminology is a special case in which complete consensus about word meaning is explicitly sought" (Lehrer 1983), to make the point that terms associated with the Javanese concept of *rasa* ("taste, feeling, affect, mood, inner meaning, faculty of taste, intuition, deep understanding") "are not meant to be scientific." The extent to which people involved in communicating music theories aspire to consensus varies greatly, as do ways of seeking or resisting consensus.

A closely related issue turns up in discussion of *categories* and classification. Zbikowski (2002, 39–42) contrasts *natural* with *artificial* or *classical* categories, the former "so named based on their emergence from the interaction of humans with their natural environment" and

CONCEPTS, MODELS, AND METAPHORS 103

the latter identified by "individually necessary and jointly sufficient conditions" or features. He calls them Type 1 and Type 2, respectively, and mentions the suggestion of Rosch and Mervis (1975) that Type 1 categories "were organized around a stable cognitive construct called a *prototype*" that allowed for distinguishing between more typical and less typical instances. To Perlman (2004, 19) these are "'non-classical,' probabilistic, or family-resemblance categories" rather than "natural." Chapter Five returns to the distinction between natural and artificial via Kartomi's work on classifications of musical instruments.

104   MUSIC THEORY IN ETHNOMUSICOLOGY

Issues, 4: Variables among Interrelated Concepts

In addition to *mode*, such terms as *tone, interval, tuning, scale, contour,* and *tone system* refer to concepts whose meanings depend on their relationships to other concepts. The perceptual realities designated by each of those concepts are likely to have different ranges of acceptable variability as musicians and listeners act and make judgments. Generalizing from her extensive experience in Sumatra, Kartomi warned (2012, xii) that tables giving a researcher's measurements of pitches can "distort local aesthetic attitudes, forcing on them an uncharacteristic concept of in-tuneness in place of the artists' and audiences' usual tolerance of pitch variability." Researchers should not assume that the measurements they make on one occasion represent a norm and can only learn the extent to which variability of pitches (or of whatever) is tolerated by gathering reliable data.

A good example of doing just that is Wim van Zanten's empirical study of "tuning behavior" among Sundanese players of the large zither *kacapi indung* who perform the vocal genre *Tembang Sunda.* Van Zanten (1986, 105) found that "the tuning process is well-articulated by the musicians in that they display a very similar tuning behavior" with respect to the three recognized *models* of tuning. He learned that a singer's melodies and those played on the bamboo flute *suling* or spike-fiddle *rebab* (but not on the large *kacapi*) could include tones from any of the models.

Klaus Wachsmann had connected measurement of results with observation of the relevant actions in his account of three stages followed by the Muganda musician Temuseo Mukasa in tuning the harp *ennanga* (1950). Mukasa began by tuning the first string to the highest pitch, close to G4, then the second string to a pitch about 240 cents lower, replicating this process for the remaining strings before testing them in groups of three to ensure that the intervals in what Wachsmann called "an equal-stepped pentatonic tuning" were close enough to a *norm* of roughly 235 to 250 cents.[31] Mukasa then checked the octaves formed by strings 1 and 6, 2 and 7, 3 and 8. When Wachsmann observed forty-seven operations performed by a maker and tuner of an *amadinda* xylophone, he found them applying the same norm (Wachsmann 1957, 12–13).

In the 1960s Kubik revisited the question of whether the pentatonic tuning of the *ennanga, amadinda* xylophone, and other Baganda

CONCEPTS, MODELS, AND METAPHORS 105

and Basoga instruments was in fact "equal-stepped" (1994, 55–58, 258–64, 406n9), concluding that "in the Kiganda musical system there is nothing like a concept of minor thirds as opposed to seconds, but musicians have in mind instead a standard interval, that may be tuned wider or smaller, but is still considered to be the same interval. It is about +/- 240 cents wide. I should like to call this standard interval a Kiganda second" (259). He found that Kiganda tunings of an "octave" (*myanjo*) must be at least slightly wider or narrower than a perfect octave (58) and subsequently proposed the term *toneme* for "intraculturally conceptualized pitch values" (Kubik 1999, 20) by analogy with *phoneme* and *lexeme* in linguistics.

From the 1960s onward empirical studies of margins of tolerance in tuning and intonation have provided a control over conventional representations of scale and mode. Jairazbhoy and Stone (1963) showed that analysis of the intonation of Hindustani vocalists and instrumentalists made from oscillograms did not support the venerable Indian conception of twenty-two *śrutis* within an octave. Rather, the twelve tones of an octave in equal temperament fall "within the tolerance allowed in the intonation of the various notes of the scales commonly used in North Indian classical music," adding that performers used the term *śruti* in discussing specific ragas that require "consciously flattening or sharpening, or more often shaking the note from slightly above to slightly below [the] usual note" (Jairazbhoy and Stone 1963, 129–30).

In their research on the singing of Palestinian Arabs, Dalia Cohen and Ruth Katz used a melograph to measure the *scatter* (range of variation) of each interval of a second as well as variability of pitch in each scale degree. Cohen found that "each *maqam* imposes a specific pattern of deviation"; its identity is maintained, in part, by seconds of different sizes due to a greater or lesser range of variation in the pitch of specific scale degrees (Carmi-Cohen 1964, 104). Cohen and Katz developed a conception of *modal framework* in which *tonal skeleton* (Cohen and Katz 1967, 161–64) or *intonation skeleton* (Cohen and Katz 2006, 327) is one factor among others, each potentially "important to a different degree, and in a different way" (Cohen 1971, 56).

Arom and his collaborators in experiments carried out in the late 1980s used a Yamaha DX 7 II FD synthesizer to alter the intervals of melodies familiar to the Central African musicians they asked to accept

106   MUSIC THEORY IN ETHNOMUSICOLOGY

or reject the altered versions. Musicians were filmed as they tried to reproduce melodies on the synthesizer; also filmed were sessions where musicians and bystanders judged the various tunings. Arom and Susanne Fürniss concluded (1992, 171) that the succession of degrees is more important than the size of intervals for BaAka singers; they added (1993, 11) that thinking of a scale as "a mental template, a kind of mental grid" is not consistent with these findings. That conclusion would have pleased Hornbostel, who suggested that "what matters in pure melody is not a precise but only an approximate interval size" (Hornbostel 1910, 479).[32]

Two other participants in Arom's project, Vincent Dehoux and Frédéric Voisin, attached plywood bars to the synthesizer keyboard, so that xylophonists of the Manza, Ngbaka-Manza, Gbaya, and Banda Gba-Mbia ethnicities could strike the bars in the normal manner and alter any programmed tunings they rejected. Dehoux and Voisin recognized (1992, 179) that, with respect to the xylophone practices of these four peoples, *scale* is best understood as "an ensemble with two dimensions," pitch and timbre, "to which we must add the factor of roughness . . . at the intersection of these two dimensions." Placing a wide bar over two white synthesizer keys tuned 30 cents apart allowed players to create a rougher tone by sounding both at once, and the researchers synthesized sounds in which the first harmonic was 15, 25, 50, 17, 85, or 100 cents sharp in order to emulate the inharmonic timbres produced by mirlitons normally attached to the resonators of xylophone bars. Preferred rates of inharmonicity were found to vary considerably among the four populations (see also Dehoux and Voisin 1993).

Both the margin of tolerance for interval sizes and the degree of interest in reproducing precise frequencies are major variables in both *scale* and *tone system*. Frequency measurements of a Pitjantjatjara song from Central Australia made by Catherine Ellis and Udo Will showed "a degree of precision never before reported for any vocal music" (Will and Ellis 1996, 212). In the 1960s Ellis had already recognized that Central Australian singers reproduce specific frequencies with remarkable accuracy, and she questioned the assumption that scales and tone systems have no relevance in purely vocal practices[33] as well as the belief that perception of pitch differences is necessarily based on frequency ratios (Ellis 1965, 127). In a series of publications extending over three decades and including a lengthy analysis of a Pitjantjatjara

CONCEPTS, MODELS, AND METAPHORS   107

Kangaroo song (Ellis 1967), she accumulated evidence that in this vocal practice scales are "governed by steps of equal numbers of [Hertz] (or multiples of steps of equal numbers of [Hertz])" (1965, 135). Ellis used frequency-duration graphs to identify "peak frequencies" emphasized by performers, sometimes with ornamentation. A restudy of the Kangaroo song, undertaken with Will and benefitting from technological advances, showed that the "peaks represent a network of fix points throughout which the melodic line is spun" (Will and Ellis 1996, 199). Within a range of about 100 Hz, this "fixed frequency" space had "a non-equidistant arrangement of frequency steps," which allowed for "exact linear transposition" of the sequence 151, 154.5 and 158 Hz to 231, 234 and 238 Hz (202). Thus, the 1965 hypothesis of "a scale governed by steps of equal numbers of [Hz]" was falsified as the conception of a linear frequency system was affirmed, with two qualifications: some transpositions do appear to maintain frequency ratios, and shifting a sequence of intervals requires "slight changes of at least some intervals to match those frequency 'slots' provided by the [non-equidistant] tonal space" (213).

Results of these case studies challenged familiar conceptions: those of 22 *śrutis* to the octave in Hindustani music, of Central African scales as "mental templates," and of frequency ratios as the sole basis for perception of pitch differences in Central Australian singing. While some results are consistent with Hornbostel's "supposition" (*Annahme*) that "only an approximate interval size" matters in "purely melodic music," Ellis and Will's findings show the opposite.

In W. Jay Dowling's "two-component model of how melodies are stored in long and short-term memory" *scale* is an "overlearned perceptual-motor scheme" and *contour* functions "independently of pitch interval sequence in memory" (Dowling 1978). He subsequently maintained (1982, 20) that "an actual melody—perceived or produced—is the result of hanging a particular contour . . . on a modal-scale structure." Ethnomusicologists can treat this thesis as a question: in situations when musicians are engaged with tunings do we find evidence that perception and production of melodic contours presuppose a modal-scale structure?[34] The case studies reviewed here provide good reasons not to attach terms like *scale* to abstract concepts severed from perception of the relevant variables.

5
Relationships among Names and Terms

Musicians cannot act without recognizing and comparing distinctive features of sounds, movements, sequences of these, and circumstances of performance. Names and terms often prove helpful for registering, remembering, and teaching *sets* of these features and exploring their interrelationships. It is hard to coin, learn, or use a name or term without some sense of how it relates or could relate to others, and musicians sometimes make their reasons for recognizing relationships among referents of names and terms explicit in words and deeds. Ethnomusicologists are apt to take terms "as clues to cognition relating to music and musicians" (Sakata 1983, 106), knowing that people also attend to actions and events not marked with terms.

Important research on music theory (e.g., Qureshi 2007 and Macchiarella 2009) has resulted from participating in and documenting "Conversation as a cultural activity" (Keating and Egbert 2004), with attention to acts and circumstances of enunciation as well as to what is spoken or written (see Pandolfo 1997, 3–6). Listening to discussion of ideas about musicking, an ethnomusicologist can quickly enough identify the terms used in articulating issues, but it is never easy to develop a sense of their interrelationships and of different ways that speakers use terms and metaphors.

With a nod to J. L. Austin's *How to do things with words* (1975 [1962]), this chapter looks at things done with words and morphemes in theorizing, such as

naming parts of a whole for various purposes

positing or exploring analogies among two or more polarities

reflecting on other actual and potential relationships among names and terms.

Music Theory in Ethnomusicology. Stephen Blum, Oxford University Press.
© Oxford University Press 2023. DOI: 10.1093/oso/9780199303526.003.0006

RELATIONSHIPS AMONG NAMES AND TERMS 109

Table 5.1 lists eight common referents of names, terms, and metaphors in theories focused on musical action; many more could be added.

The existing literature is richer in lists of terms than in transcripts of statements, conversations, and narratives that document usage. Transcripts and translations of *feedback interviews* in which participants in a performance discuss their reactions to a recording of the event are rarely included in publications, despite the good example of Ruth M. Stone's study of performance events among the Kpelle of Liberia (1982, 138–57). Chapter Two mentioned Ignazio Macchiarella's "polyvocal study" (*studio a più voci*) of Sardinian multipart singing (2009), which offers extensive extracts from his conversations with four singers, and Qureshi's translations of "orally transmitted words that are generated not declaratively but interactively" (2007, 3).

Table 5.1. Common referents of names, terms, and metaphors in music theories

1. Distinctive attributes of movements and sounds

2. Locations (in the vocal apparatus, on an instrument, in a performance space, etc.)

    where sounds with specific qualities are produced; or the sounds produced at those locations

3. Distinctive attributes of performance occasions and situations

4. Participants in one genre of performance or composition, each charged with

    specific responsibilities and disposing of a range of options; the roles or parts performed by these participants and the requisite skills

5. Moments, or phases, in a sequence of actions; patterns appropriate to those moments or phases

6. Individual components recognized within a larger whole, such as a *stroke, sound/tone, interval* (distance between two tones, moments, locations), *phase, section*

7. Aggregates such as a system of intervals, roster of components, coordinated set of parts, or inventory of locations or sounds

8. Items in a repertory of two or more sequences of action, or types of performance event

110 MUSIC THEORY IN ETHNOMUSICOLOGY

Kubik (2010, 7–8) proposed a rigorous standard for what he terms an "intra-culturally oriented study" in which "all information . . . would be written or transcribed in the dialect of the place, preserving informants' individual styles of expression" while "the researcher's own observations . . . would be written in his/her own language." Adoption of that standard could foster the development of intracultural scholarship sensitive to local languages and dialects while supporting multicultural and cross-cultural studies based on reliable data. Four contributions to a Festschrift for Kubik include transcripts of interviews alongside translations or commentaries.[1] An alternative, used by Benamou (2010, 159–70) for two Indonesian conversations on the Javanese concept of *rasa*, is to publish English translations "with key terms left in the original."

The value of "preserving informants' individual styles of expression" alongside translations of their words should increase as archives digitize more ethnomusicological holdings (including fieldnotes) and make them available on websites.[2] With adequate documentation, ethnomusicologists can try to judge how well concepts we think with in our mother tongues relate to theories and practices of musicians who speak, read, and think in languages that may appear to lack words for those concepts. Ideally, researchers would be able to check transcripts of conversations and interviews against audio or video recordings of the events, and could register rhythmic, melodic, and gestural dimensions of exchanges between researcher and subject. As George Steiner has written (2011, 13), "Argument, even analytic, has its drumbeat" (see Lortat-Jacob 1998b on "musical analysis of a spoken text").

Sets of Names and Terms

Sets of names or terms for sounds, actions, events, and sequences of these are common results of theorizing concerned with their attributes and functions, grouped together for such purposes as identifying sounds available on an instrument and movements that produce or respond to them, comparing their distinctive qualities, and spelling out possible sequences.

RELATIONSHIPS AMONG NAMES AND TERMS   111

Al-Fārābī outlined relationships of names to sounds in his *Great book on music* (*Kitāb al-mūsīqā al-kabīr*) of the tenth century CE: some names are based on qualities (*kayfiyyat*) of sounds as perceived by the ear, some are based on "resemblances" (*ashbāh*) between aural perceptions and those involving vision or touch, and some are composed of phonemes imitating musical sounds (Fārābī 1967, 1069–70; English translation in Madian 1992, 270–71; French translation in Erlanger 1935, 57). Al-Fārābī registered four names linked to techniques of vocal production and noted the absence of names for other techniques.

His typology is still useful. Names with an iconic relation to a sound frequently stand for both the sound and how to produce it. Syllables for each sound and action in a set of two or more are often composed of two or three phonemes representing successive moments of an event: a consonant for the attack, a vowel for the emergent timbre, and possibly a second consonant for the termination. Variants of the syllables *dum* and *tak* are widely used from North Africa to Central Asia to represent an undamped stroke at the center of a circular membranophone or idiophone and a sharper hit on the rim. Larger sets of syllables for drum strokes exploit similar contrasts among initial and final consonants of syllables (see Tenzer 2000, 261–69, on drumming in Balinese *gamelan gong keybar*). Such sets of names for timbres linked to actions result from analytic thinking that labels attributes of an event's successive phases in combinations musicians need to learn and remember. The names register phonemic contrasts, with or without terms for *attack*, *consonant*, *continuation*, *vowel*, or *termination* to make the implicit theory more explicit.

A name composed of two or three phonemes may also designate both a specific scale degree and its location on an instrument. The solmization system explained to Giannattasio by Dionigi Burranca, a master of the Sardinian triple-clarinet *launeddas*, uses the contrast between a retroflex plosive and an alveolar plosive (written respectively as *dd* and *d*) to distinguish the tones of two conjunct tetrachords. On instruments with the tuning (*kunsertu*) known as *fiorassiu in do*, these are *ddo dda dde do* (equivalent to *sol la si do* in conservatory solmization) and *do da de di* (equivalent to *do re mi fa*); scale degrees within a tetrachord are distinguished by the vowels *-o*, *-a*, *-e*, and *-i* in that

112 MUSIC THEORY IN ETHNOMUSICOLOGY

order. Tones of the lower tetrachord are available on the mid-length pipe *mankosa manna*, those of the upper tetrachord (plus *ddo*) on the smaller pipe *mankosedda* (Giannattasio 1985, 216).

Names for strokes of the hand learned by players of the Chinese *qin* (a seven-string zither) designate motions involving one or more of three oppositions: inward or outward, upward or downward, use of thumb or a specific finger of left or right hand (Yung 1984 and 1997, 79–86; Gulik 1969, 126–38). Modifications of syllables for individual tones can convey information about the next event in a sequence, as in the notations of seven compositions inscribed on rocks at Kudumiyāmalai, Tamil Nadu, South India, dating from the seventh or eighth century CE. Widdess (1979 and 1995, 106–15) made a strong case for the hypothesis that vowels in the seven conventional solmization syllables (*sa ri ga ma pa dha ni*) were modified so that six sequences ($u + e, e + a, a + i, u + a, e + i, u + i$) would signify a melodic ascent and six contrasting sequences ($i + a, a + e, e + u, i + e, a + u, i + u$) a descent. The sequences, like those for the *launeddas*, respect the register of the vowels' second formants, *u* being the lowest and *i* the highest. David W. Hughes (2000) recognized this principle in several sets of syllables used in East Asia and elsewhere (which he called *acoustic-iconic mnemonic systems*), with melodic ascent represented by vowels with higher second formants.

Phonemic contrasts may also serve to convey information about qualities of a pattern's successive attacks and the requisite motions. Well-known examples are the elaborate systems of syllables used by Hindustani and Karnatak drummers to generate "syllabic chains in which (1) the same stroke may be represented by a number of different syllables depending on the context; and (2) the same syllable may be chosen to represent different, although sonically appropriate, sounds" (Rowell 1992, 142). With further research we may learn to recognize systems less elaborate than (or not spelled out as explicitly as) those of the Hindustani *bols* (from Hindu-Urdu *bolnā* "to speak") and Karnatak *śolkaṭṭu* (literally "words bound together" in Tamil).[3] Richard Wolf describes relationships of syllable to stroke and tone articulated by South Asian musicians (Wolf 2014, 20–22, 61–74, 91–114, and *passim*), with numerous examples of "the grounding of drum patterns in verbal, motivic, and beat patterns"

RELATIONSHIPS AMONG NAMES AND TERMS 113

(113) and a table of "various kinds of pattern names and their relationships" (62–64).

Syllables composed of two or three phonemes often represent what Kubik (1990, 132) terms *kinemes*, "the smallest discernable action units that seem to be significant for the performer." He analyzes mnemonic formulas for several so-called *time-line* patterns (Kubik 2010, 65–84) to test his hypothesis of "a firm and fairly standardized relation between speech-sounds, timbres and motor action, valid probably throughout wide areas of West and Central Africa" (1972a, 176), while noting that "Considerable comparative research will have to be carried out to find a reliable answer to this question" (2010, 83).[4] In a study of *verbal representation of instrumental sounds* among the Luvale of northwestern Zambia, Tsukada Kenichi (1997, revised 2002) found evidence of a "principle of inverse representation" whereby "high" (*helu*) and "light" (*lelu*) syllables designate a drum's "low" (*heshi*) and "heavy" (*lemu*) sounds, and vice versa; his notations coordinate sequences of syllables with types of stroke and areas of the membrane to which they are directed.

Sequences of syllables that represent time-lines and other patterns result from analysis of such features as (1) actions of the hand or hands, (2) differences in timbre and duration, (3) silence or continuation of a sound with no new attack, (4) number of attacks and silent pulses in a time-line, and (5) articulation of a time-line into two segments of unequal duration. Kubik was right that the topic invites comparative research. The work of Yung, Widdess, Hughes, Wolf, and Tsukada should also inspire further attempts to identify and enumerate distinctions among sounds and motions that musicians articulate in syllables used for teaching and remembering patterns. As Kubik's terms *toneme* and *kineme* (emulating *phoneme*) suggest, these are likely to be systematic to some extent, whether devised on the spur of the moment or learned as a set of conventional names. Thomas Porcello's research on the "structured, technical lexicon of timbre" that he experienced in American recording studios extends work on this topic into what are now major sites of musical production in much of the world. His outline of four types of "Structure of onomatopoeic forms" (Porcello 2004, 327) provides a framework with which to describe other sets of syllables and words, and to compare those used in recording studios

114   MUSIC THEORY IN ETHNOMUSICOLOGY

with older sets devised for teaching and remembering patterns (see also Porcello 1996).

To name only five common types, a set of terms for parts of a whole may designate actions required for a ceremony to fulfil its purpose, skills expected of performers in a given role, essential constituents of an art, emotions commonly experienced in musicking, and desirable attributes of a performance or composition. Reasons for identifying a whole and enumerating a fixed or variable number of its parts, and the principles (if any) by which they are ordered, are sometimes self-evident. Lines in an oral epic may answer the implicit question, "What skills or attributes does this role or genre require?" Susan S. Wadley (1989, 75) quotes the opening invocation of the northern Indian oral epic *Dholā*: "'Oh (Goddess), I have need of four things: beat, throat, voice and wisdom,' . . . (*Cāri cīz mange mile; tāl kanṭh svar gyān.*)." Oft-repeated maxims may enumerate the skills that those performing a particular role are expected to have mastered. For a singer (*kwangdae*) of the Korean vocal genre *p'ansori*, these are the "four great laws of the kwangdae": presence, narrative, voice, gesture (Pihl 1994, 96–97 and Song 1976). In northeastern Iran a bard (*bakhshi*) should have a good hand (*panje*) for playing the *dotār* (a long-necked lute with two strings), a good voice (*sedā*) for singing verses, and clear speech (*bayān*) for presenting prose portions of narratives; some bards add expertise in conducting or animating a gathering of listeners (Youssefzadeh 2002, 58, 60). The analogous roster of skills for an Azerbaijani bard (*aşıq*), whose instrument is the long-necked lute called *saz*, includes all four of these plus a fifth, dancing, which bards of northeastern Iran and neighboring Turkmenistan avoid in order not to lose status.

Polarities, Complementarities, and Analogies

Distinctions among sounds and movements may take the form of binary oppositions that register *presence or absence* of a given feature: plus or minus, on or off, one or zero, genes activated or not by proteins, *Da!* "there" or *Fort!* "away" in the games of Sigmund Freud's grandson (Freud 1920, 12–15; Bonnet 2005).[5] Oppositions of *more or less* may extend in positive and negative directions from a neutral center or may define extremes of a continuum without positing a neutral center. Polarities of a third type are complements that coexist or can be joined to yield a desired result—as in some understandings of *theory* and *practice*. Attention to complementarities (many of which are *not* polar opposites) can lead to heightened awareness of how "It's all connected," a recognition shared by many ethnomusicologists (e.g., McAllester 2006, 203) and voiced elsewhere in the world before Alexander von Humboldt propagated it in Europe.

All humans experience differences between presence and absence, greater or lesser relevance of a given quantity or quality, and complementarity. The same words (e.g., *male* and *female*) may refer to differences of all three types, and as constituents of music theories any of them can evoke rich fields of analogy. Theorizing about musical activity depends heavily on polarities that can posit analogies among modes of perception and areas of experience and that can also suggest further relationships of analogy among multiple polarities: male/female, penetrating/absorbing, mobile/stable, figure/ground, acute/grave, high/low, tense/lax, hard/soft, compact/diffuse, clear/muddy, refined/coarse, contracting/expanding, closed/open, small/large, short/long, light/heavy, happy/sad, fast/slow, strong/weak, young/old, close/distant, attractive/repulsive, hot/cool, inward/outward, and so on. Human ears are sensitive to these discriminations, which are productive sources of conceptual metaphor and generate vocabularies for theorizing about sound and musicking. Definitions that improve on the thirteen "specific oppositions" of Robert Cogan's "phonological theory" of timbre (1984, 133–40)[6] could provide a basis for describing perceptions to which words for these polarities refer.

Enumeration of a fixed number of constituents (such as four, seven, eight, or twelve) often results from pursuit of analogies among parts of more than one whole: scale degrees correlated with a roster of emotions or constellation of celestial bodies, for example.[7] The polarity of summer and winter solstices is easily extended to take in both equinoxes, and further division yields the eight seasons correlated with directions and material sources of musical sound in the ancient Chinese doctrines summarized by Needham and Robinson (1962, 153–60; also Kartomi 1990, 37–39). The seasons and directions are defined by polarities, but the roster of sources of musical sound is not.

116 MUSIC THEORY IN ETHNOMUSICOLOGY

Classification schemes based on multiple polarities and other "characters of division" are treated throughout Kartomi's *On concepts and classifications of musical instruments* (1990), the first survey of this major concern of music theory worldwide. Figures in her book display formats for representing four common types of classification: *taxonomies* (with characters of division that "are 'natural' to the culture or group"), *keys* (which align "dichotomous oppositions in several steps"), and *paradigms* and *typologies*, both of which represent the intersection of multiple dimensions (Kartomi 1990, 17–22). The latter two differ in the same way taxonomies and keys do: "A paradigm is normally a natural culture-emerging phenomenon, whereas a typology is always the construct of the observer" (21). Kartomi notes (17) that certain paradigms (the Chinese correlation of seasons, directions, and sources of sound among them) can be represented as mandalas. Paradigms and typologies are not necessarily structured around polarities or symmetrical divisions, nor are the formats scholars use in analyzing relationships among terms limited to those constructed around polarities, prominent though the latter have been (and remain) in theories of music.

Writing on classification of individual maqāms within the *Irāqi maqām*, S. Q. Hassan lists three polarities in general use among performers and eight more discussed by a major theorist, al-Sheykh Jalāl al-Hanafi, "who deduced them from his observation of musical practice." She notes that four of al-Hanafi's categories "use metaphoric descriptions and are often personal": strong/weak, small/big, light/heavy, and easy/difficult (S. Q. Hassan 2008, 109–13; summarized in Blum 2015a, 62–63). In other words, musicians and listeners engaged with the vocal genre can find those distinctions relevant to their experience of different maqāms without agreeing on the details.

Sets with three, five, or seven constituents invite consideration of complementary relationships that are not always reducible to polarities. Tripartite models can distinguish successive moments of a brief event or successive phases of a performance or composition. Japanese *jo-ha-kyu* "introduction, scattering, rushing" (Malm 1986, 347) or "introduction-exposition-denouement" (Malm 1959, 110) is applied on many rhythmic levels and "has the tenacity of the theory of question and answer, arsis and thesis in Western music" (ibid., 102). The Japanese sequence bears comparison with three terms developed by the composer-theorist Olivier Messiaen (1908–92) for analysis of rhythm: *anacrouse-accent-désinence* (Messiaen 1994, 48–49).

The Chinese aesthetic theory outlined in the *Rhymeprose on literature* of Lu Chi (261–303 CE) stresses the interdependence of five attributes that control one another's tendencies to excess: *ying* "response," *ho* "harmony," *pei* "gravity of feeling," *ya* "restraint in expression," and *yen* "richness of texture." DeWoskin (1983, 189), citing Jao Tsung-i's thesis that Lu Chi's terminology comes from "the tradition of music theorizing," analyzes the constraints placed on each quality by one or two of the others in terms of three polarities: "variety versus sameness," "unison versus harmony," and "accord, correspondence, and harmony versus loneliness and profundity of individual sentiment" (205).[8]

Recognizing three constituents of a larger whole was a fundamental premise of musical thought in ancient India and ancient Greece. The Sanskrit *Nātya śāstra* (ca. 200 CE) names tones (*svara*), time-cycles (*tāla*), and words (*pada*) as the components of *gāndharva* (ceremonial music) and also identifies song (*gāna*), instrumental music (*vādya*), and acting (*nātya*) as constituents of drama.[9] Two prominent tripartite models in Plato's dialogues were taken up or alluded to in later theoretical writings: *logos, harmonia,* and *rhythmos* as constituents of *melos* (*Republic* 398D; cf. Aristotle's *Poetics* 1447a) and a model, applicable to "all arts," of measuring (*metrein*), numbering (*arithmein*), and weighing (*isthanai*) (*Republic* 602D; *Philebus* 55E; *Laws* 757B and *Euthyphro* 7BC).[10] The first triad furnished a point of departure for the European theorists and musicians of subsequent centuries who argued about the proper relations among two or all three constituents (as noted in Strunk 1950, xvi).

A single term may designate musical perception or judgment engaging two or more senses without implying a polar opposite. Barbara Tedlock glosses the Zuñi term *tso'ya* as "multicolored, chromatic (in the musical sense), clear, bright, sharp, new, dynamic, varied and beautiful." She contrasts uses of *tso'ya* in evaluating perceptions that are visual, auditory, or both with uses of such alternatives as *attani* "powerful, taboo, dark, muffled, shaggy, old, static and fearful" and *k'okshi* "attractive or good" (Tedlock 1986, 189–90). Neither alternative is the polar opposite of polysemous *tso'ya*; rather, "the contrary of *tso'ya* . . . is *kwa' tso'ya* or 'not multicolored, not clear, not beautiful.'" Zuñi participants in a discussion of 116 recorded songs judged 30 of them to be *k'okshi* but only four to be *tso'ya* (Tedlock 1980, 32). Tedlock (1986, 193) interprets *tso'ya* and *attani* as complements referencing contrasting aesthetics, the former associated with "cosmological systems that symbolize the cardinal points with a succession of different colors," the latter with shamanism and bear possession. She registers the presence of both *The beautiful and the dangerous* "within and between all lives" (Tedlock 1992, xi).

Alessandra Ciucci (2012, 109–16) lists several ways that the term *ḥərsh* "coarse, or rough" and its derivatives in Moroccan Arabic can "refer to beauty or quality" as perceived through one or more senses and recalled in memory. The *ḥaṣbawiya* style of the vocal genre *'aiṭa*, as performed in the 'Abda region of Morocco's Atlantic Plains, takes its name from the semantically related word *ḥaṣba* "crushed rock, pebble, or gravel," and a woman who wished to hear *'aiṭa ḥaṣbawiya* told Ciucci that "I want to smell the soil, taste the countryside." The powerful association of both style and voice with the region's rocky soil enables what Ciucci describes as experience of the countryside and celebration of rurality (see also Ciucci 2022).

Raimund Vogels (2004) suspects that ethnomusicologists have encountered many instances of "intermodal aesthetic judgments" without writing about or even reflecting on them much.[11] Ellis draws attention to terms in Australian languages that refer to distinctive characteristics of both a melody and a taste (in the Andagarinja dialect of Pitjantatjara) or both a melody and a scent (in Aranda) (Ellis 1969; Ellis et al. 1978, 69). Much theorizing about sources and meanings of musical sounds has presumably encompassed efforts to identify implications of polysemous expressions, probe affinities sensed among multiple polarities, or register discrete increments along a continuum between such extremes as highest pitch to lowest or fastest tempo to slowest.[12] The literature offers numerous examples of things done with multivalent polarities or polysemous terms like Zuñi *tso'ya* and Moroccan Arabic *ḥərsh*, and intermodal aesthetic judgment is generally involved.

RELATIONSHIPS AMONG NAMES AND TERMS   119

In the words for sounds based on "resemblances" (*ashbāh*) between aural perceptions and those engaging other senses, al-Fārābī saw evidence of the capacity of sounds to signify "passions" (*infiʿalat*) of the soul. Certain words for attributes of sounds will "refer to the imagery (*takhayyūl*) that the human has of sounds" (translated Madian 1992, 271 from Fārābī 1967, 1071). Al-Fārābī contrasted distinctions among the "quantities" (*kammiyyat*) of sounds, whether produced by instruments or voices, with the "qualities" (*kayfiyyat*) of vocal sounds alone: while the former can be measured only as degrees of acuity (*ḥidda*, equivalent to Greek *oksytēs*) or gravity (*thiqal*, Greek *barytēs*), music's power to communicate human emotions depends on distinctions in vocal timbre. His list of terms for distinctive qualities of vocal sounds includes such oppositions as those between *ṣafāʿ* "clarity" and *kūdrah* "muddiness," *malāsa* "smoothness" and *khushūna* "coarseness," *nāʿmah* "softness," *shiddah* "forcefulness," and *ṣalāba* "hardness"—all of which allow for perceptions that are not limited to hearing (Fārābī 1967, 1063–70; Madian 1992, 261–71; Erlanger 1935, 57–58).

A focus on a single master polarity may help performers control relationships among units on several structural levels. That appears to be a major function of the polarity of blackness (*lǝ-kḥāl* in Hassānīya Arabic) and whiteness (*lǝ-byāḍ*) in the music of Mauritanian griots (*īggāwan*, sing. *īggīw*): in performance, blacker units on each level must precede whiter units, just as in human life associations of blackness (youth, strength, honor, etc.) come before those of whiteness (old age, nostalgia, pleasure, etc.) (Guignard 1975, 96–97). Each term of the polarity denotes a cluster or configuration of attributes consistent with the opposition of taut versus loose strings on the *tidnit* (lute) of male musicians (Norris 1968, 71).[13] Viewed against the long history of music theory in Arabic and its dialects, the Mauritanian black/white polarity retains connotations of earlier oppositions between "expansive" (*al-bastī*) and "contracting" (*al-qabḍī*), "strong" (*al-muqawwiya*) and "soft" (*al-mulaiyina*) with which theorists classified tetrachords and melodic frameworks according to their "effect" (Arabic *ta'thir*, analogous to Greek *ēthos*) on the soul (see the summary in Blum 2013, 108–11 and 117–18).

120 MUSIC THEORY IN ETHNOMUSICOLOGY

The accounts of vocal production given to Anthony Seeger by Suyá Indians of Mato Grosso, Brazil, were based on a polarity with applications in several areas of life. Explaining that the throat (*so kre*) "begins just behind the teeth and lips and extends down to the collar bone," Suyá singers distinguished two positions—base (*kradi*) and top (*sindaw*)—and the very different sensations of vocalizing with a "big throat" or a "small throat," respectively (A. Seeger 1987, 100). These opposing ways of vocalizing were one of several contrasts between two performance genres with quite different functions: respectively, the unison song (*ngère*) in which voices must blend, and the shout song (*akia*) in which voices must not blend so that a man's "classificatory sister" can recognize the song he sings from a distance. Positions in the "throat" were correlated with locations of performance: the central plaza or residential houses for *ngère*, the plaza or outside the village for *akia* (A. Seeger 1979, 380). *Kradi* and *sindaw* also designate such complements as, respectively, first and second halves of a song, lower and upper parts of a palm trunk, beginning and end of the sky in the east and west, and moieties of the east and west sides of the men's house (A. Seeger 1987, 19).

Implicit scenarios for performance or *group plans* (Magrini 1989, 1998) are often based on polarities and complementary terms. Participants in the annual rice-wine drinking ceremony of the highlanders on the island of Palawan in the Philippines experience the timbral contrast of two small suspended gongs in the *basal* gong ensemble throughout the ceremony. The sounds of the two small suspended gongs called *sanang* (literally "happiness") are identified as *märägujas*, "a beautiful high tone and a bright thin sound," and *sämärang*, "a lower tone, and a 'dull' or 'thick' sound" (Revel-Macdonald and Maceda 1987). Using a thicker stick to produce a heavier sound on the boss and a thinner stick to strike the rim, the two players exchange roles about every thirty seconds in a shared experience of the contrast between a higher/bright/thin and a lower/dull/thick sound.[14]

When polarities refer to actions of performers, one term may be *marked* as *on* rather than *off*, with a narrower referential scope than the other in certain circumstances.[15] Sounds in a *foreground*, like the *sanang* gong's *märägujas*, are easily experienced as marked in relation

RELATIONSHIPS AMONG NAMES AND TERMS 121

to those of a *background*. Among the many terms that denote *figures* performed against a *ground* are *utom* in instrumental music of the T'boli people of the southern Philippines, a more variable part whose relationship to the supporting *tang* can be realized in a number of ways (Mora 1987, 202–3; Kartomi 1990, 238–39). The terminology that enables discussion of *utom*, as the "main design" above a background in composition and performance, is also relevant in other areas of activity such as verbal argument and weaving (Mora 2005a, 52). The fact that *utom* must be ornamented gives it a strong affinity with terms in two other T'boli polarities: *lemeny* "refined" as opposed to *megel* "hard," and *lemnek* "detailed" rather than *lembang* "broad" (2005a, 110–15). Mora derived what he termed "A Filipino epistemology of adeptness in performance" (2005b) from conversations with individuals identified as knowledgeable from having "acquired knowledge through personal revelation" and having been "ritually ordained" (2005b, 81). One such adept told Mora that the spirit-guide "who visits me is the custodian of the utom I play" (2005a 101).

The T'boli complementarity of *utom* and *tang* is a prime example of the "bilateral relationship" between *melody* and *drone* that Maceda saw as fundamental to Southeast Asian musical practices. Another is the "musical dualism" of Mandailing ceremonial ensembles in Sumatra, which "occurs between the rigidly unvarying tunings and rhythmic patterns of the drums and metallophones . . . and the ornamented, variably intoned, and rhythmically free wind and vocal parts" (Kartomi 2012, 261). Maceda (1986, 13–14) understood *drone* as any "constantly repeating phrase of one or more pitches played by one or several instruments for the duration of the music." He took a particular interest in compound drones like that of the Mandailing ceremonial ensembles and constructed a typology of six relationships between melody and drone (Maceda 1974) that brings out commonalities among many Southeast Asian musical practices.

In a study of "African elements in twentieth-century United States Black folk music," David Evans outlined a *binary aesthetic framework* to display affinities within two clusters of terms, one including *hot, hard, rough, dirty, down home* and the other their opposites—*cool, mellow, smooth, clean, modern*, and so on (Evans 1978, 104 and 1981, 65–66). He argued that this framework facilitated the "great flexibility

122 MUSIC THEORY IN ETHNOMUSICOLOGY

and variety" in style so abundantly evident throughout the history of African American music.[16]

Charles Keil, in an overview of music terminology in the Tiv language (1979, 25–52), likewise found it "important to note that 'hot' and 'cool' are both positive qualities and in this sense analogous to Afro-American descriptions of hot and cool jazz" (45). In the Tiv "dynamics vocabulary—low-soft-slow-smooth (cool) versus high-loud-fast-strong (hot)," Keil recognized "a male/female dialectic whose higher synthesis is the celebration of fertility or life" (51). Eric Charry notes more recently (2000, 327) that two Mande "words used for tempo conform well with general African and African American usage: *sumaya* (cool) for slow; and *kalan* or *kandi* (hot) for fast."

Given a roster of distinctive features among sounds, one can isolate combinations that are useable. William P. Malm (1986, 9–11) outlined the possible varieties of a *pon* tone on the Japanese *ko tsusumi*, a small hourglass drum, as identified by Ikuta Shigeru in a 1917 monograph on that drum. A *pon* sound can be big (*ōne*) or small (*kone*); long or short; expanding, confined, or contracted; complete or incomplete. Only four possibilities, all of them long and complete, remain after rejecting those that are either incomplete or both short and contracted. The two big tones, which produce a "trailing sound" (*yoin*), are contrasted as either expanding or confined and compared to a tree peony and a chrysanthemum, respectively; the expanded small tone is compared to a cherry blossom, the confined small tone to a plum blossom.

Modeling Relationships among Terms

Ethnomusicologists interested in how and for what purposes people recognize or posit relationships among names or terms and the concepts they designate can participate in theorizing as a process by imagining and trying out *potential* relationships.[17] In an essay on implications of three Brazilian Portuguese terms (*rítmo*, *balançáo*, *circularidade*), for example, Chris Stover attempts "to incorporate the words and concepts used by high-level practitioners to build a theoretical scaffolding" of his own (Stover 2019, abstract). Reflection on how terms are used, or might be used, generally requires attention

RELATIONSHIPS AMONG NAMES AND TERMS   123

to more than one type of relationship or grouping, and this chapter concludes with remarks on terms for several types of relationship or grouping: lexical sets, key words, clusters, combinations, categories, topics, constellations, configurations, and semantic fields.

Benamou concludes his study of the extensive Javanese "lexicon of musical affects" associated with *rasa* (glossed as "taste, feeling, affect, mood, inner meaning, faculty of taste, intuition, deep understanding," xxiv) with a section on "Why *rasa* talk matters" (2010, 199–217). He identifies fourteen "most common lexical sets" (each centered on a "key word") and six "basic terms" that he "arranged along several continua" and "grouped . . . into a number of binary oppositions," some of which "link up with a large number of related dualisms" (63–65). One of his tables (66) lists oppositions relating to the dichotomy *humble/brash* and others relating to *heavy/light*, with a note that oppositions in each set may or may not be related to each other. He speculates that the heavy/light polarity (Javanese *anteb/ènthèng*) is "perhaps the most fundamental of all" (70). Benamou displays associations of the six basic terms as six circular *clusters* within which binary oppositions are no longer relevant. He tested his "intuitive selection" of fourteen key words from which he derived the fourteen lexical sets by "a rough statistical analysis of the recorded and written corpus" (63), which confirmed his intuition. Researchers attempting an analysis of interrelated polarities and clusters of terms can benefit from Benamou's detailed account of his procedures.

Combinations and categories

Three questions concerning relationships among terms in a speech community's vocabulary are

(1) How does one morpheme, syllable, or word function in various *combinations*?

(2) What *categories* do members of a speech community or interested researchers recognize in the vocabulary of musicking?

(3) Does a *constellation* or *configuration* of terms and metaphors refer to attributes of one or more instruments and actions performed with them?

124 MUSIC THEORY IN ETHNOMUSICOLOGY

In their study of musical instruments in First Nation communities of Canada and the United States, Diamond, Cronk, and von Rosen (1994, 68) justified the first of these questions with the observation that "Concentration on the smallest units of meaning—the morphemes of language—is consistent with Anishnabe and Innu elders' and hunters' emphases." William K. Powers started with one of Lakota's "instrumental prefixes" in a study of "Oglala song terminology": the morpheme *ya* serves as a prefix to verbs and adjectives for "actions performed by means of the mouth" (1980, 28). Hugo Zemp likewise opened his presentation and analysis of musical terminology in the Dan language of West Africa with a discussion of combinations that include the syllable for "voice" (Zemp 1971, 73–92). Keil began his outline of "Tiv music terminology" (1979, 25–52) with a one-syllable word, *dugh*, "apparently the Tiv equivalent of our verb 'compose.'" After listing a dozen nouns that can follow *dugh*, Keil observed that it often functions when "something that already exists is taken from a prepared context so that a new effect is suddenly achieved" (31).

The authors of an illuminating outline of "words describing musical activities and techniques" in the Pitjantjatjara-speaking areas of central Australia approached that topic via thirteen English-language *categories*, for twelve of which they identified one or more *key words* ("rhythm" being the thirteenth): accentuation, beating, ceremony, dancing, dreaming, humming, melody, painting, rhythm, singing, text, verse, and voice register. Links among activities and techniques in these thirteen categories are significant in Pitjantjatjara discourse, and the concepts indexed by the key words are prominent in Ellis's outline of "the Pitjantjatjara musical system" (1985, 82–111). A list of onomatopoeic words supports the four authors' thesis that "categorising and naming according to sound . . . is consistent with the concept of 'naming' a place by using the correct stylised sung form of the name; with 'singing' a person by manipulating his behaviour through the medium of song; with taboos on the use of the name of the dead, since their spiritual power can be tapped through the correct sounding of the name" (C. J. Ellis, A. M. Ellis, Tur, and McCardell 1978, 78).

Other scholars group words for musical activities and techniques in a smaller number of categories or topics. Zemp's chapter on the Dan "vocabulary of musical interest" (1971, 69–92) has sections on genres and performers, sources of sound (focused on voices), modes of performance, taxonomy and symbolism of instruments, and musical surrogates for speech. David W. Ames and Anthony V. King describe their *Glossary of Hausa music and its social contexts* as "a kind of shorthand ethnography of musical life" (1971, vii); the sections on instruments and their parts, classes of performers, and performance treat aspects of music theory. Lester B. Monts's treatment of the same topics for the Vai language (1990) extends to Vai uses of terms from the Mende and Gda languages.

Configurations, constellations, and semantic fields

Zemp's study of "Aspects of 'Are'are musical theory" (1979) covers three fundamental topics in the music of bamboo panpipe ensembles ('*au rokoroko*): *interval, musical segment,* and *polyphonic organization.* Lessons that Zemp drew from his experience in Melanesia remain pertinent for research on musical terminology: "that a linguistic study of interval denominations should be linked to the observation of tuning practices and playing techniques, that the vocabulary dealing with polyphony should be correlated to learning processes and the spatial configuration of musicians, etc." (1979, 32). In an explication of "concepts of musical form and construction" among the Kaluli, Feld (1982, 163–81) likewise reported on experiences that were decisive to his understanding of Kaluli music theory. Both Zemp and Feld carefully delineated a *configuration* of concepts and metaphors basic to music-making in a given environment. Feld (1986a, 155) also understood eight metaphors for the body, voice, pulse, speech, and sound of the Kaluli drum as constituting a *constellation* that offers insight into "the links between sound and meaning." He concluded that "Kaluli musical theory . . . verbally surfaces in metaphoric expression," systematically joining two *semantic fields*, sound and water. Feld noted further that, in 'Are'are theory, bamboo ('*au*) likewise offers a "metaphoric means for shaping the expression of sonic experience and the theory of its formal organization" (1982, 164–65).

Feld's conclusion is consistent with a general point made by Eve Feder Kittay in *Metaphor: Its cognitive force and linguistic structure*

126   MUSIC THEORY IN ETHNOMUSICOLOGY

(1987 and *OSO*), where she describes *semantic fields* as "constituted by content domains that have been articulated by lexical fields" (1987, 230). Kittay views metaphor as produced through "a process in which the structure of one semantic field induces a structure on another content domain" (259). Applying those terms to Feld's interpretation of Kaluli music theory, the structure of the semantic field of water "induces a structure" on the content domain of sound (see also Kittay 1992). Another example is the derivation of metaphor for tonal hierarchies from a lexical field of hierarchical relations within a civil order—ruler, minister, people, affairs, and things in the Chinese *Yue Ji*, for example.[18] Some content domains are areas of activity or reflection where speakers of a language make relatively few discriminations.

A content domain of *affect* or *emotion* can be articulated by words for recognized emotions and superimposed on content domains of music, dance, and other arts—the tonal and rhythmic resources of music, for example, or the gestures, expressions, and movements of dance. Results of that process may become theories, doctrines, or classifications with a long history, like that of the Indian theories of *rasa* (emotional flavor or essence) from the *Nātyaśāstra* to the present. Rowell (1992, 329) remarks on the affinity of the eight *rasa*s (to which a ninth, serenity, is sometimes added) and the eight *sthāyi bhāva*s "permanent emotions" (see also Schechner 2003, 333–67, on "Rasaesthetics"). Rosters of emotions or affects are often limited to eight or nine fundamental terms, a recent instance being the nine "primary affects" of Silvan Tomkins's work on *Affect, imagery, consciousness* (1962–92). Tomkins classifies six of the nine as "negative," in sharp contrast to the *Nātyaśāstra*'s "cosmopolitan neutrality" as Vinay Dharwadker (2015, 1381) observes in comparing its theory of emotion with those of Darwin, William James, and Tomkins. Dharwadker (1400–1) notes correspondences in Darwin and Tomkins between several of the *Nātyaśāstra*'s eight relatively stable emotional states and some of its thirty-three "smaller emotions, which appear and disappear quickly but contribute to the articulation of other emotions" (1384).

Attempts to superimpose a lexical field for emotions on content domains of music and other arts do not always produce settled doctrines. "I doubt that there is a unitary theory [of expression] to be had" was one of Benamou's conclusions after analyzing Javanese "*rasa* talk" (2010, 158). Writing on the so-called *theory of affects* in seventeenth-century Europe, George J. Buelow (2001 and *OMO*) noted the interest of music theorists in "categorizing and describing types of affect as well as the affective connotations of scales, dance movements, rhythms, instruments, forms and styles." But whether the intensive interest of seventeenth-century European theorists in affect resulted in "a unitary theory" is another matter. Ethnographers and historians of music theory generally find it difficult to assess the range of agreement and controversy around representations of affect and emotion in music and musicking. Many who theorize about the human significance of musicking have posed questions about actual and possible relationships of music and emotion, which continue to offer a promising area for further inquiry and comparative study (see Juslin and Sloboda, eds. 2010).[19]

Continuing Issues

Recommendations:

1. Patience, with long-term commitment to language communities, attention to all languages currently used in each community, and readiness (even eagerness) to recognize and correct errors and misunderstandings.
2. Registering words for both actions and their results.
3. Attention to everyday uses of words that also function as musical terms. Which of their connotations are most relevant to musicking?
4. Recognition of implications that terms may not share with equivalents in English and other languages.
5. Reflection on potential uses of various results of theorizing.
6. Experimentation with possible ways of representing relationships among terms, and of using the representations.

Terms and metaphors in common (or less common) use among musicians that lack close equivalents in the researchers' own vocabularies often have analogues in the musical terminology of

128 MUSIC THEORY IN ETHNOMUSICOLOGY

neighboring communities, and attention to shared terminologies is increasingly evident in surveys of a region's musical practices.

Studies mentioned in this chapter describe specific varieties of what Ter Ellingson termed *non-graphic notations*: the unique *solmization* of the Sardinian *launeddas* (Giannattasio); sequences of *kinemes* (Kubik); *acoustic-iconic mnemonic systems* (Hughes); *verbal representations of instrumental sounds* (Tsukada); and *grounding of drum patterns in verbal, motivic, and beat patterns* (Wolf).

Sonic analysis and work on music cognition are likely to increase our understanding of musicians' reasons for choosing to work and play with specific oppositions among timbres or polysemous terms and metaphors like *twang* (Neal 2018), *heaviness* (see Berger and Fales 2005 for a pioneering analysis of "acoustic features that correlate with the perception of heaviness in heavy metal guitar timbres"), and *groove*. A team of researchers has demonstrated that metaphors for *groove* used by producers of electronic dance music refer to their actions in manipulating "sound, timing, and sound-timing interactions" (Brøvic-Hanssen et al. 2022, 1, 14).

6

Actors, Actions, and Outcomes

I see exploration of how people attempt to understand actions and results of musicking as a necessary contribution of ethnomusicologists to music theory as a general discipline, leaving open the question of "general in what sense?" At a time of growing awareness of longstanding (as well as recent) interconnections among human cultures, I can neither support nor oppose beliefs that the proper concern of music theory is with universals when so much historical and ethnographic research on music continues to perpetuate cultural biases strengthened and sustained through colonialism and imperialism. Success in identifying universals would require concerted efforts to overcome those biases while working to create favorable circumstances for participants in the world's musical practices to make choices freely arrived at rather than dictated by external interests.

Agawu suggests that from the publications of Ames and King, Monts, Keil, and others "we can begin to glimpse an African musical metalanguage," one commonality being the prominence of "action words associated with performance" (Agawu 2016a, 149; see also 32–35, 81–85).[1] On that topic, work of Africanists offers valuable perspectives for research on musicking and theorizing in the rest of the world, as does work on several issues addressed in *Reclaiming the human sciences through African perspectives* (Lauer and Anyidoho, eds. 2012). This chapter, on formulating and communicating concepts of musical action, revisits some of the concerns of earlier chapters.

Terms for roles and skills of performers and for their actions in performances, along with terms for possible sequences, intended results, and errors to be avoided, facilitate efforts to imagine how participants understand the actions brought into play in performance genres, including those represented through *mimesis*. While cultural practices vary in the extent to which people use such terms in communicating expectations of *who* should act in *what* manner

Music Theory in Ethnomusicology. Stephen Blum, Oxford University Press.
© Oxford University Press 2023. DOI: 10.1093/oso/9780199303526.003.0007

130 MUSIC THEORY IN ETHNOMUSICOLOGY

during a performance event, names of performance roles alone can index sequences of action carried out by those enacting or preparing to take on the role. Regulating the timing of participants' actions in a performance can rely more on visual and tactile cues than on words. In discussion, musicians may concentrate on results of musicking while leaving implicit the actions that can produce those results, or they may be more concerned with actions than with results.

Interaction of Participants in Musicking

Tullia Magrini presumably meant for the term *group plan*, mentioned in Chapters Four and Five, to cover the full range of differences in the habits and expectations shared by groups engaged in musicking. *Multipart music making* and *dialogic exchange* are less comprehensive terms, each with a vast extension nonetheless. The first of these has the merit of a focus on "the co-presence of at least two intentionally perceived sound emissions" that directs attention to "what individuals do when they sing/play together in organized ways" (Macchiarella 2012, 9–11).[2] That focus could support work on an area of inquiry envisioned in André Schaeffner's concise survey of "The Music of Black Africa" (1946, 465): "the psychology of all polyphony."[3] Types of organization that participants in a specific practice might resist or reject are often implicit in descriptions of those "organized ways."

The many varieties of dialogic exchange include "multimedia dialogue" between dancers and drummers (Polak 2012, 265) as well as exchanges between leaders and followers or competitors in song duels, or among members of an ensemble during "rehearsal-composition sessions" (Turino 1993, 72–78).[4] Turino's account of interaction among members of flute or panpipe ensembles in Conima, Peru, as they prepare new pieces for a competition at a fiesta begins with an "initial brainstorming phase" when men quietly play brief musical ideas that others may take up or ignore. Once the men have worked out the three conventional sections of a new piece, a "correctional phase" starts with individuals again quietly playing changes others may take up or ignore. At this stage "musicians may enter into a discussion" of

ACTORS, ACTIONS, AND OUTCOMES   131

the acceptability of the alterations, though they may sense "an implicit consensus" without any discussion (Turino 1993, 77).

Ethnomusicologists interested in how participants in musicking learn what is expected can start by recording verbs for the relevant actions, registering cues exchanged among performers, or both. Ken Gourlay's description (1972) of a vocal *cueing system* developed by the Karimojong people of Uganda is an early study of cues given during social or ceremonial gatherings as participants signaled their desire to lead a song and as leaders would vary length of a solo, introduce a new chorus, or end a song. Ceremonies had a dance-leader (*ekewpaton*) who controlled the timing of events, whereas sociability in non-ceremonial gatherings required exchanging the role of leader. A decade later, Ruth M. Stone (1982) looked closely at uses of cues in her study of performance events among the Kpelle of Liberia. Cognitive scientists interested in how people learn to listen and identify cues that invite, require, or discourage a response, and in how they conceptualize that process, should be interested in the work of ethnomusicologists who have learned to recognize cues by participating in ensembles. Good examples are Gerstin's study of Martinican *bèlè* mentioned in "Issues, 2" and Polak's account (2007) of social interaction in drum/dance performances at celebrations in Bamako, Mali.

Starting with paired concepts like *initiate/respond*, researchers can assemble more specific words in each category, noting their relation to gestures and movements of performers. In his study of *Tiv song*, Keil (1979, 38–39) found that "starting a song in Tivland is a process that can be described in a variety of vivid ways," while verbs for responding are "fewer in number but equally interesting." Musicians may mention several applications of a pair of terms like Persian *sowāl-javāb* "question and response" (from Arabic), which a bard (*bakhshi*) in northeastern Iran illustrated for me with exchanges experienced by bards themselves or represented in the prosimetric narratives they performed (examples in Blum 1996 and 2009, 222–24).[5]

In discussing the funeral song *buñansaŋ* with men of the Fogny subgroup of the Diola people in the Basse-Casamance region of Senegal, J. David Sapir learned verbs for four of the lead singer's actions: "*fɔñ* 'to sing out the melody' (literally 'to resound'); *kịt* 'to begin'; *sankɛn* 'to speak' or *salɛn* 'to praise', both referring to the solo's verse; and *buj*

132   MUSIC THEORY IN ETHNOMUSICOLOGY

'to kill' or *nɛn* 'to place', two verbs for 'to terminate the solo section.'" Performers used the verbs in statements about what should happen and how the singing could go off course: "Now in order to kill the song he will turn and lead to where the song is (i.e. to the *fʌñ*) ... Should you speed up and forego the killing it will not be good. The singer ... looks for the road by which he is to kill so that everyone in the ensemble will hear the song and remember it" (Sapir 1969, 178). Sapir outlined eight possible orderings of the four actions yielding "smooth and harmonious interchange between solo and ensemble" (181, 190–91).

Multipart Vocalizing

Researching the vocal genre *ganga* of Herzegovina and parts of Bosnia for a 1977 dissertation, Ankica Petrović decided that "the guiding factor in selecting the units of analysis" should be "the categories recognised and used by the people involved in performing and listening to ganga." She found singers "keen to speak about this style of music, because it is for most of them their favourite kind of singing" (100). Petrović diagramed "the way in which people distinguish the singers' musical roles" with verbs: in the opening section the first singer "takes the lead" (*vodi*) or "starts," (*počinje*) and the second, third, or later the first "takes over" (*preuzima*), "replies" (*edgovara*), "receives" (*dočekuje*), or "pursues till the end" (*goni do kraja*); in the second section the chorus "chops" (*sjeca*), "sobs" (*jeca*), "perform accompaniment" (*gangaju*), "accompany" (*prate*) or emulate the one-string fiddle (*gusle*) (Petrović 1977, 107). Singers and listeners who "knew about the significance and aesthetic value of every tone, pattern, fluctuation, vibration, and melisma" made Petrović aware of "tiny nuances of style, which were unrecognized by the previous researchers" (Petrović 1995, 65). Rice (1988, 5) had the same experience in southwestern Bulgaria, finding that "verbal explanations of the singers' own conceptualizations were crucial to an understanding of details" of their three-part singing.

Categories recognized and used by singers are a major concern of both the Research Centre for European Multipart Music Making in Vienna and the ICTM Study Group on Multipart Music (see

ACTORS, ACTIONS, AND OUTCOMES   133

"Approaches to a *Lexicon of local terminology on multipart singing in Europe*" in Ahmedaja, ed. 2011, 233–458).[6] Earlier comparative studies by Karl Brambats (1967) and George Marcu (1983) took the use of similar verbs in musical practices of disparate regions of Europe as evidence of shared theoretical constructs (a *model* to Brambats, a *system* to Marcu). Brambats was struck by similarities in terms for the second soloist's function in singing with two soloists and a choral drone:

> The following basic "model" seems to emerge from the Latvian, Balkan and Georgian material: the leader recites or chants the text of the song, is joined by a second soloist who "folds," "turns," "breaks," "cuts," etc. the song, using some peculiar, "unnatural" yodel-like techniques of voice production, and this process is covered up by a vigorous drone. This model can be realized just as well in a narrow or in a wide tonal space, with different scale structures and rhythmic patterns. It could be grafted upon a variety of melodic styles.
>
> (Brambats 1983, 29)

Multipart singing of Sardinian men (*cantu a cuncordu*) is the subject of the "polyvocal study" (*studio a più voci*) Macchiarella carried out in collaboration with four singers in Santulussurgiu and of an earlier monograph by Lortat-Jacob on singing for Holy Week in Castelsardo (1996 in Italian, 1998a in French). Macchiarella (2014) describes "three and a half years of negotiated dialogue through a collective writing" that began with lengthy discussions followed by reading and discussion of his first draft, then the second, and so on until all could endorse the final version. One chapter of the resulting book (2009, 136–85) is a debate among the four singers, compiled by Macchiarella from recordings of the discussions; footnotes in the collective text of the other three chapters register points of disagreement. The singers bore sole responsibility for producing the accompanying CD. Just as Petrović found singers "keen to speak about . . . their favourite kind of singing," for Macchiarella's collaborators *cantu a cuncordu* was "a crucial element of their social life: it was something 'to think about constantly', something of 'inestimable value' for their 'personal life', a 'reason for living.'"

134　MUSIC THEORY IN ETHNOMUSICOLOGY

Lortat-Jacob's techniques of analysis explored implications of statements, stances, and actions of men who exercised one or more of four vocal roles: from lowest to highest register *bassu*, *contra*, *bogi* ("voice" in Castellanese Sardinian), and *falzittu* (produced with a chest voice, despite the name). Each voice has a distinctive manner of production, stays within a range of a fifth, and emphasizes two, three, or four vowels whose spectra are appropriate to the harmonic fusion desired. When singers make the necessary adjustments, fusion of the spectra of their four fundamental tones produces a resultant tone termed *quintina* and said to represent the Virgin Mary. Singers must maintain positive interpersonal relationships and may keep their distance from a potential partner to avoid friction.

Lortat-Jacob speaks of performers' "intuitive knowledge" while also quoting one expert singer's remarks on the vowels he favors or avoids when singing *bogi* or *falzittu* (1996, 130; 1998a, 128–29). An outline of the system of voice-types (1996, 134; 1998a, 134) covers preferred vowels, ambitus, nasality, tension, vibrato, ornamentation, spectrum, and quality. A roster of twenty principles that constitute a "wholly implicit grammar" of Castellanese polyphony includes a schema of the "harmonic possibilities authorized by the system" (1996, 145–53; 1998a, 155–66). A table comparing the physique and personality traits of men in each vocal role (1996, 184; 1998a, 204) displays tendencies rather than social norms.

Interlocking Parts

Discussion of how to develop techniques of analysis consistent with implications of performers' words and gestures benefits when two or more scholars work on closely related practices. In addressing the question of how the responsibilities of performers whose parts interlock are conceptualized with reference to the whole, Kubik made good use of Luganda terminology learned during his studies with a court musician of Buganda, Evaristo Muyinda, at various times between 1959 and 1962 (e.g., the terms for xylophone playing techniques in Kubik 1994, 54–55). Luganda terms for roles of performers are related etymologically to names of the parts performed by a prescribed

ACTORS, ACTIONS, AND OUTCOMES 135

number of players. Music for the twelve-key *amadinda* xylophone requires three, with specified playing areas on each side of the instrument. The *omunazi* leads off with *okunaga* "to hit, to start striking," the *omwawuzi* enters at a specified moment with *okwawula* "to separate, differentiate," which interlocks with the *okunaga*, and the *omukoonezi* listens closely to the other two parts in order to add *okukoonera* (perhaps from *okukona*, "to knock"), which doubles the lowest two pitches (*entengezzi*) as they are sounded in the other two parts (Kubik 1969, 37; Anderson 1968, 135–36). The interlock of *okunaga* and *okwawula* in compositions of the *amadinda* repertory can be realized by four of the six players in the tuned-drum ensemble *entenga* (one of whom also plays the *okukoonera*), or by a single performer's right and left hands on the harp *ennanga*, for which many compositions are thought to have been created with a vocal part (*okuyimba*) that matches some of the *okunaga* and *okwawula*'s pitches.

Kubik's publications on the Baganda repertory of pieces with interlocking parts (1960, 1962, 1969, 1972b, 1983) were preceded by Joseph Kyagambiddwa's 1956 book and joined by writings of Lois Anderson (1968, 1984), Peter Cooke (1970), and Ulrich Wegner (1993, to which Cooke 1994 responds). Kyagambiddwa (1956, 216–17) saw melodic and harmonic similarities of five songs on related topics as evidence that "in creating their music, the ancient Baganda used reason and theoretical knowledge, rather than instinct." Kubik speculated that techniques of composition facilitated the emergence of *resultant patterns* formed by certain neighboring pitches in the interlocking pulse streams of *okunaga* and *okwawula*, which proceed too quickly for ears to grasp each stream as a whole. He attempted "to discover statistically how the second or contrasting part [*okwawula*] was normally set out to fit into the first one [*okunaga*]" and suggested that large intervals between adjacent tones as the parts interlock facilitated the emergence of resultant patterns (1969, 32). He also suggested (1994, 54) that the preferred way of striking the keys, *okusengejja* ("to sort things out, to clarify") might favor creation of the *inherent melodies* or *inherent patterns* which he had first (1960, 12–14) called *subjective* or *inherent rhythms*. Cooke argued "that the instrumental structures are closely related to the musico-phonological structures of the songs" and inherent rhythms "are to a large extent a coincidental feature of

136 MUSIC THEORY IN ETHNOMUSICOLOGY

the process" that Cooke termed "instrumentalising song" (1970, 62, 77). Kubik found Cooke's view complementary to his own, seeing the "key phrases" of songs and "expected inherent note-patterns" as "the principal criteria watched for by the musicians when combining their instrumental parts" (1972b, 115).

In a critique of Kubik's thesis, Wegner (1993, 218) asked, "How is it possible that the Muganda percipient extracts a melody from the interlocking structure of a composition, and during the same musical event perceives inherent patterns that mirror *parts* of just the same melody musically and textually on different levels of organization?" Wegner expected a satisfactory answer to posit *schemata* internalized by musicians and listeners, and after evaluating the responses of nine Baganda musicians to recordings modified to alter the relationship of *okunaga* and *okwawula*, he concluded (228) that "cognitive relevance within Kiganda music culture" of resultant or inherent patterns has not yet been demonstrated." Perhaps Wegner's "How is it possible" question could be answered by experiments showing that Muganda percipients shift their attention to different results of the auditory streaming process in the course of a performance.

Kubik's 1962 article was the first overview of "The phenomenon of inherent rhythms in East and Central African music," with examples of "rhythm patterns which automatically emerge from the total musical complex" produced on a guitar, a lamellaphone, or a pair of conical drums as well as on the *ennanga* and the Kiganda *akadinda* xylophone. Subsequent researchers have explored the capacities of specific instruments and ensembles to produce inherent patterns (Tracey 1961, 51; Berliner 1978, 88–94; Fiagbedzi 1980; Locke 1978, 315–16). Valuable analytic work on the idiom of the Shona *mbira dza vadzimu* (also called *uhare*) has been published by Berliner (1978, 2020), Tracey (1989), Brenner (1997), Grupe (2004), Berliner and Magaya (2020). At least one mbira player is normally required for each of the complementary parts called *kushaura* and *kutsinhara*, though a single player may occasionally draw on both parts in a solo (Berliner 1978, 106; Grupe, 124). Unlike *okunaga* and *okwawula*, *kushaura* and *kutsinhara* invite variation from players. Although Grupe did not claim to have based his analyses of mbira players' motions and the resultant sounds on an implicit or partly explicit theory, he made good use of discussions with

ACTORS, ACTIONS, AND OUTCOMES   137

players, who had much to say about *kutsinhara* parts (126–34) among other topics.

Ritual and Ceremony

Few if any human activities are more dependent on group plans than rituals and ceremonies. A researcher who shares Rouget's interest in musicians as "ritualizers" (1996, 82) and in what Rouget termed "the choreographic-musical architecture" (1996, 11) of a ritual or ceremony will need the help of participants with specialized knowledge, who are not always prepared or permitted to discuss certain topics.[7] Highly pertinent to the theorizing of ritual specialists and researchers alike is the premise that "When analyzing sound's effectiveness, it is important to consider the integration of all the requisite semiotic parameters" (Perman 2008, 197). After identifying variables that participants in rituals interrelate in specific ways, researchers can try to imagine

Table 6.1. Variables subject to prescriptions in ritual (modified from Yung 1996, 17–18, with one additional variable)

1. pattern of loudness
2. timbre or quality of sound
3. regularity or irregularity of explicit or implicit pulse
4. intonation
5. rhythmic patterns
6. tonal patterns
7. tempo
8. absolute pitch
9. verse structure: syllables in a phrase, phrases in a line, lines in a unit
10. verse structure: patterns of phonic elements such as rhyme, alliteration, linguistic tones, length or accentuation of syllables
11. number and location of differentiated streams of musical activity required or allowed at specific moments

138 MUSIC THEORY IN ETHNOMUSICOLOGY

reasons for selecting those ways rather than alternatives. Some of the reasons may become clear from words spoken or sung during a ritual or from participants' accounts of the appropriate actions.

Bell Yung's introduction to a collection of essays on music in Chinese ritual lists ten "musical elements" subject to prescriptions (Yung, Rawski, and Watson eds. 1996, 13–31). Table 6.1 reproduces his list with alterations that treat those elements as variables with a view toward studies of ritual beyond the many worlds of Chinese culture; I also add an eleventh variable, "number and location of differentiated streams of musical activity required or allowed at specific moments in the ritual" (examples in Wolf, Blum, and Hasty 2019, 16–17).

The list in Table 6.1 bears comparison with the outline of thirteen English-language categories for Pitjantjatjara "musical activities and techniques" summarized in Chapter Five (Ellis et al. 1978). Simply listing "musical elements" or "musical activities" can be a useful step toward considering "the integration of all the requisite semiotic parameters" (see also Nketia 1989; Wong 2001; Perman 2020).

Richard Schechner's sensitivity to affinities of ritual and drama, in both of which he discerns a "basic structure of gathering/performing/dispersing" (2003, 189),[8] should prove helpful to ethnomusicologists on such questions as how those involved theorize the staging of rituals for observers who do not otherwise participate, and how participants imagine and theorize their roles as rituals acquire new functions. Dave Pier's study of *Ugandan music in the marketing era* (2015) compares "performance roles Africans were enticed to play in today's globalization culture" with roles that were "enacted in embodied rituals of great aesthetic/social intensity" and of great antiquity in the African Great Lakes region (2015, 6–11). Experience of ritual, ceremony, drama, and genres of activity deriving from them should convince ethnomusicologists not to give verbal ways of knowing and verbal outcomes of theorizing priority over all others. In an afterword to a book on issues raised by a "multimedia ethnography" of a southern Italian festival, Feld urges readers to reverse the order of the familiar practice of reading texts before turning to associated images or recordings: "no media controls primal authority either when it comes to memorability or explanation" (Feld in Ferrarini and Scaldaferri 2020, 419). Good advice for engaging with the multimedia

ACTORS, ACTIONS, AND OUTCOMES 139

ethnography of that southern Italian festival (Scaldaferri and Feld, eds. 2019) and much else.

Process models

Modeling normal sequences of action in a ritual or in preparations for musicking (such as pre-performance composition) is a widespread genre of theorizing, in which hermeneutic or pedagogical motives may encourage simplifications that can be helpful or misleading depending on how they are used (cf. Rice 1988). A well-known passage in the Chinese *Book of Documents* (two versions of which were developed in the second century BCE) outlines a sequence of stages from expression of intent in a poem to song and to harmonized notes: "Poetry expresses the mind, the song is a (drawing-out =) chanting of its words, the notes depend upon (the mode of) the chanting, the pitch-pipes harmonize the notes" (translated in Karlgren 1950, 7; another translation and the Chinese text in Kaufmann 1976, 23, 195). This generative process was described in later writings, such as the "Great Preface" (25 CE) to the *Book of Odes* (from inward feeling to speaking to sighing to singing to dancing) and the commentary by K'ung Ying-ta (574–648): "What is in the heart is intent, once out of the mouth it is speech; words intoned are poetry, notes chanted are song; and when these [notes] have been distributed among the eight [kinds of instrumental] sounds, we call the result music" (translated in Saussy 1993, 78). The model provided a rationale for two hermeneutic principles: investigating each phase can lead to knowledge of the next and examining outcomes of the process can reveal the state of government. As formulated in Chapter 27 of the *Record of Rites*, the so-called Classic of Music (second century BCE): "One investigates sounds in order to know the tone [*yin*]; investigates tones in order to know music; investigates music in order to know government" (translated in Saussy 1993, 88, and with the Chinese text in Kaufmann 1976, 33, 199).

Agawu (1995, 27–30, 180–85) devised "a conceptual model for rhythmic expression in West Africa" that resembles the ancient Chinese sequence, with five stages in a circle from gesture to spoken word to vocal music to instrumental music to dance as stylized gesture,

140 MUSIC THEORY IN ETHNOMUSICOLOGY

and so on. Probing the model's limitations (1995, 180–85) he wisely acknowledged that relationships among some "stages" are reciprocal rather than unidirectional.

Two components may suffice for a concise model. An attitude of "Now I'll tell you what it's really all about" often underlies statements like that of Baba Naim, a Persian-speaking musician of northern Afghanistan, who informed Mark Slobin "that all music is divided into *raft* ('going') and *āmad* ('coming'), and that the amad is the more stable and important of the two" (Slobin 1976, 164). In a dissertation on creative processes of Ewe composers of "new song" (*hayeye*), George W. K. Dor (2000, 271) quotes one composer's explanation of why text should come before tune: "Text advises me on how the tune should go." Another Ewe composer's statement that "Something has to affect the composer emotionally to compose" (272) suggests a model activated by emotional expression like that in the *Book of Documents*. Dor also heard composers mention exceptions to the text before tune model, when "finding words to match the tones" follows "origination of a melody" (275).

Studies of how music is now produced in much of the world are increasingly concerned with numerous interactions of participants with one another and with technologies. Albin Zak (2001, 24–25) describes three "modes of creative activity" in the "multifaceted creative process" of rock: songwriting, arranging, and cutting tracks, which do not follow a widely shared model of the appropriate sequence. Theorizing in the course of musicking can disregard any existing models of how to sequence the usual actions. It may concentrate on what Louise Meintjes (2003, 173) describes as a "poetic, performative, and unsettled process of imaging in sound" that "challenges any moves toward linearity in the analysis of the productive process." "When culturally scripted figures are selected and molded by socially situated individuals," she adds, "power and expression come to reside formatively but unstably in each other." This book has treated *theorizing* as an activity that often includes "poetic, performative, and unsettled" processes like these. Opportunities to witness such processes or experience their outcomes are privileges for which an ethnomusicologist must be grateful.

Notes

Chapter 1

1. Theorizing often starts with attention to *affordances* as discussed by James J. Gibson: "To identify an affordance is to have achieved access to a panoply of expectations that can be exploited, reflected upon (by us and maybe some other animals), used as generators of further reflections, etc." (Dennett 2017, consulted January 23, 2017). I use *options* to include the affordances people identify along with other possibilities imagined and not immediately rejected in the course of such "further reflections."

2. As discussed in Chapter Two, Catherine Ellis (1985) drew important lessons for her work as researcher and educator from Bateson's conception of three levels of learning.

3. Theoretical statements in many languages recognize that musical sound depends on motion; see, for example, the opening of the text known as *Divisio canonis* (once attributed to Euclid), which survives in Greek (Barbera 1991, 114–15), Latin (ibid., 228–31), and Arabic (Neubauer 2004–5, 335–37).

4. In the Fourth Homeric Hymn (lines 483–84), Hermes gives Apollo the lyre he has just invented, telling him that the instrument "teaches all manner of things that delight the mind" so long as the player "enquires of it cunningly."

5. The oldest surviving documents of music theory are cuneiform tablets containing instructions for proper tuning of a harp or lyre, allowing for reconstruction of an "Old Babylonian" system of seven heptatonic scales presumably in place ca. 1800 BCE, and a "New Babylonian" system of fourteen named intervals described as paired strings (Kilmer 1997, 141–43).

6. The sections relating to music in the main texts on ritual are assembled with English translation and commentary in Kaufmann 1976. Scott Cook 1995 offers a different translation of the music section of the *Li Ji* "Record of Rites," also with commentary.

7. How different arts of representation (*mimēsis*) make use of rhythm, language, and relationships among tones (*harmonía*), separately or in

142 NOTES

combination (and simultaneously or in succession), is the initial topic of the lecture notes that make up Aristotle's *Poetics*: rhythm alone in dance, rhythm and tone-relationships in instrumental performance, all three in tragedy, comedy, dithyrambic and nomic poetry. Although these are the three constituents of *mousikē* in other writings of Plato and Aristotle, the term is avoided in this instance.

8. Music is discussed in chapters 28–33 of the *Nāṭyaśāstra* (translated in Ghosh 1961, 1–200; contents outlined in Nijenhuis 1977, 6–7).

9. In Oskár Elschek's overview of the "systematics, theory, and development" of music research (1984 in Slovak, 1992 in German), the chapter on "music aesthetics" has sections on East Asia, South and Southeast Asia, and the Middle East (1984, 157–69; 1992, 234–52), but the chapter on "music theory" (1984, 229–54; 1992, 331–60) does not.

10. David Carson Berry's definition in *The Grove Dictionary of American Music* and *Grove Music Online* replaces that in the 1980 and 2001 editions of the *New Grove* by Claude V. Palisca: "Theory is now understood as principally the study of the structure of music."

11. See Paul Berliner's account of Shona musicians' interactions with their mbiras (Berliner 1978, 127–31, 144–45) and Akin Euba's description of "the drummer's perception of his instrument as containing a living force which directs the creative process" in *Yoruba drumming: The dùndún tradition* (Euba 1990, 392–93).

12. In the preface to a new edition of their 1985 book *Leviathan and the air-pump* (2011, xliii, xlix), Steven Shapin and Simon Schaffer revisit their widely discussed thesis that "solutions to the problem of knowledge are solutions to the problem of order," which are *"the same problem"* (their italics) since "To have knowledge is to belong to some sort of ordered life; to have some sort of ordered life is to have shared knowledge."

13. PASMAE's website attributes this change to "recognition of the fact that for Africans music encompasses more than simply a Western view of 'music' " (www.pasmae.africa, accessed December 5, 2020). In the United States, the Society for Asian Music sponsored a journal that challenged conventional academic divisions between music, dance, and drama with articles on their interrelationships (Blum 2011, 5 on *AsM* 1/1, 1969, 1).

14. In his *Essai sur l'origine des langues où il est parlé de la mélodie et de l'imitation musicale*, Jean-Jacques Rousseau (1781) developed a conception of systems of meaningful melodic inflections crucial to human communication and expression (Blum 1986 and 1991, 13–14), a topic further explored by many subsequent theorists, including Boleslav Yavorsky (1908) and Boris Asaf'yev (1930).

NOTES   143

15. "Emotional expression" is the first of ten functions of music discussed by Alan P. Merriam in *The anthropology of music* (1964, 209–27). A table of twelve functions drawn up by Hodges (2019, 31) compares Merriam's list with those of Gregory (1997) and Clayton (2009).

16. Two meanings of Arabic *adab* are relevant here: (1) *belles-lettres* includes the "anecdotal writings" Shiloah regarded as a significant body of Arabic writings on music theory, and (2) norms of etiquette that masters of music and other disciplines transmit to their students.

17. In his reflections on "The politics of recognition," Charles Taylor uses *language* "in a broad sense, covering not only the words we speak, but also other modes of expression whereby we define ourselves, including the 'languages' of art, of gesture, of love, and the like."

18. The title J. S. Bach gave to his *Inventions and Sinfonias* promises "a clear way not alone (1) to learn to play clearly in two voices, but also, after further progress, (2) to deal correctly and well with three *obbligato* parts; furthermore, at the same time not alone to have good *inventiones* [ideas], but to develop the same well, and above all to arrive at a singing style in playing and at the same time to acquire a strong foretaste of composition" (translated in David and Mendel, eds. 1966, 86).

19. From his encounters with Southeast Asian musicians at the *Exposition universelle* of 1889, Debussy came to believe that their knowledge was conveyed through continuing performance, with modifications, of "very old songs, combined with dances," resulting in Vietnamese music-dramas with more gods and fewer stage-sets than Wagner's *Ring* and a Javanese counterpoint "beside which Palestrina's is child's play" (Debussy 1971 [1913], 223, my translation).

20. Scholars working in the field they knew as *musical ethnography* found uses for Ukrainian, Russian, and Polish equivalents of the term *ethnomusicology* (and the adjective *ethnomusical*) as early as the 1920s (Stęszewski 1992; Lukaniuk 2010).

21. Discussion of tone-systems, a major topic of Hornbostel's earlier studies of recordings from Japan, India, and Tunisia, is conspicuous by its absence in his 1909 analysis of Nyamwezi songs, which has four subheadings: *Melos*; Harmony; Rhythm, structure (*Aufbau*), and tempo; Singing style (*Vortragsweise*). In later publications on African music he added Polyphony and separated "Form" from "Rhythm."

22. The term *ethnophilosophy* has also been used for constructs that encapsulate what an observer takes to be assumptions and modes of thinking shared by members of larger or smaller communities. Paulin Hountondji (1983 [1976], 33–34) refers to "Western 'ethnophilosophy'" that was "not

144 NOTES

addressed to Africans but to Europeans, and particularly to . . . colonials and missionaries," and reserves the term *African philosophy* for a "set of texts written by Africans and described as philosophical by their authors themselves."

23. "la théorie indigène est dans une relation beaucoup plus directe avec la réalité indigène que ne le serait une théorie élaborée à partir de nos categories et de nos problems."

24. Perlman (2004, 7) "deliberately avoid[s] speaking of 'musical thought' but prefer[s] to talk of musicians' *thinking*" on the grounds that "treating their conceptualizations as creative activity has several advantages," gained by focusing our study of music theories on "processes of creative thought" (15). I speak of *theorizing* for the same reasons.

25. H. H. Eggebrecht's essay on "Musikalisches Denken" (Musical Thinking) offers an overview of that development, viewing musical thinking as "the actual source, the origin, not only of musical products but also of music theory" (1975, 233: "die eigentliche Quelle, der Ursprung, nicht nur der musikalischen Produkte, sondern auch der Musiktheorie . . .").

26. Pandora Hopkins developed a conception of "aural thinking" (P. Hopkins 1982) derived in part from Rudolf Arnheim's work on *Visual thinking* (Arnheim 1969).

27. The project's website (consulted June 21, 2021) lists three "formative orientation points": improving access to heritage, diversifying discussions on its curation, and transferring agency to "stockholders of their heritage." It was funded for three years by the Joint Programming Initiative on Cultural Heritage and Global Change, part of the EU's Horizon 2020 Research and Innovation Programme.

28. I adopt the phrase "internal decolonization" from A. G. Hopkins 2018, 40.

29. "Open Letter to the Board, the Council, and the Membership of the Society for Ethnomusicology," circulated August 20, 2020, and available on *ethnomusicology.org*.

30. Harold S. Powers (1980b, 422–23) used these terms in surveying the history of the concept *mode*; both processes are further discussed in Chapter Four.

31. Representations of "the West" that merit discussion spell out specific factors, as Joseph Henrich does in *How the West become psychologically peculiar and particularly prosperous* (2020), where WEIRD stands for those who are Western, educated, industrialized, rich, and democratic.

32. Merriam (1969, 81) reports a discussion of reasons for preferring one interior design to another in his detailed account of "Drum-making among

the Bala (Basognye)." Music theories are often concerned with properties and capacities of materials.

33. In a review of *CCMT*, Andrew J. Chung (2022, 176) nicely summarizes the relevance of Chakrabarty's book to work in music theory: "provincializing music theory as it is practiced in the Euro-Western academy must entail situating its concepts as both illuminating *and* inadequate for grasping a wide diversity of musical practices, but would also espouse an openness to how other provincialized music theories productively complicate what we think of as our music-theoretical knowledge."

34. Many pedagogues who have attempted a scientific and systematic presentation of music theory have had far less experience of science than Sindoesawarno, who studied engineering and taught high school mathematics (Sumarsam 1995, 141).

35. The entry on "Musicology" by Egon Wellesz in the fifth edition of *Grove's Dictionary of Music and Musicians* outlines several Greek and Latin classifications in a useful "Historical synopsis of the systems of musical theory" (1954, 1021–25).

36. The discussion of sense perception and reasoning in *De institutione musica* is a simplification of what Boethius wrote elsewhere. Andrew Hicks points out (2017, 163) that in his commentary on Aristotle's *On interpretation* Boethius maintains that "sense perception and mental images (*imaginatio*) are natural substrates for the soul's perception" on which "the more robust intellect . . . fleshes out in intellective, cognitive terms what had been indistinctly presumed by the mental image."

37. Like al-Fārābī, Felipe Hernández-Armesto (2019, 17) sees imagination as crucial to our ability to think, though he criticizes Aristotle for failing to recognize that "memory and imagination overlap," notably when "[m]isrememberering recasts reality as fantasy, experience as speculation."

38. Eggebrecht (1991, 14) formulated that thesis as follows: "This relationship of theory and practice is characteristic of Western music: received theory precedes practice and lives within it as theoretical thinking, endowing it with a capacity for theory, which can be acquired from practice through that relation. In this sense theory and practice are inseparably bound up with one another in music" ("Dies ist das für die abendländische Musik eigentümliche Verhältnis von Theorie und Praxis: Theorie als überkommene geht der Praxis voraus, wohnt sich als theoretisches Denken ihr ein, macht sie theoriefähig und kann in bezug auf sie aus ihr gewonnen werden. In diesem Sinne sind in der Musik Theorie und Praxis unlöslich miteinander verbunden"). See also Sachs 1997.

146 NOTES

39. "la etnomúsica es una rama de la creación musical que se caracteriza por la ausencia de interés especulativo." Jürg Stenzl (1981) defines "music cultures without theory" as those that use *names* for various purposes but have not yet developed *terms*. My Chapter 5 treats sets of names as outcomes of theorizing.

40. Grocheio's criteria of "usage and sociality" recall the familiar typology of three rhetorical styles: grandiloquent, plain, and intermediate (as in Cicero's *Orator*, 19–21). He offered his typology as an alternative to the three varieties of *musica* "recognized by those schooled in it" according to Boethius (trans. Bower 1989, 9–10): the cosmic (*mundana*), the human (*humana*), and that of instruments (*instrumentalis*).

41. Weber's treatment of rationalization in his sociology of music was largely ignored for most of the twentieth century (Kaden 1997, 1621–22) with the important exception of T. W. Adorno (1903–69), whose critique of rationalization was based on resistance to domination. The prominence of technologies in musical life of the twenty-first century may prompt renewed attention to Weber's sociology of music.

Chapter 2

1. The importance of institutions in production and promulgation of music theories, and the weight of ideologies in their production and communication, are now more widely recognized by historians of Western music than they were at the time of Gushee's essay. Papers from two conferences organized by Dörte Schmidt and Thomas Christensen at the Wissenschaftskolleg zu Berlin (2010) and the University of Chicago (2014) will appear in a forthcoming publication (see also Schmidt, ed. 2005).

2. In a paper on "The disunity of ancient Chinese music theory," Lars Christensen (2020) translates and comments on Chen Yang's critique of eleven earlier approaches to tuning in his *Book of music* (1101 CE).

3. Andrew Weintraub (1993, 37) provides a good example from his 1988–89 fieldwork in west Java: "In contrast to the institutional model, I found that Sundanese musicians outside the conservatory articulate theory by using metaphor, 'folk etymology,' or an allusion to some other aspect of culture."

4. John Miller Chernoff (1979, 99–111, 132–41) was among the first US scholars to report at length on a musician's ideas about how knowledge is communicated, after extensive conversations with the Dagomba drummer Ibrahim Abdulai.

NOTES 147

5. Sepideh Raissadat's dissertation in progress will describe her work with the great Iranian singer Parisa (b. 1950), initially for three and a half years then for another two after finishing high school.

6. Compare Perlman's remark (2004, 127) that "The attempt [of Javanese gamelan musicians] to bring together their piecemeal, disarticulated knowledge of particular cases within a synoptic view can inspire creative thinking, stimulating musicians to understand their music in new ways."

7. Baily describes one string-tying ceremony on the Hindustani model (121–23) as an occasion for Herati musicians to socialize and perform. It failed to initiate a relationship of mutual devotion between the teacher and the would-be student; the latter never received the promised lessons in "popular music" and asked the teacher to return the silk gown given him at the ceremony.

8. Baily modified a distinction made by Peter Caws, who argued that social structure is dependent on operational and representational models "attributed to members of the society studied," in contrast to a researcher's "explanatory models" (Caws 1974, 1). Brinner (1995, 115–16) also finds the distinction useful.

9. Some documents name this topic as a major part of a musician's pedagogy without providing details of the techniques involved. According to the Fatimid court musician Ibn al-Ṭaḥḥān (d. after 1057 CE), apportionment (*qisma*) of tones to song lyrics was one of four domains (*ḥudūd*, sing. *ḥadd*) named by the ʿAbbāsid court musician Isḥāq al-Mawsilī (d. 850 CE) as fundamental to the art of song (Neubauer 1998, 367, 403).

10. See also Routledge's *World Music Pedagogy* series (Campbell, ed. 2018–21).

11. The Centre for Aboriginal Studies in Music (CASM), established in collaboration with traditional leaders from Indulkana in northern South Australia, is now a department within the University of Adelaide's Elder Conservatorium of Music, which "provides specialised tertiary level university based music programs for Aboriginal and Torres Strait Islander musicians, and is a key centre for Australian Indigenous music production" (www.music.adelaide.edu.au, consulted July 23, 2016).

12. SADC stands for South African Development Community. According to its website (www.ciimda.org, consulted July 8, 2016, no longer online), CIIMDA was active in Botswana, Malawi, Mozambique, Namibia, Swaziland, and Zambia as well as in the Republic of South Africa.

13. *The Cambridge History of Western Music Theory* (Christensen, ed. 2002) is organized according to a similar tripartite scheme: Speculative Traditions, Regulative Traditions, and Descriptive Traditions.

148 NOTES

14. *Robert Lowery's method for Jazz improvisation* was published posthumously online by his student Gerald Chavis (2019).

15. Noting the equation of *oral tradition* with absence of writing, Nino Pirrotta suggested that "in the case of instrumental music one might almost call it a manual one" (Pirrotta and Povoledo 1982, 22).

16. Saussy is well aware of how often dichotomies in Sterne's "litany of orality" turn up in discussion of oral literature. In a book subtitled *Orality and its technologies*, he notes (2016, 61) that in some theories of oral composition (including the Parry-Lord theory discussed in Chapter Four), "The equivalence of paper with premeditation, and of hearing with immediacy, remain in the background."

17. Online collections of oral literature are listed on the website of the World Oral Literature Project: oralliterature.org/info/links.html (accessed September 19, 2020).

18. See, for example, Yonatan Malin's paper on a "profound form of orality in which the sacred text is imbued with the memory of individual voices" (2019, abstract). Bruno Deschênes and Yuko Eguchi (2018, 70) use the term *embodied orality* for efforts at "understanding how the body learns, assimilates, and personalizes what is being taught" in performing arts, even when techniques of vocalizing are not being taught.

19. "Immer ist die Schrift das stärkste Mittel, die Musik zu intellektualisieren, einer theoretische Einstellung zu erzwingen. Die Schrift erhält die Theorie, deren Niederschlag sie ist, am Leben."

20. Zabana Kongo and Jeffrey Robinson (2003, 106–8) summarized "key premises" of Polanyi's theory in presenting "The case for improvisation in education" at the 2003 conference of the Pan African Society for Musical Arts Education. See also the chapter on tacit knowledge in *The Cambridge handbook of expertise and expert performance* (Cianciolo et al. 2006).

21. "nicht nur sämtliche sprachlichen Äußerungen über Musik zu berücksichtigen, sondern außerdem die unausgesprochene, 'implizite' Theorie zu rekonstruieren, die in der Kompositionsgeschichte enthalten ist, in den literarischen Dokumenten aber fehlt (aus Gründen, die dann ihrerseits zu den Themen einer umfassenden Geschichte der Musiktheorie gehören würden)."

22. Compare Rouget's observation (1996, 347) that "il y a bien des choses que l'on fait sans le savoir et bien des systèmes que l'on pratique sans pouvoir en dire la théorie" ("There are lots of things one does without knowledge and lots of systems one works with without being able to articulate the relevant theory"). With respect to *capability*, Bateson argues (1972, 142–43) that

human knowledge of systems is inevitably partial: "it is not conceivably possible for any system to be totally conscious" inasmuch as "No organism can afford to be conscious of matters with which it could deal at unconscious levels." Musicians are well aware of this.

23. Seebass's paper for the Bologna round table is a model study of stages and processes in the history of Indonesian music theory (see also Seebass 1986).

24. As Brinner writes in conclusion (1995, 320), "I hope that the theoretical concepts and frameworks developed in this book will inspire others to look at the totality of musical thought and practice in a community—however large or small—in terms of cognitive and interpersonal challenges, potentials, and accomplishments."

25. Ben-Amos (1984, repr. 2020, 91) distinguishes "Seven strands of *tradition*" in the writings of US folklorists, noting that "none is more adequate than the other, none is more proper than the other." As a result of the diverse and shifting interests of folklorists, the term may refer to lore, canon, process, mass (material transmitted by "tradition bearers"), culture, *langue* (adopting Saussure's distinction of *langue* and *parole*, a language and its uses in specific instances), and performance.

Chapter 3

1. "il faut observer le non-emprunt, le refus de l'emprunt même utile. Cette recherche est aussi passionnante que celle de l'emprunt." André Schaeffner (1936, 357) recognized the need for attention to this point in research on "diffusion" of musical instruments.

2. Reports from participants in the 1932 Congress appeared in the *Zeitschrift für vergleichende Musikwissenschaft* (1933) and elsewhere (comprehensive bibliography in Vigreux, ed. 1992). Farmer's minutes and final report of the Commission on History and Manuscripts as well as his "Itinerary of visit to Cairo" have been edited (I. J. Katz 2015, 149–90, 216–50), and Robert Lachmann's letters to his parents on his experience at the Congress are translated (R. Katz 2003, 303–27).

3. Participants in the colloquium discussed the criteria for selecting the performers and repertory to be recorded and analyzed the recordings of Algerian, Tunisian, Iraqi, and Egyptian musicians (Vigreux, ed. 1992, 51–68, 69–86, 123–45, 155–79, respectively). Lambert and Cordereix 2015 is an edition of the recordings on eighteen CDs with a text by Bernard Moussali.

150 NOTES

4. Al-Hifnī (1896–1973) had recently returned from completing his doctorate in Leipzig and became a prominent figure in Egyptian musical life. Yekta Bey (1871–1935), along with Sachs, Farmer, Hornbostel, and Bartók, belonged to what I have called "the first generation of ethnomusicologists" (Blum 1991, 3–9).

5. In Egypt *al-mūsīqa al-ʿarabiyya* referred both to "Arab music" in this broad sense and to a recent "category of secular urban music" (El-Shawan 1979, 86). El-Shawan's study of the category (1981, 88–141) opens with an informative survey of developments in the decades preceding the 1932 Congress.

6. In his *Système générale des intervalles des sons*, Joseph Sauveur (1701 [1973, 30]) derived his description of "the Oriental system, which is followed by the Turks and Persians" from a French translation of the *Kitāb al-adwār* of Ṣafi al-Dīn al-Urmawī (d. 1294), whom Sauveur considered "an Arab author" since he wrote in Arabic. In Sauveur's accurate table, "the Oriental system" becomes "the Arab scale" (*gamme des Arabes*). It retained that name in Laborde's *Essai sur la musique ancienne et moderne* of 1780 (see Marcus 1989, 809, for Laborde's comparison of "the Arab scale" with "the European scale of equal semitones").

7. Michael D. Rosse's dissertation *The movement for the revitalization of 'Hindu' music in Northern India, 1860–1930* devotes a chapter to the Gandharva Mayavidyalaya (Rosse 1995, 152–74) and briefly discusses earlier conferences (175–76). One of Paluskar's most important collaborators, Gurudev Patwardhan, published a detailed drumming notation in a manual translated and discussed in its historical context by Kippen (2006).

8. Lemaire's accomplishments are discussed by Darvishi (1995, 29–33, 53–61) and Khoshzamir (1979, 37–45), who calls him "the most influential musician in the history of modern music in Iran" (40). Lemaire published piano arrangements of melodies from the court music repertoire (excerpts in Darvishi 1995, 60–61) as well as a theory text in French with Persian translation. The French solfège syllables replaced the system found in earlier treatises among performers of what is now called Persian *traditional* or *classical* music.

9. Names for seven primary scale degrees can be documented from the fourteenth and fifteenth centuries, when they also served as names for modes built on that degree, like Persian *segāh*/Arabic *sikāh* on the third degree of the general scale (Shiloah 1979, 84, 127, 308).

10. At a 1961 conference on *Preservation of the learned and popular forms of traditional music of the Orient and the Occident* in Tehran, Vaziri

NOTES   151

maintained that all national musics of Asia could be preserved in notations using his two signs for "intermediate tones" that are less than a sharp or less than a flat, since musicians could learn by ear "the exact value of the intermediate tones" (Vaziri 1964, 255). Alain Daniélou (1907–94) responded by advocating "a standardized system of notation" that would indicate "the real intervals used in the performances, the precise form of the ornaments and the amplitude of the vibrations" (Daniélou 1964, 312).

11. "In Azerbaijan music, as in European schools of music, an octave contains 7 diatonic and 12 chromatic grades. The only difference is that the octave grades in European music are *equally* tempered, but in Azerbaijan music . . . the octave grades are tempered *unequally*" (Hacıbäyli 1945 [1985, 21]). This spelling of Hacıbäyli's name uses the modern Azeri alphabet; others come from transliteration systems for Cyrillic and retain Russified versions of his surname like Hadzhibegov, Hajibekov, or Hajibeyov (in *NG*).

12. In the cultivation of Chinese street opera in Singapore, as described by Lee Tong Soon (2009, 62–68, 78–85), it is the professional troupes that were long associated with religious rites and the amateurs whose organizations offer training that makes use of music notation. The latter have flourished as public interest in the former declined. Members of the amateur troupes, who are better educated and wealthy enough to employ teachers from abroad, enjoy official support as bearers of Chinese cultural heritage.

13. When I asked the 'ud player and composer Anouar Brahem in April 1990 about his relationship with the guardians of musical heritage at the Rashidiya Institute, he told me he had chosen to study the *maqāmāt* with a "marginal" musician, Ali Sriti (1919–2007).

14. During fieldwork at the Uzbek State Conservatory between 2002 and 2005, Tanya Merchant (2006, 70) found that this "pedagogical model" remained in place as Uzbekistan became an independent nation following the breakup of the USSR. Merchant was impressed by the conservatory students' "significant grounding in the analysis of the structure of the *Shashmaqom*" (71), whereas Levin (1984, ii) had found younger performers rather weak on that score. Even conservatory students who were not majoring in "traditional music" were required to take a course in *maqom*, given its greatly enhanced importance to the "nationalist project" of post-Soviet Uzbekistan (Merchant 2021, 236).

15. Levin also helped in translating a section on rhythmic theory from Karomatov's book on Uzbek instrumental music (Karomatov 1983).

16. Mark and Greta Slobin dropped "ideological passages that interrupt the main narrative" in translating Beliaev's conservatory textbook on *Central Asian Music* (Beliaev 1975, vii).

152 NOTES

17. Ella Zonis (1964, 308–9) described difficulties in producing an authoritative version of the Persian *radif* in her review of the publication (Barkeshli and Ma'rufi 1963).

18. Lê Tuân Hùng (1994, 243) quotes Hô Chi Minh's conviction that a "modern national" language for music and other arts required "a synthesis of indigenous and 'progressive' non-indigenous means of expression."

19. In addition to the AAWM journal and conferences, both the Society for Ethnomusicology and the Society for Music Theory have interest groups on Analysis of World Music.

20. See also the essays in Moisala et al. eds. 2017 and the *assemblage theory* outlined by Manuel DeLanda (2013 [2006]).

21. Hoyningen-Huene (2013) sees "nine dimensions of science" as constitutive of *systematicity*: description, explanation, prediction, defense of knowledge claims, critical discourse, epistemic connectedness, an ideal of completeness, knowledge generation, and the representation of knowledge. Music theoretical writing rarely aspires to be *systematic* in all nine respects, which may be just as well.

22. Folklorists often make this assumption explicit. A. R. Ramanujan (1986, 41) speaks of "a folklore system in one village . . . where each genre is fitted to others, fitted, dovetailed, contrasted—so that we cannot study any of them alone for long." Likewise, Dan Ben-Amos (2020, xx) sees *folklore* as "a system of communicative acts. All of its elements, including its cognitive, expressive, and characterizing features, are interdependent, and variations in one characterizing feature activate modifications in others."

23. Joseph Sauveur's "Système générale des intervalles des sons," mentioned in Ch. 3, n6 and Ch. 4, n2, is a landmark in the early history of comparative musicology.

24. See, for instance, the lengthy entries on *systema* and *système* in the music dictionaries of Brossard (1703, 156–68) and Rousseau (1995 [1768], 1070–1104).

25. In all three editions of *The study of ethnomusicology*, Nettl maintained that "the main interest of ethnomusicology is in total musical systems" (1983, 252; 2005, 140; 2015, 148), adding however that "the idea of the world of music consisting of a large number of discrete systems, more or less acceptable for the past, may not work in the present, when there is much less to keep the musics of the world apart" (Nettl 1983, 51; compare the altered wording in Nettl 2005, 59, and 2015, 71). In the first edition (1983, 253–54), Nettl distinguished between cultures that "had developed systematic ways of teaching their music, sometimes in the process separating it from its cultural context" and those that had not, adding that a researcher's

NOTES 153

"ability to enter the entire cultural system" would probably be more important in the latter.

26. Charles Seeger sketched a "model of the systems of human communication" that included tactile, auditory, and visual "instances" (1994 [1976], 342). He defined *system* as "an item of attention regarded as a unit, a one, a singularity, a gestalt," which "may be regarded equally in terms of structure and in terms of function" (345).

27. "Si l'on veut bien se souvenir que nous sommes encore très loin de connaître tous les systèmes originels qui régissent la mélodie, le rythme, la forme, sans oublier la polyphonie . . ."

28. "que l'on ait affaire à des échelles, des rythmes ou des structures, ces pierres à bâtir se révèlent, vues de près, déterminées par un principe intelligible, duquel découle un ensemble plus ou moins étendu de procédés ou, si l'on préfère, un *système*."

29. Work that adopts, extends, or critiques Brăiloiu's procedures has been published by Baud-Bovy (1956, 1968) on Greek folksong; Estreicher (1964) on the rhythmic system of the Bororo Peul; Labussière (1976) and Fatemi (2003) on rhythmic systems of children; and Reiche (1991), Cler (1994), and Dauer (1994) on *aksak* rhythms. Brăiloiu's efforts to enumerate the principles of "autonomous" rhythmic systems can be fruitfully compared with Arom's writings on "metric and rhythmic principles in Central Africa" (e.g., Arom 1998).

30. "le propre de la pensée mythique est de s'exprimer à l'aide d'un répertoire dont la composition est hétéroclite et qui, bien qu'étendu, reste tout de même limité."

31. Kubik (1996, 6) remarks that "The insider/outsider distinction focuses upon the *person* of the observer or researcher and his share in the culture to be studied. The emic/etic distinction focuses upon *standpoints*, regardless of the kind of person involved. It is thus much more abstract than the first."

32. Bateson's definition of *information* as "Any difference that makes a difference" (Bateson 1979, 228) requires representation (hence coding) of such differences "inside some information-processing entity" (68). The discussion of differences that make a difference by William James (1842–1910) accords well with theorizing directed toward action: "There can *be* no difference anywhere that doesn't *make* a difference elsewhere—no difference in abstract truth that doesn't express itself in a difference in concrete fact and in conduct consequent upon that fact, imposed on somebody, somehow, somewhere, and somewhen" (James 1987a [1907], 508, his italics).

154 NOTES

33. The analogous term in German, *Tonsystem*, has at least four senses: the repertory of tones (*Tonvorrat*) available in a given practice, a tuning, a schema on which tone relations are based, or a structure common to a group of melodies (Dahlhaus 1966, 533).

Chapter 4

1. For example, H. T. Norris's edition and translation of "Two Arabic manuscripts on the subject of Mauritanian music and Saharan folk poetry" (Norris 1968, 155–93) has numerous footnotes to both text and translation, some of which report explanations given to Norris by the Mauritanian scholar Mukhtār wuld Hāmidun.

2. A music-theoretical analogue to Leibniz's "alphabet of human thoughts" was the "Système générale des intervalles des sons" that Joseph Sauveur proposed as the "foundation" (*principe*) of the new science of *acoustics* in a 1701 address to the Academy of Sciences in Paris. Making available a means "of ascertaining all ratios that constitute the specific systems on which instruments have been constructed . . . and of comparing these different systems with one another," Sauveur intended his *general system* to serve as "a kind of philosophical language, composed entirely of monosyllables, in which the significance of words depends on the number, nature, and ordering of letters, and in which each word carries a specific meaning for this reason" (Sauveur 1973 [1701], 129, 137).

3. *HmT* is available online through *RILM Music Encyclopedias* (rme-rilm-org.ezproxy.gc.cuny.edu) and the Digitale Bibliothek of the Münchener DigitalisierungsZentrum (daten.digitale-sammlungen.de, accessed January 13, 2021). An entry on "Gaku" is the sole gesture toward inclusion of East Asian languages.

4. See, for example, "Approaches to a *Lexicon of local terminology on multipart singing in Europe*" (Ahmedaja ed. 2011, 235–458).

5. The final section of Powers's article on mode was expanded with new sections by other authors in the 2001 edition of *NG*; those interested in his views should consult the first edition (1980).

6. Distinctions emphasized by Powers include location on a "spectrum between abstract scale and fixed tune," association with solo or ensemble performance, serving as a set of models for making music or a set of categories within an existing repertory, closed and symmetrical systems like the Medieval church modes or open-ended collections like the *rāgas*.

NOTES 155

Other differences are whether individual names are used in spelling out sequences to be observed in ritual, theater, and other activities; and whether the entities are organized hierarchically with such categories as "principle," "derivative," "branch."

7. Hood (1971, 324) made a tentative list of four "basic features of Mode": "(1) a gapped scale, that is, a scale made up of both small and large intervals; (2) a hierarchy of principal pitches; (3) the usage of vocal or ornamental pitches; and (4) extramusical associations with the seasons, hours of the day or night, and so forth."

8. Such differences did not prevent music theorists writing in Persian during the seventeenth, eighteenth, and nineteenth centuries from positing correspondences between specific *maqām*s and *rāga*s. M. T. Massoudieh's inventory of Persian manuscripts on music (1996) lists several works that discuss such correspondences (e.g., nos. 38, 50, 203, and 108).

9. I attribute the problems with *modality* "as an inherent musical property" to efforts of nineteenth- and twentieth-century music historians and theorists to imagine an earlier system with properties comparable to those attributed to *tonality* as a system whose properties provide a basis for *tonal* music.

10. "non soltanto una scala caratteristica di questo modo, ma anche quell'insieme di convenzioni varianti da una musica all'altra."

11. Thrasher (2008, 80–112) uses *mode* in much the same sense as Pian, though he calls heptatonic collections of pitches *scales* in order to distinguish them from the pentatonic modes.

12. English *rhythmic mode* has found its way into ethnomusicology from histories of music in Medieval Europe (e.g., Sawa 1989 and 2009). In their study of Australian *Wangga songmen and their repertories*," Marett, Barwick, and Ford use the term for named patterns "defined primarily by the combination of tempo . . . with the patterns articulated by the clapsticks" and "used by songmen to differentiate their repertory from others" (2013, 47).

13. Javanese *pathet* is frequently glossed as *mode* (Walton 1987; Perlman 1998 and 2004) or *modal system* (Sumarsam 1995 where it is also glossed as *modal practice* and *modal classification*). Christina Sunardi (2017, 63) contrasts the usage of one eastern Javanese musician in which *laras* replaces *pathet* as a term for mode with Central Javanese usage where *laras* designates tuning system. In 1988–89 Weintraub found that "the concept of *patet* . . . does not currently enjoy widespread acceptance among Sundanese gamelan musicians" (1993, 29).

156 NOTES

14. The Parry-Lord collection became widely known as a repertory of "Serbo-Croatian epic" and only recently has the Albanian verse they collected been published (Scaldaferri 2021).

15. Like Lord and Ampene, Euba's student George Dor (2000, 285) finds that "usage of the term improvisation remains problematic" when it implies lack of preparation. Many who use the term feel constrained to distance themselves from that implication; the music theorist Steve Larson (2005, 258), for instance, felt "confident in describing [Bill] Evans's apparently 'instantaneous' improvisation as the result of years of preparation."

16. Models for making or receiving music often include moments or phases when external assistance is crucial or desirable. Reception of songs from spirits was a prominent topic in early ethnomusicological research on compositional processes of Native Americans (Nettl 1954; Merriam 1964, 165–84).

17. Leo Treitler saw multiple notated realizations of a model as fundamental to musical production and transmission in Europe from the twelfth to the fourteenth century: "the performer, or the notator, not reproducing the piece in performance exactly from score or from memory, not copying it directly from a written antecedent, but reconstructing it each time on the basis of a model, and under the influence of local and individual principles guiding the reconstruction" (Treitler 2003, 86–87).

18. "Als übergeordnete Kategorien für all das was wir sonst unter Begriffe wie Komposition, Improvisation, Aufführungspraxis, usw, subsumieren, könnte man auch 'Modell und Ausführung' betrachten" (Grupe 2004, 243). Nettl (1974, 19) gave the term *model* precisely this extension.

19. "un ensemble ambigu et complexe de perceptions, d'idées, et de schéma comportementaux, fruit d'un savoir cumulatif qui, si d'un côté il se cristallise en règles et modèles formels, de l'autre conserve sa dynamique dans les modalités de traitement."

20. Descriptions of modes do describe models, but not one *type* of model that might serve to define *mode* cross-culturally.

21. Paul Ricoeur (1975, 61) related Aristotle's observation that metaphors bring things "before our eyes" by signifying them as "engaged in an activity" to the discussion of drama as an imitation of human action in *Poetics*, 1448a. Ricoeur adds that "The ontological function of metaphorical discourse may well be to present humans 'as acting' and all things 'as active': all the dormant potential of existence appears *as* manifest, all latent capacity of action *as* effective" ("Présenter les hommes '*comme agissant*' et toutes choses '*comme en acte*', telle pourrait bien être la fonction *ontologique* du discours métaphorique. En lui, toute potentialité dormante

NOTES 157

d'existence apparaît *comme* éclose, toute capacité latente d'action *comme* effective"). This is a good reason for theorizing about music-making to be highly metaphorical.

22. In the late 1960s Milton Babbitt (1972, 171) remarked that "The loosely scrutinized metaphor of music as a language and, almost unbelievably, as a universal language, has reasserted itself in a new and demanding guise as structural linguistics and, most particularly, transformational grammars, which suggest tantalizingly the possihility of helpful analogies or even the means of sharply clarifying the probably deep distinctions between music and language." Powers (1980c) has reviewed "language models" in music analysis, Feld and Fox (1994) the English-language anthropological literature on relations of music and language.

23. See Blumenberg's chapters on "background metaphorics" (1998, 92–111, trans. 2010, 62–76) and on "probability" (1998, 118–42, trans. 2010, 81–98).

24. In the English translation by Bergin and Fisch, Vico's treatment of "poetic logic" in paragraphs nos. 400–11 includes metaphors and topics (paragraph numbers supplied by the translators).

25. Ethnomusicologists and music historians can point to work with textiles as a common source domain for metaphors depicting composition, performance, or making instruments as weaving or stitching. Examples are the observations that "the technique of making a drum was similar to the technique of weaving" and "Beating the drum is also a form of weaving" in the conversations on Dogon religious ideas between Ogotemmêli and Marcel Griaule (1965, 65).

26. Michael Spitzer defines musical metaphor as "the relationship between the physical, proximate, and familiar, and the abstract, distal, and unfamiliar" (2004, 4) and treats the relationship as "bidirectional"—from physical to abstract for listeners and theorists as receivers of music, and from abstract norms of musical poetics to a finished work for composers. Spitzer's treatment of reception and production as two "realms" seems to me unwise, with respect both to the European compositions he discusses and to a wider range of practices.

27. Euclid's *Geometry* begins by defining *sēmeion* "point" as "that which cannot be divided" (Euclid 1947, i, 153, 155). In what survives of his *rhythmics*, Aristoxenus equates a *sēmeion* of bodily movement with a tone (*phthongos*) in melody and a syllable in speech as he defines *protos chronos* as "the duration in which there can in no way be placed either two notes or two syllables or two gestures" (Barker 1989, 187). His translators have used *signal* (Pearson in Aristoxenus 1990, 7, 9) and *gesture* (Barker 1989, 187) as

158   NOTES

well as *point* (Barker, 186) for *sēmeion*. Sawa (2009, see index) discusses multiple uses of the point metaphor in Arabic music theory.

28. As Perlman remarks (2004, 30), writers disagree on whether to treat metaphor as a form of analogy or analogy as a form of metaphor. The prominence of Lakoff's and Johnson's work in American musical scholarship favors the latter view, though the long history of responses to Aristotle's remarks on the subject is reason enough to also consider the former.

29. Ethnomusicological publications concerned with experiences of time include Judith Becker's "Time and tune in Java" (1979), Merriam's "African musical rhythm and concepts of time-reckoning" (1981), Ellis's "Time consciousness of Aboriginal performers" (1984), Araújo's "Acoustic labor in the timing of everyday life" (1992), and Wolf's *The black cow's footprint: Time, space, and music in the lives of the Kotas of South India* (2005). See also Scherzinger 2019.

30. Translated by Hans Heinrich Braun from Weber 1904 [1968, 194]: "[Der Idealtypus] ist ein Gedankenbild . . . welches die Bedeutung eines rein idealen *Grenz* begriffes hat, an welchem die Wirklichkeit zur Verdeutlichung bestimmter bedeutsamer Bestandteile ihres empirischen Gehaltes *gemessen*, mit dem sie *verglichen* wird."

31. Alexander J. Ellis (translator of Helmholtz's *On the sensations of tone*) proposed *cents* as a logarithmic measure of interval sizes: assigning 100 cents to every semitone in equal temperament allows for easier comparison of interval sizes than do frequency ratios expressed in Hertz.

32. For Hornbostel, "purely melodic music" is meant to be heard and performed without imagining implied harmonies.

33. Jaap Kunst, for example, argued that when a musical practice is "purely vocal . . . we cannot speak of 'scales' in the ordinary sense of the word, let alone of 'tone systems'" (Kunst 1973 [1949], 11).

34. Dowling's four "levels of psychological analysis" (Dowling and Harwood 1986) could also provide ethnomusicologists with an *ideal type*, allowing for recognition of discrepancies (as discussed in the final section of Chapter Four).

Chapter 5

1. Moya Aliya Malamusi's "Rise and development of a Chileka guitar style in the 1950s" includes transcripts of conversations in Chichewa with English translation (1994, 44–72), and Artur Simon transcribes and translates

NOTES 159

his interview with Avi Pwasi in Bura, a Chadian language of northeast Nigeria (1994, 90–145). Maurice Djenda appends a French translation to a facsimile of notes he took during a conversation on Mpyεmŏ religion with Joseph Leka, an elderly sage. Tiago de Oliveira Pinto adds comments on the player's actions to the Portuguese text of excerpts from his interview with a berimbau player (1994, 475–78).

2. Some archives are making selected holdings available online, and important interviews are occasionally published on compact discs (e.g., conversations of Hormoz Farhat with the Persian musician and teacher Nur 'Ali Borumand in Farhat and As'adi 2005).

3. See Nelson 2008 for an introduction to Karnatak *śolkaṭṭu* and Kippen 1988, 143–59, for the Hindustani *tablā* bols taught in the Lucknow *gharānā*, whose students "must learn a variety of techniques for the same spoken *bols*."

4. Kubik's glosses *time-line* (1994, 44) as "a specific category of struck motional patterns, characterized by an asymmetric inner structure, such as 5 + 7 or 7 + 9." J. H. K. Nketia (1974, 132) gave the term a greater extension: "an accompanying rhythm and a means by which rhythmic motion is sustained. . . . It may be designed as a rhythmic pattern in additive or divisive form, embodying the basic pulse or regulative beat as well as the density referent." Both Nketia and Kubik realized that what they termed asymmetric or additive patterns are coordinated with beats occurring at equal intervals of time.

5. Alfons Dauer (1985, 19, 28, 31, 33–36, 53) uses the labels *off* and *on* for "departures from and returns to the tonal center" in music of wind ensembles from various regions of Africa.

6. Sandell (1990) and Smoliar (1995) offer pertinent criticism of Cogan's "phonological theory."

7. Emmie te Nijenhuis (1974, 40) lists Sanskrit treatises that refer to "the ancient Indian system whereby each note of the octave (*saptaka*) was related to a particular deity, social class, sentiment (*rasa*), colour, finger of the hand, verse-metre" and so on. One section of the Arabic treatise on music of the Ikhwān al-Ṣafā (Brethren of Purity, second half of tenth century CE) is devoted to "tetrads" (*murabba'āt*), "groups of four features corresponding to each other: the position of the celestial bodies, the zodiac, seasons, winds, humours, elements, colors, perfumes, the four strings of the 'ud, etc." (Shiloah 1979, 232).

8. In his study of the *sizhu* "silk and bamboo" instrumental music of South China, Thrasher (2008, 40–41) comments on the "clear musical manifestations, historical and contemporary" of two of the five terms, *ho*

160 NOTES

(*he* in the *pinyin* system of romanization) and *ya*, which he glosses as "harmony, concordance" and "elegant, refined," respectively.

9. *Nātyaśāstra*, chapter 28.11, trans. Ghosh 1961, 3: "The Gāndharva is of three kinds: that of the notes (*svara*), that of the Tāla and that of the verbal theme (*pada*)."

10. This triad also appears in the Apocryphal *Wisdom of Solomon* (11:21). I have not seen a survey of its uses in music theory. In Book One of his *Harmonie universelle* (1636), Marin Mersenne maintained that "puis que toutes choses consistent en poids, en nombre & en mesure, & que les Sons represente ces trois proprietez, ils peuuent signifier tout ce que l'on voudra, si l'on en excepte la Metaphysique . . ." (i, 43).

11. Interests of comparative musicologists in the 1920s included "The Unity of the Senses" (Hornbostel 1925 and 1927) as well as synesthesia (Wellek 1928–29), and Merriam devoted a chapter of *The anthropology of music* to synesthesia (1964, 85–101).

12. In the second volume of *Ilmu Karawitan* "Knowledge about gamelan music," Sindoesawarno "describes a descending order of weight of sounds, from the heaviest to the lightest sound" in the sequence of solmization syllables: *dong* (heaviest, most important), *dung, dang, dèng, ding* (Sumarsam 1995, 143).

13. The Greek distinction of "tense" and "lax" genera, and the opposition of tone and semitone as *sýntonos* "hard" and *malakós* "soft," made in the second century CE by Claudius Ptolemy, were assimilated into Arabic theory and extended by al-Kindi (d. ca. 866 CE) to characterize major thirds as *qawwī* "strong," *khashin* "rough," and *mudhakkar* "masculine," minor thirds as *nāqis* "weak," *laiyin* "soft," and *mu'annath* "feminine" (Neubauer 1994, 391). The equivalent polarity in European music theory is Latin *dūrus* "hard"/*mollis* "soft," which survives in the names of major and minor keys in German, French, and other languages. On the semantics of that polarity in European music history, see Keym and Hinrichsen, eds. 2020.

14. The two *sanang* are led by the player of the drum *gimbal*, who chooses from among five named rhythms. A *basal* ensemble also includes at least one *agung*, a larger suspended gong that plays one of three named rhythms and may be joined with counterpoint on one or two additional *agung*. Like a *sanang*, an *agung* is also *mäsning* "higher-pitched" or *mälämbäg* "lower-pitched" (Revel-Macdonald and Maceda 1987 [1992]; *basal* ensemble on the CD, track 13).

15. In the linguistic theory of N. S. Trubetzkoy and Roman Jakobson, when one term of an opposition is "marked" by a specific property, the unmarked term

may refer to absence of that property or to a class of entities whose members may or may not possess it. See Hatten 1994, 34–44, on implications of the relationship marked/unmarked in European art music.

16. Evans's emphasis on complementarity responded to Robert Farris Thompson's articles (1966, 1973) on "an aesthetic of the cool." Thompson was one of the first Africanists to list terms in several languages relating to a broad aesthetic category. Evans's binary framework may turn out to be particularly relevant to musical practices of South Africa, given the intensive engagement of South African musicians with African American innovations.

17. C. S. Peirce saw "a potentiality for future growth as essential to present meaning" (Short 2007, x). More recently, "the potentiality of the virtual" is a major theme in the philosophy of Gilles Deleuze, including his "two philosophies of music" (Gallope 2010, 78–91).

18. The translations of the *Yue Ji* by Scott Cook (1995, 30–32) and Walter Kaufmann (1976, 33, 113–14) both have valuable commentary. Cook (31) quotes a statement from the *Zheng Xuan*: "the lower (*zhuo*, 'murky') ones [tones] are revered and the higher (*qing* 'clear') ones are lowly." Kaufmann elsewhere (1967, 54–56) lists several analogues to the pentatonic hierarchy of the *Yue Ji*, among them a family of man, wife, son, son's wife, and their offspring.

19. Another example of comparative inquiry, in addition to Dharwadker 2015, is Benamou's comparison of approaches to the topic of *musical affect* in the practices of Javanese gamelan and Western classical music (Benamou 2003).

Chapter 6

1. By *metalanguage* Agawu means "a language about another language" (2016, 147), in this instance language "as the interpreting system of music" (148). In Nattiez's usage, mentioned in the Preface, *meta-theory* interprets "ethnotheories" in a metalanguage.

2. In his chapter on *polyphony* for *CCMT*, where he wished "to view polyphony from as great a distance as we could" (2019, 640), Tenzer found *multipart music making* an appropriate term for research on "older, smaller societies."

3. "l'extraordinaire variété de rapports entre le choryphée ou soliste et le choeur offer matière à une analyse très féconde pour la connaissance de la technique polyphonique, voire de la psychologie de toute polyphonie."

NOTES

4. Izaly Zemtsovsky's thought-provoking reflections on "Dialogie musicale" (1993) offer a point of departure for comparative study.

5. My recording of this conversation with 'Ali Aqa Almajoqi is catalogued as AWM SC 11746 in the Archive of World Music, Eda Kuhn Loeb Music Library, Harvard University.

6. Other collections of work by members of these groups are Ahmedaja and Haid, eds. 2008; Ahmedaja, ed. 2013; Ahmedaja, ed. 2017; Morgenstern and Ahmedaja, eds. 2022.

7. Rouget received crucial assistance from King Gbèfa's two most knowledge-able wives as he studied the King's court music over a period of thirty-five years (1952–87). André Schaeffner (1895–1980), his great predecessor in ethnomusicological studies of ritual, saw studies of ritual as crucial to work in organology (e.g., Schaeffner 1951) and cultivated a deep interest in "pre-theater ritual" (Schaeffner 1965; see Rouget 1982, 6–7).

8. Among the sets of terms that articulate Schechner's "basic structure" are Japanese *jo/ha/kyu* (mentioned in Chapter Five), central concepts of the *Noh* drama, as Schechner would have known.

References

Abbreviations

AAWM   *Analytical Approaches to World Music* (www.aawmjournal.com)

AfM   *African Music*

AsM   *Asian Music*

CCMT   *The Oxford Handbook of Critical Concepts in Music Theory*, edited by Alexander Rehding and Steven Rings. New York: Oxford University Press, 2019.

CSE   *Chicago Studies in Ethnomusicology*. Chicago: University of Chicago Press.

EM   *Ethnomusicology*

GEWM   *Garland Encyclopedia of World Music*. New York: Garland Publishing, 1998–2002.

MGG 2 Sachteil   *Die Musik in Geschichte und Gegenwart*, second edition, Sachteil, 9 vols. Kassel: Bärenreiter, 1994–98.

MTO   *Music Theory Online* (www.mtosmt.org)

NG 2   *The New Grove Dictionary of Music and Musicians*, second edition, edited by Stanley Sadie and John Tyrrell. London: Macmillan, 2001. Also available through *OMO*

OMO   *OxfordMusicOnline* (includes access to *NG 2* and *CCMT*)

OSO   *Oxford Scholarship Online*

RdM   *Revue de Musicologie*

SRE   *Selected Reports in Ethnomusicology*, UCLA

WoM   *The World of Music*

YTM   *Yearbook for Traditional Music*

164 REFERENCES

Abraham, Otto, and E. M. von Hornbostel. 1902–03. Studien über das Tonsystem und die Musik der Japaner. *Sammelbände der Internationalen Musikgesellschaft* 4/2, 302–60. Reprinted with English translation in Hornbostel 1975, 1–84.

Abraham, Otto, and E. M. von Hornbostel. 1909. Vorschläge für die Transkription exotischer Melodien. *Sammelbände der Internationalen Musikgesellschaft* 11/1, 1–25. English translation, "Suggested methods for the transcription of exotic music," *EM* 38/3 (1994), 425–56.

Advielle, Victor. 1885. *La musique chez les Persans en 1885*. Paris: the author.

Agawu, Kofi. 1995. *African rhythm, a Northern Ewe perspective.* Cambridge: Cambridge University Press. Accompanying CD.

Agawu, Kofi. 2003. *Representing African music: Postcolonial notes, queries, positions*. New York: Routledge.

Agawu, Kofi. 2016a. *The African imagination in music*. New York: Oxford University Press.

Agawu, Kofi. 2016b. Tonality as a colonizing force in Africa. In *Audible empire: Music, global politics, critique*, edited by Ronald Radano and Tejumola Olaniyan, 334–55. Durham, NC: Duke University Press.

Agawu, Kofi. 2017. Against ethnotheory. In *The dawn of music semiology: Essays in honor of Jean-Jacques Nattiez*, edited by Jonathan Dunsby and Jonathan Goldman. Rochester: University of Rochester Press.

Ahmedaja, Ardian, ed. 2011. *European voices II. Cultural listening and local discourse in multipart singing traditions in Europe*. Schriften zur Volksmusik, 23. Vienna: Böhlau. Accompanying CD and DVD.

Ahmedaja, Ardian, ed. 2013. *Local and global understandings of creativities. Multipart music making and the construction of ideas, contexts and contents*. Newcastle upon Tyne: Cambridge Scholars Publishing.

Ahmedaja, Ardian, ed. 2017. *European voices III. The instrumentation and instrumentalization of sound: Local multipart music practices in Europe: in commemoration of Gerlinde Haid*. Schriften zur Volksmusik, 25. Vienna: Böhlau.

Ahmedaja, Ardian, and Gerlinde Haid, eds. 2008. *European voices I. Multipart singing in the Balkans and the Mediterranean*. Schriften zur Volksmusik, 22. Vienna: Böhlau.

Allen, Matthew Harp. 2008. Standardize, classicize, and nationalize: The scientific work of the Music Academy of Madras, 1930–52. In *Performing pasts: Reinventing the arts in modern South India*, edited by I. V. Peterson and D. Soneji, 99–129. New Delhi: Oxford University Press.

Alorwoyie, G. Foli, with David Locke. 2013. *Agbadza: Songs, drum language of the Ewe*. St. Louis: African Music Publishers.

Alter, Andrew. 1994. Gurus, shishyas and educators: Adaptive strategies in post-colonial North Indian music institutions. In *Music-cultures in contact:*

REFERENCES   165

Convergences and collisions, edited by M. J. Kartomi and S. Blum, 158–68. Sydney: Currency Press and Basel: Gordon and Breach.

Ames, David W., and Anthony V. King. 1971. *Glossary of Hausa music and its social contexts*. Evanston: Northwestern University Press.

Amoozegar-Fassaie, Farzad. 2018. Ethical dimensions of music-making in Iran: Beauty in Islamic revelations, mysticism and tradition. Ph.D. dissertation, University of California, Los Angeles.

Ampene, Kwasi. 2005. *Female song tradition and the Akan of Ghana: The creative process in nnwonkorɔ*. SOAS Musicology Series. Aldershot: Ashgate. Accompanying CD.

Anderson, Fred, and Paul Steinbeck. 2002. *Exercises for creative musicians*. Chicago: Many Weathers Music.

Anderson, Lois Ann. 1968. The "miko" modal system of Kiganda xylophone music. Ph.D. dissertation, University of California, Los Angeles.

Anderson, Lois Ann. 1984. Multipart relationships in xylophone and tuned drum traditions in Buganda. *SRE* 5, 121–44.

Appiah, Kwame Anthony. 2016. There is no such thing as Western civilization. *The Guardian*, 9 November. Online at theguardian.com.

Appiah, Kwame Anthony. 2018. *The lies that bind: Rethinking identity*. London: Liveright.

Araújo, Samuel. 1992. Acoustic labor in the timing of everyday life: A critical contribution to the history of samba in Rio de Janeiro. Ph.D. dissertation, University of Illinois at Urbana-Champaign.

Archer, William K., ed. 1964. *The Preservation of Traditional Forms of the Learned and Popular Music of the Orient and the Occident. La preservation des formes traditionnelles de la musique savante et populaire dans les pays d'Orient et d'Occident*. Urbana: Center for Comparative Psycholinguistics, Institute of Communications Research, University of Illinois.

Aristides Quintilianus. 1963. *De musica libri tres*, edited by R. P. Winnington-Ingram. Leipzig: B.G. Teubner.

Aristotle. 1930–35. *Metaphysics*, with a translation by Hugh Tredennick. Cambridge, MA: Harvard University Press and London: Heinemann. Loeb Classical Library, 271, 287. 2 vols.

Aristotle. 1957. *On the soul, Parva naturalia, On breath*, with a translation by W. S. Hett. Loeb Classical Library, 288. Cambridge, MA: Harvard University Press and London: Heinemann.

Aristoxenus. 1990. *Elementa rhythmica: the fragment of Book II and the additional evidence for Aristoxenean rhythmic theory*, edited and translated by Lionel Pearson. Oxford: Clarendon Press.

Arnheim, Rudolf. 1969. *Visual thinking*. Berkeley and Los Angeles: University of California Press.

Arom, Simha. 1974. Une méthode pour la transcription de polyphonies et polyrythmies de tradition orale. *RdM* 59/2, 165–90.

166 REFERENCES

Arom, Simha. 1976. The use of play-back techniques in the study of oral polyphonies. *EM* 20/3, 483–519; https://doi.org/10.2307/851046.

Arom. Simha. 1985. *Polyphonies et polyrythmies d'Afrique Centrale: Structure et méthodologie.* Société d'Études Linguistiques et Anthropologiques de France. Paris: Centre National de la Recherche Scientifique.

Arom, Simha. 1990. Réflexions préliminaires. In International Musicological Society, *Atti del XIV congresso della Società Internazionale de Musicologia: Trasmissione e recezione delle forme di cultura musicale*, I, *Round Tables*, edited by A. Pompilio, D. Restani, L. Bianconi, and F. Alberto Gallo, 187–90. Turin: E.D.T.

Arom, Simha. 1991. *African polyphony and polyrhythm: Structure and methodology.* Translated by Martin Thom, Barbara Tuckett, and Raymond Boyd. Cambridge: Cambridge University Press. Translation of Arom 1985.

Arom, Simha. 1994. Intelligence in traditional music. In *What is intelligence?*, edited by J. Khalfa, 137–60. Cambridge: Cambridge University Press.

Arom, Simha. 1998. 'L'arbre qui cachait la forêt': Principes métriques et rhythmiques en Centrafrique. *Revue Belge de Musicologie* 52, 179–95.

Arom, Simha, and Susanne Fürniss. 1992. The pentatonic system of the Aka pygmies of the Central African Republic. In *European studies in ethnomusicology: Historical developments and recent trends. Selected papers presented at the VIIth European Seminar in Ethnomusicology, Berlin, October 1–6, 1990*, edited by M. P. Baumann, A. Simon, and U. Wegner, 159–73. Intercultural Music Studies, 4. Wilhelmshaven: Florian Noetzel.

Arom, Simha, and Susanne Fürniss. 1993. An interactive experimental method for the determination of musical scales in oral cultures: Application to the vocal music of the Aka pygmies of Central Africa. *Contemporary Music Review* 9/1–2, 7–12.

Asad, Talal. 1997. Remarks on the anthropology of the body. In *Religion and the body*, edited by Sarah Coakley, 42–52. Cambridge: Cambridge University Press.

Asaf'yev, Boris. 1930. *Muzikal'naya forma kak protsess.* Moscow: Gosudarstvennoye Isdatel'stvo, Muzikal'noiy Sektor. English translation in James Robert Tull, B.V. Asaf'ev's *Musical form as a process*: Translation and commentary, 183–564. Ph.D. dissertation, Ohio State University, 1976.

Austin, J. L. 1975 [1962]. How to do things with words. Second edition, edited by J. O. Urmson and Marina Sbisà. Cambridge, MA: Harvard University Press.

Ayangil, Ruhi. 2008. Turkish music in Western notation. *Journal of the Royal Asiatic Society* 18/4, 401–47.

Ayangil, Ruhi. 2010. Western notation: A debatable matter in Turkish *makam* music contributed by Giuseppe Donizetti Pasha. In *Giuseppe Donizetti Pascià: Traiettorie musicali e storiche tra Italia e Turchia/Giuseppe Donizetti Pasha: Musical and historical trajectories between Italy and Turkey*, edited by Federico Spinetti, 39–58. Bergamo: Fondazione Donizetti.

REFERENCES 167

Babbitt, Milton. 1972. Contemporary music composition and music theory in contemporary intellectual history. In *Perspectives in musicology*, edited by Barry S. Brook, Edward O. D. Downes, and Sherman Van Solkema, 151–73. New York: Norton. Reprinted in *The collected essays of Milton Babbitt*, 270–307. Princeton: Princeton University Press, 2003.

Baily, John. 1981. A system of modes in the urban music of Afghanistan. *EM* 25/1, 1–39.

Baily, John. 1985. Music structure and human movement. In *Musical structure and cognition*, edited by Peter Howell, Ian Cross, and Robert West, 237–58. London: Academic Press.

Baily, John. 1988a. *Music of Afghanistan: Professional musicians in the city of Herat*. Cambridge Studies in Ethnomusicology. Cambridge: Cambridge University Press.

Baily, John. 1988b. Anthropological and psychological approaches to the study of music theory and musical cognition. *YTM* 20, 114–24.

Baily, John. 1991. Some cognitive aspects of motor planning in musical performance. *Psychologica Belgica* 31/2, 147–62.

Baily, John. 1992. Music performance, motor structure, and cognitive models. In *European studies in ethnomusicology: Historical developments and recent trends. Selected papers presented at the VIIth European Seminar in Ethnomusicology, Berlin, October 1–6, 1990*, edited by M. P. Baumann, A. Simon, and U. Wegner, 142–58. Intercultural Music Studies, 4. Wilhelmshaven: Florian Noetzel.

Baily, John. 2008. The (Afghan) *rubab* as the embodiment of modal thinking in Afghanistan. In *Intercultural comparison of maqām and related phenomena: Proceedings of the Fifth Meeting of the ICTM Study Group 'maqām', Samarkand, 26–30 August 2001*, edited by Jürgen Elsner and Gisa Jähnichen, 29–32. Berlin: trafo.

Bakan, Michael. 1999. *Music of death and new creation: Experiences in the world of Balinese gamelan beleganjur*. CSE.

Baker, David. 1969. *Jazz improvisation: A comprehensive method of study for all players*. Chicago: Maher Publications.

Bakhle, Janaki. 2005. *Two men and music: Nationalism in the making of an Indian classical tradition*. New York: Oxford University Press.

Bakhtin, Mikhail M. 1986. *Speech genres and other late essays*. Translated by Vern W. McGee, edited by Caryl Emerson and Michael Holquist. Austin: University of Texas Press.

Barbera, André. 1991. *The Euclidean division of the canon: Greek and Latin sources*. Lincoln: University of Nebraska Press.

Barker, Andrew, ed. 1989. *Greek musical writings*, II, *Harmonic and acoustic theory*. Cambridge Readings in the Literature of Music. Cambridge: Cambridge University Press.

168 REFERENCES

Barkeshli, Mehdi and Musā Ma'rufi. 1963. *La musique traditionelle de l'Iran/ Radif-e musiqi-ye Irān*. Tehran: Honarhā-ye Zibā-ye Keshvar. Text in French and Persian.

Bartók, Béla. 1931. *The Hungarian folk song*. London: Oxford University Press. First published in Hungarian, 1924.

Barwick, Linda, Allan Marett, and Guy Tunstill, eds. 1995. *The essence of singing and the substance of song: Recent responses to the Aboriginal performing arts and other essays in honour of Catherine Ellis*. Oceania Monograph 46. Sydney: University of Sydney.

Basso, Ellen B. 1985. *A musical view of the universe: Kalapalo myth and ritual performances*. University of Pennsylvania Publications in Conduct and Communications. Philadelphia: University of Pennsylvania.

Bastos, Rafaele José de Menenzes. 1978. *A musicológica Kamayurá: para una antropologia da comunicaçao no Alto-Xingu*. Brasilia: Fundaçao Nacional do Indio.

Bastos, Rafaele José de Menenzes. 1986. Música, cultura e sociedade no Alto-Xingu: A teoria musical dos indios Kamayurá. *Latin American Music Review* 7/1, 51–80.

Bateson, Gregory. 1972. *Steps to an ecology of mind*. New York: Ballantine.

Bateson, Gregory. 1979. *Mind and nature, a necessary unity*. New York: E.P. Dutton.

Baud-Bovy, Samuel. 1956. La strophe de distiques rimés dans la chanson greque. In *Studia Memoria Belae Bartók Sacra*, edited by B. Rajeczky and L. Vargyas, 355–73. Budapest: Akadémiai Kiadó. English translation, "The strophe of rimed distichs in Greek song," in *Studia memoria Belae Bartók sacra*, 3rd ed., 359–76. London: Boosey & Hawkes, 1959.

Baud-Bovy, Samuel. 1968. Équivalences métriques dans la musique vocale grecque antique et moderne. *RdM* 54, 3–15.

Baxandall, Michael. 1971. *Giotto and the orators: Humanist observers of painting in Italy and the discovery of pictorial composition, 1350–1450*. Oxford: Clarendon Press.

Becker, Judith. 1979. Time and tune in Java. In *The imagination of reality: Essays in Southeast Asian coherence systems*, edited by A. L. Becker and A. Yengoyan, 197–210. Norwood, NJ: Ablex.

Beliaev, Viktor M. 1975. *Central Asian Music: Essays in the history of the music of the peoples of the U.S.S.R.*, edited by Mark Slobin, translated by Mark and Greta Slobin. Middletown, CT: Wesleyan University Press.

Bellah, Robert N. 2011. *Religion in human evolution: From the Paleolithic to the Axial Age*. Cambridge, MA: Belknap Press of Harvard University Press.

Ben-Amos, Dan. 1984. The seven strands of *tradition*: Varieties in its meaning in American folklore studies. *Journal of the Folklore Institute* 21/2–3, 97–131. Reprinted in Ben-Amos, 2020, 64–98.

Ben-Amos, Dan. 2020. *Folklore concepts: Histories and critiques*. Bloomington: Indiana University Press.

REFERENCES 169

Benamou, Marc. 2003. Comparing musical affect: Java and the West. *WoM* 45/3, 57–76.

Benamou, Marc. 2010. *Rasa: Affect and intuition in Javanese musical aesthetics.* AMS Studies in Music. New York: Oxford University Press. Audio tracks available online at www.oup.com/us/rasa.

Berger, Harris M., and Cornelia Fales. 2005. "Heaviness" in the perception of heavy metal guitar timbres: The match of perceptual and acoustic features over time. In *Wired for sound: Engineering technologies in sonic culture*, edited by P. D. Greene and T. Porcello, 181–97. Middletown, CT: Wesleyan University Press.

Berger, Karol. 2000. *A theory of art.* Oxford and New York: Oxford University Press.

Berliner, Paul F. 1974. The Soul of mbira: An ethnography of the mbira among the Shona people of Rhodesia. Ph.D. dissertation, Wesleyan University.

Berliner, Paul F. 1978. *The Soul of mbira: Music and traditions of the Shona people of Zimbabwe.* Berkeley and Los Angeles: University of California Press.

Berliner, Paul F. 1994. *Thinking in jazz: The infinite art of improvisation.* CSE.

Berliner, Paul F. 2020. *The Art of mbira: Musical inheritance and legacy, featuring the repertory and practices of Cosmas Magaya and associates.* CSE.

Berliner, Paul F., and Cosmas Magaya. 2020. *Mbira's restless dance: An archive of improvisation.* CSE.

Berry, David Carson. 2013. Theory, 1. Introduction. In *The Grove dictionary of American music*, edited by Charles Hiroshi Garrett. New York: Oxford University Press and *OMO*.

Bielawski, Ludwik. 1959. System metrorytmiczny polskich melodii ludowych. *Muzyka* 4/4, 123–46.

Bielawski, Ludwik. 1979. Instrumentalmusik als Transformation der menschlichen Bewegung. Mensch –Instrument—Musik. *Studia instrumentorum musicae popularis* 6, 27–33.

Black, Max. 1962. Metaphor. In *Models and metaphors*, edited by Black, 25–47. Ithaca: Cornell University Press. First published in *Proceedings of the Aristotelian Society* 55 (1954), 273–94.

Blacking, John. 1971. Towards a theory of musical competence. In *Man: Anthropological essays in honour of O.F. Raum*, edited by E. J. de Jager, 19–34. Cape Town: Struik.

Blacking, John. 1981. The Problem of "ethnic" perceptions in the semiotics of music. In *The Sign in music and literature*, edited by Wendy Steiner, 184–94. Austin: University of Texas Press.

Blacking, John. 1990. Performance as a way of knowing: Practice theory and the theory of practice in Venda traditional music-making. In *Atti del XIV congresso della Società Internazionale de Musicologia: Trasmissione e recezione delle forme di cultura musicale*, I, *Round Tables*, edited by A. Pompilio, D. Restani, L. Bianconi, and F. Alberto Gallo, 214–20. Turin: E.D.T.

170 REFERENCES

Blake, Daniel. 2013. Performed identities: Theorizing in New York's improvised music scene. Ph.D. dissertation, CUNY Graduate Center.

Blake, Daniel. 2016. Space Is the Place: Composition in New York City's improvised music scene. *American Music Review* 45/2, 1–7.

Blum, Stephen. 1975. Towards a social history of musicological technique. *EM* 19/2, 207–31.

Blum, Stephen. 1986. Rousseau's concept of *sistême musical* and the comparative study of tonalities in nineteenth-century France. *Journal of the American Musicological Society*, 38/2, 349–61.

Blum, Stephen. 1991. European musical terminology and the music of Africa. In *Comparative musicology and the anthropology of music: Essays in the history of ethnomusicology*, ed. Bruno Nettl and Philip V. Bohlman, 3–36. CSE.

Blum, Stephen. 1996. Musical questions and answers in Iranian Xorasan. *EM: Annuario degli Archivi di Etnomusicologia* 4, 145–63.

Blum, Stephen. 2001. Composition. *NG* 2, vol. 6, 186–201 and *OMO*.

Blum, Stephen. 2009. Modes of theorizing in Iranian Khorasan. In *Theorizing the local: Music, practice, and experience in South Asia and beyond*, edited by Richard K. Wolf, 207–24. New York: Oxford University Press.

Blum, Stephen. 2011. A society and its journal: Stories of hybridity. *AsM* 42/1, 3–23.

Blum, Stephen. 2013. Foundations of musical knowledge in the Muslim world. In *The Cambridge history of world music*, edited by Philip V. Bohlman, 103–24. Cambridge: Cambridge University Press.

Blum, Stephen. 2015a. Transmission of music theory through lists of terms enhanced with proper names. In *"Muğam aləmi" IV Beynəlxalq Musiqişünaslıq Simpoziumnun Materialları/Proceedigs of the IV International Musicological Symposium "Space of Mugham"*, edited by S. Agaeva, 59–69. Baku: "Şərq-Qərb" Nəşriyyat Evi.

Blum, Stephen. 2015b. Afterword. In *Musical exodus: Al-Andalus and its Jewish diaspora*, edited by Ruth F. Davis, 199–206. Lanham, MD: Rowman & Littlefield.

Blumenberg, Hans. 1998 [1960]. *Paradigmen zu einer Metaphorologie*. Frankfurt am Main: Suhrkamp. First published as *Archiv für Begriffsgeschichte* 6, Bonn: Bouvier, 1960. Translated by Robert Savage as *Paradigms for a metaphorology*, Ithaca: Cornell University Press, 2010.

Boethius, Anicius Manlius Severinus. 1966 [1867]. *De institutione arithmetica libri duo, De institutione musica libri quinque, accredit Geometria quae fertur Boetii*, edited by Gottfried Friedlein. Frankfurt am Main: Minerva. First published Leipzig: Teubner, 1867.

Boethius, Anicius Manlius Severinus. 1989. *Fundamentals of music*, translated by Calvin M. Bower, edited by Claude V. Palisca. Yale Music Theory Series. New Haven: Yale University Press.

Bonnet, Gérard. 2005. Fort-Da. In *International dictionary of psychoanalysis*, edited by Alain De Mijolla, 1, 599–600. Detroit: Macmillan Reference USA.

REFERENCES 171

Bor, Joep, Françoise Nalini Delvoye, Jane Harvey, and Emmie te Nijenhuis, eds. 2010. *Hindustani music: Thirteenth to twentieth centuries*. New Delhi: Manohar.

Born, Georgina. 1995. *Rationalizing culture: IRCAM, Boulez, and the institutionalization of the musical avant-garde*. Berkeley: University of California Press.

Bourdieu, Pierre. 1977. *Outline of a theory of practice*, translated by Richard Nice. Cambridge Studies in Social Anthropology. Cambridge: Cambridge University Press. Revised version of Bourdieu 1972.

Bourdieu, Pierre. 2000 [1972]. *Esquisse d'une théorie de la pratique, précédé de trois études d'ethnologie Kabyle*. Paris: Editions du Seuil. First published Geneva: Librairie Droz, 1972.

Bower, Calvin M. 2002. The transmission of ancient music theory into the Middle Ages. In *The Cambridge history of Western music theory*, edited by Thomas Christensen, 136–67. Cambridge: Cambridge University Press.

Brăiloiu, Constantin. 1951. Le rythme aksak. *RdM* 30, 71–108. Reprinted in Brăiloiu 1973, 301–40. English translation in Brăiloiu 1984, 133–67.

Brăiloiu, Constantin. 1952. Le giusto syllabique. Un système rythmique populaire roumain. *Anuario Musical* 7: 117–58. Revision of an article published in *Polyphonie* 2 (1948), 26–57. Reprinted in Brăiloiu 1973, 151–94. English translation in Brăiloiu 1984, 168–205.

Brăiloiu, Constantin. 1954a. Le rythme enfantin: notions liminaires. *Les Colloques de Wégimont* 1: 64–96 and separately as *La rythmique enfantine*. Reprinted in Brăiloiu 1973, 265–99. English translation in Brăiloiu 1984, 206–38.

Brăiloiu, Constantin. 1954b. Le vers populaire roumain chanté. *Revue des Études Roumaines* 2, 7–74. Reprinted in Brăiloiu 1975, 195–264.

Brăiloiu, Constantin. 1959. Réflexions sur la création musicale collective. *Diogène* 25, 83–93. Reprinted in Brăiloiu 1973, 135–47. English translation in Brăiloiu 1984, 102–09.

Brăiloiu, Constantin. 1973. *Problèmes d'ethnomusicologie*, edited by Gilbert Rouget. Geneva: Minkoff.

Brăiloiu, Constantin. 1984. *Problems of ethnomusicology*, edited by A. L. Lloyd. Cambridge: Cambridge University Press.

Brambats, Karl. 1967. The vocal drone in the Baltic countries: Problems of chronology and provenance. *Journal of Baltic Studies* 14/1, 24–34.

Brandom, Robert B. 1994. *Making it explicit: Reasoning, representing, and discursive commitment*. Cambridge, MA: Harvard University Press.

Braxton, Anthony. 1985. *Tri-axium writings*. n.p.: Synthesis Music.

Brenner, Klaus-Peter. 1997. *Chipendani und Mbira: Musikinstrumente, nichtbegriffliche Mathematik und die Evolution der harmonischen Progressionen in der Musik der Shona in Zimbabwe*. Abhandlungen der Akademie der Wissenschaften in Göttingen, Philologisch-Historische Klasse, 3. Folge,

172 REFERENCES

221. Göttingen: Vandenhoeck und Ruprecht. Two accompanying CDs. English summary, 367–74.

Brinner, Benjamin. 1995. *Knowing music, making music: Javanese* gamelan *and the theory of musical competence and interaction*. CSE.

Brossard, Sébastien de. 1703 [1964]. *Dictionaire de musique, contenant une explication des termes grecs, latins, italiens, & françois les plus usitez*. Paris: C. Ballard. Facsimile reprint, Amsterdam: Antiqua.

Brøvig-Hanssen, Ragnhild, Bjørnar Sandvik, Jon Marius Aareskjold-Drecker, and Anne Danielsen. 2022. A grid in flux: Sound and timing in electronic dance music. *Music Theory Spectrum* 44/1, 1–16.

Brown, Steven. 2000. The "musilanguage" model of music evolution. In *The origins of music*, edited by Nils L. Wallin, Björn Merker, and Steven Brown, 271–300. Cambridge, MA: MIT Press.

Bruner, Jerome. 1986. *Actual minds, possible worlds*. Cambridge, MA.: Harvard University Press.

Buelow, George J. 2001. Rhetoric and music, 4. Affects. *NG 2* and *OMO*.

Buenconsejo, Jose S., ed. 2003. *A search in Asia for a new theory of music. A symposium organized by the University of the Philippines, Center for Ethnomusicology as the 7th International Conference of the Asia Pacific Society for Ethnomusicology (APSE)*. Quezon City: University of the Philippines Center for Ethnomusicology.

Byler, Darren. 2021. *Terror capitalism: Uyghur dispossession and masculinity*. Durham, NC: Duke University Press.

Campbell, Patricia Shehan. 1991. *Lessons from the world: A cross-cultural guide to music teaching and learning*. New York: Schirmer.

Campbell, Patricia Shehan, ed. 2018–21. World Music Pedagogy Series. New York and London: Routledge. 7 vols.

Campbell, Stuart, ed. and trans. 1994. *Russians on Russian music, 1830–1880: An anthology*. Cambridge: Cambridge University Press.

Capwell, Charles. 2010. Representing Hindi music to the colonial and native elite of Calcutta. In *Hindustani music: Thirteenth to twentieth centuries*, edited by Jop Bor, F. N. Delvoye, J. Harvey, and E. te Nijenhuis, 285–311. Delhi: Manohar.

Carmi-Cohen, Dalia. 1964. An investigation into the tonal structure of the *maqamat. Journal of the International Folk Music Council* 16, 102–06.

Carpitella, Diego. 1975. Sistema metrico e sistema ritmico nei canti populari. In *Actes du 1er congrès de sémiotique musicale*, edited by Gino Steffani, 40–43. Pesaro: Centro di Iniziativa Culturale.

Caws, Peter. 1974. Operational, representational, and explanatory models. *American Anthropologist* 76/1, 1–10.

Certeau, Michel de. 1984. *The practice of everyday life*, translated by Steven Rendall. Berkeley: University of California Press. First published as *L'invention du quotidien*, 1. *Arts de faire*. Paris: Union générale d'édition, 1980.

Chailley, Jacques. 1960. *L'imbroglio des modes*. Paris: A. Leduc.

REFERENCES 173

Chakrabarty, Dipesh. 2000. *Provincializing Europe: Postcolonial thought and historical difference*. Princeton: Princeton University Press.

Charry, Eric. 2000. *Mande music: Traditional and modern music of the Maninka and Mandinka of western Africa*. CSE.

Chavis, Gerald. 2019. *Robert Lowery's method for Jazz improvisation*. Victoria, BC: Press Music Publishing. Available online and in print, https://qpress.ca.

Chemillier, Marc. 1995. La musique de la harpe. In Éric de Dampierre, *Une esthétique perdue: harpes et harpistes du Haut-Oubangui*, 99–226. Paris: Presses de l'École Normale Supérieure, and Nanterre: Société d'Ethnologie.

Chemillier, Marc. 2007. *Les mathématiques naturelles*. Paris: Odile Jacob.

Chernoff, John Miller. 1979. *African rhythm and African sensibility: Aesthetics and social action in African musical idioms*. Chicago: University of Chicago Press.

Christensen, Lars. 2020. The disunity of ancient Chinese theory. Paper presented online at annual meeting of Society for Music Theory.

Christensen, Thomas, ed. 2002. *The Cambridge history of western music theory*. Cambridge: Cambridge University Press.

Chung, Andrew J. 2022. Review of CCMT. *Music Theory Spectrum* 44/1, 173–86.

Cianciolo, Anna T., Cynthia Matthew, Robert J. Sternberg, and Richard K. Wagner. 2006. Tacit knowledge, practice intelligence, and expertise. In *The Cambridge handbook of expertise and expert performance*, edited by K. Anders Ericsson et al., 613–32. Cambridge: Cambridge University Press.

Cicero, Marcus Tullius. 1971. *Brutus with an English translation by G.L. Hendrickson; Orator with an English translation by H.M. Hubbell*. Loeb Classical Library, 342. Cambridge, MA: Harvard University Press and London: Heinemann.

Ciucci, Alessandra. 2012. Embodying the countryside in 'aita hasbawiya. *YTM* 44, 109–28.

Ciucci, Alessandra. 2022. *The voice of the rural: Music, poetry, and masculinity among migrant Moroccan men in Umbria*. CSE.

Clarke, Eric F. 2005. *Ways of listening: An ecological approach to the perception of musical meaning*. Oxford and New York: Oxford University Press.

Clayton, Martin. 2009. The social and personal functions of music in cross-cultural perspective. In *The Oxford handbook of music psychology*, second edition, edited by S. Hallam, I. Cross, and M. Thaut, 35–44. Oxford: Oxford University Press.

Cler, Jérôme. 1994. Pour une théorie de l'aksak. *RdM* 80/2, 181–210.

Cogan, Robert. 1984. *New images of musical sound*. Cambridge, MA: Harvard University Press.

Cohen, Dalia. 1971. The meaning of the modal framework in the singing of religious hymns by Christian Arabs in Israel. *Yuval: Studies of the Jewish Music Research Centre* 2, 23–57.

174 REFERENCES

Cohen, Dalia, and Ruth Katz. 1967. Remarks concerning the use of the melograph in ethnomusicological studies. *Yuval: Studies of the Jewish Music Research Centre* 1, 155–68.

Cohen, Dalia, and Ruth Katz. 2006. *Palestinian Arab music: A maqām tradition in practice.* CSE. Chicago: University of Chicago Press. Accompanying CD.

Cook, Nicholas. 2002. Epistemologies of music theory. In *The Cambridge history of western music theory*, edited by Thomas Christensen, 78–105. Cambridge: Cambridge University Press.

Cook, Nicholas. 2014. *Beyond the score: Music as performance.* Oxford: Oxford University Press.

Cook, Scott. 1995. *Yue ji . . . Record of music*: Introduction, translation, notes, and commentary. *AsM* 26, 1–96.

Cooke, Peter. 1970. Ganda xylophone music: Another approach. *AfM* 4/ 4, 62–80.

Cooke, Peter. 1994. Call and response: A reply to Ulrich Wegner. *EM* 38/3, 475–79.

Coplan, David. 1985. *In township tonight! South Africa's black city music and theatre.* London: Longman.

Cox, Arnie. 1999. The metaphoric logic of musical motion and space. Ph.D. dissertation, University of Oregon.

Cox, Arnie. 2016. *Music and embodied cognition: Listening, moving, feeling, and thinking.* Musical Meaning and Interpretation. Bloomington: Indiana University Press.

Dahlhaus, Carl. 1966. Tonsysteme. In *Die Musik in Geschichte und Gegenwart*, edited by Friedrich Blume, 13, 533–47. Bärenreiter: Kassel. Reprinted in *MGG 2 Sachteil*, 9, 638–46.

Dahlhaus, Carl. 1984. *Die Musiktheorie im 18. und 19. Jahrhundert*, I. *Grundzüge einer Systematik.* Geschichte der Musiktheorie, 10. Darmstadt: Wissenschaftliche Buchgesellschaft.

Dahlhaus, Carl. 1985. Was heisst 'Geschichte der Musiktheorie'? In *Ideen zu einer Geschichte der Musiktheorie: Einleitung in das Gesamtwerk*, edited by Frieder Zaminer, 8–39. Geschichte der Musiktheorie, 1. Darmstadt: Wissenschaftliche Buchgesellschaft.

Daniélou, Alain. 1964. Report on the discussions. In *The Preservation of Traditional Forms of the Learned and Popular Music of the Orient and the Occident. La preservation des formes traditionnelles de la musique savante et populaire dans les pays d'Orient et d'Occident*, edited by William K. Archer, 307–18. Urbana: Center for Comparative Psycholinguistics, Institute of Communications Research, University of Illinois.

Darvishi, Mohammad Rezā. 1995. *Negāh be gharb: Bahsi dar ta'sir-e musiqi-ye gharb bar musiqi-ye Irān* [Westward look: A discussion on the impact of Western music on the Iranian music]. Tehran: Māhur.

Dauer, Alfons. 1983 [1966]. Musiklandschaften in Afrika. In *Musik in Afrika*, edited by Artur Simon, 41–48. Veröffentlichungen des Museum für Völkerkunde Berlin, n.F. 40. Berlin: Museum für Völkerkunde. First published In *Afrika heute*, Sonderbeilage 23, 1966.

Dauer, Alfons. 1985. *Tradition afrikanischer Blasorchester und Entstehung des Jazz*. Beiträge zur Jazzforschung, 7. Graz: Akademische Druck- u. Verlaganstalt. 2 vols.

Dauer, Alfons. 1994. Asymmetrische Rhythmik in europäischer Musik. Ein vergessener Aspekt westlicher Musiktheorie? In *For Gerhard Kubik: Festschrift on the occasion of his sixtieth birthday*, edited by A. Schmidhofer and D. Schüller, 519–48. Vergleichende Musikwissenschaft, 3. Frankfurt am Main: Peter Lang.

David, Hans T., and Arthur Mendel, eds. 1966. *The Bach reader: A life of Johann Sebastian Bach in Letters and Documents*. Revised edition. New York: Norton.

Davies, Norman. 1996. *Europe, a history*. Oxford and New York: Oxford University Press.

Davis, Ruth F. 1986. Modern trends in the ma'lūf of Tunisia, 1934–1984. Ph.D. dissertation, Princeton University.

Davis, Ruth F. 2004. *Ma'lūf: reflections on the Arab Andalusian music of Tunisia*. Lanham, MD: Scarecrow Press.

Debussy, Claude. 1971 [1913]. Du goût. In Debussy, *Monsieur Croche et autres écrits*, edited by François Lesure, 221–24. Paris: Gallimard.

De Ferranti, Hugh. 1991. Composition and improvisation in Satsuma biwa. *Musica asiatica* 6, 102–32.

De Ferranti, Hugh. 1996. Text and music in *biwa* narrative: The *zatō biwa* tradition of Kyushu. Ph.D. thesis, University of Sydney.

Dehoux, Vincent, and Frédéric Voisin. 1992. Analytic procedures with scales in Central African xylophone music. In *European studies in ethnomusicology: Historical developments and recent trends. Selected papers presented at the VIIth European Seminar in Ethnomusicology, Berlin, October 1–6, 1990*, edited by M. P. Baumann, A. Simon, and U. Wegner, 174–88. Intercultural Music Studies, 4. Wilhelmshaven: Florian Noetzel.

Dehoux, Vincent, and Frédéric Voisin. 1993. An interactive experimental method for the determination of musical scales in oral cultures: Application to the xylophone music of Central Africa. *Contemporary Music Review* 9/1–2, 13–19.

DeLanda, Manuel. 2013. *A new philosophy of society: Assemblage theory and social complexity*. London: Bloomsbury. First published by Continuum International, 2006.

Deleuze, Gilles. 1962. *Nietzsche et la philosophie*. Paris: Presses Universitaires de France.

Deleuze, Gilles, and Félix Guattari. 1980. *Capitalisme et schizophrénie: Mille plateaux*. Paris: Éditions de Minuit. Translated by Brian Massumi as *A thousand plateaux: Capitalism and schizophrenia*. Minneapolis: University of Minnesota Press, 1987.

176 REFERENCES

Dennett, Daniel C. 2017. Affordance. Contribution to *2017: What scientific term or concept ought to be more widely known?* www.edge.org (consulted January 23, 2017).

Deschênes, Bruno, and Yuko Eguchi. 2018. Embodied orality: Transmission in traditional Japanese music. *AsM* 49/1, 58–79.

De Souza, Jonathan. 2017. *Music at hand: Instruments, bodies, and cognition.* Oxford Studies in Music Theory. New York: Oxford University Press.

Deutsch, Diana. 2013. The processing of pitch combinations. In *The psychology of music*, edited by D. Deutsch, 249–325. London: Academic Press.

DeWoskin, Kenneth. 1983. Early Chinese music and the origins of aesthetic terminology. In *Theories of the arts in China*, edited by Susan Bush and Christian Murck, 187–214. Princeton: Princeton University Press.

Dharwadker, Vinay. 2015. Emotion in motion: The Nāṭyashāstra, Darwin, and affect theory. *PMLA* 130/5, 1381–1404.

Diamond, Beverley. 2008. *Native American music in Eastern North America.* Experiencing Music, Expressing Culture. New York: Oxford University Press.

Diamond, Beverley, M. Sam Cronk, and Franziska von Rosen. 1994. *Visions of sound: Musical instruments of First Nations communities in Northeastern America.* CSE.

Djenda, Maurice. 1994. De la croyance religieuse des Mpyɛmõ. In *For Gerhard Kubik: Festschrift on the occasion of his sixtieth birthday*, edited by A. Schmidhofer and D. Schüller, 73–82. Vergleichende Musikwissenschaft, 3. Frankfurt am Main: Peter Lang.

Donald, Merlin. 1991. *Origins of the modern mind: Three stages in the evolution of culture and cognition.* Cambridge, MA: Harvard University Press.

Dor, George Worlasi Kwasi. 2000. Tonal resources and compositional processes of Ewe traditional music. Ph.D. dissertation, University of Pittsburgh.

Douglas, Gavin. 2001. State patronage of Burmese traditional music. Ph.D. dissertation, University of Washington.

Douglas, Gavin. 2019. The boundaries of the self in Burmese performing arts. Paper presented at 64th Annual Meeting of the Society for Ethnomusicology, Indiana University, November 9, 2019.

Dowling, W. Jay. 1978. Scale and contour: Two components of a theory of memory. *Psychological Review* 85, 341–54.

Dowling, W. Jay. 1982. Musical scales and psychophysical scales: Their psychological reality. In *Cross-cultural perspectives on music*, edited by Robert Falck and Timothy Rice, 20–28. Toronto: University of Toronto Press.

Dowling, W. Jay, and Dane L. Harwood. 1986. *Music cognition.* Orlando: Academic Press.

Duranti, Alessandro. 2009. The relevance of Husserl's theory to language socialization. *Journal of Linguistic Anthropology* 19/2, 205–26.

Durga, S. A. K. 1992. Bharata's methodology in Nāṭyaśāstra (a treatise on dramaturgy). In *Von der Vielfalt musikalischer Kultur: Festschrift für*

Josef Kuckertz, zur Vollendung des 60. Lebensjahres, edited by Rüdiger Schumacher, 147–56. Anif/Salzburg: Ursula Müller-Speiser.

During, Jean. 2006. The Intervals of the Azerbaijani Mugam: Back to the Sources. Paper presented at International Symposium on the Ottoman Period, Bursa. Persian translation, "Fawāsel-e maqām-e āzarbāijāni: bāzgasht be sarcheshme-hā." *Fasl-nāme Māhur* 12/45 (2010), 9–17.

During, Jean and Sabine Trebinjac. 1991. *Introduction au muqam ouïgour.* Papers on Inner Asia, 17. Bloomington: Indiana University Research Institute for Inner Asian Studies.

Eggebrecht, Hans Heinrich. 1975. Musikalisches Denken. *Archiv für Musikwissenschaft* 32, 228–40.

Eggebrecht, Hans Heinrich. 1991. *Musik im Abendland. Prozesse und Stationen vom Mittelalter bis zur Gegenwart.* Munich: Piper.

Eisenstadt, S. N. 2003. *Comparative civilizations and multiple modernities: A collection of essays.* Leiden: Brill.

Ellingson, Ter. 1992. Notation. In *Ethnomusicology: An introduction,* edited by Helen Myers, 153–64. The Norton/Grove Handbooks in Music. New York: Norton.

Ellington, Duke. 1973. *Music is my mistress.* Garden City: Doubleday.

Ellis, Catherine J. 1965. Pre-instrumental scales. *EM* 9/2, 126–37.

Ellis, Catherine J. 1967. The Pitjantjatjara kangaroo song from Karlga. *Miscellanea Musicologica* 2, 171–268.

Ellis, Catherine J. 1969. Structure and significance in Aboriginal song. *Mankind* 7, 3–14.

Ellis, Catherine J. 1984. Time consciousness of Aboriginal performers. In *Problems and solutions: Occasional essays in musicology presented to Alice M. Moyle,* edited by Jamie C. Kassler and Jill Stubington, 149–85. Sydney: Hale & Iremonger.

Ellis, Catherine J. 1985. *Aboriginal music, education for living: Cross-cultural experiences from South Australia.* St. Lucia, Queensland: University of Queensland Press.

Ellis, Catherine J. 1994. Powerful songs, their placement in Aboriginal thought. *WoM* 36/1, 3–20.

Ellis, C. J., A. M. Ellis, M. Tur, and A. McCardell. 1978. Classification of sounds in Pitjantjatjara-speaking areas. In *Australian Aboriginal concepts,* edited by L. R. Hiatt, 68–80. Australian Aboriginal Studies, 87. Canberra: Australian Institute of Aboriginal Studies.

El-Shawan, Salwa. 1979. The socio-political context of al-mūsīka al-'arabiyya in Cairo, Egypt: Policies, patronage, institutions, and musical change (1927–77). *AsM* 12/1, 86–128.

El-Shawan, Salwa. 1981. Al-mūsīka al-'arabiyya: A category of urban music in Cairo, Egypt, 1927–1977. Ph.D. dissertation, Columbia University.

Elschek, Oskár. 1984. *Hudobná veda súčasnosti. Systematika, teória, vývin.* Bratislava: VEDA.

178 REFERENCES

Elschek, Oskár. 1992. *Die Musikforschung der Gegenwart: ihre Systematik, Theorie und Entwicklung.* Acta ethnologica et linguistica, 64; Series Musicologica, 4. Vienna-Föhrenau: E. Stiglmayr.

Eppstein, Ury. 1985. Musical instruction in Meiji education: A study of adaptation and assimilation. *Monumenta Nipponica* 40/1, 1–37.

Eppstein, Ury. 1994. *The beginnings of Western music in Meiji era Japan.* Studies in the History and Interpretation of Music, 44. Lewiston, NY: Edwin Mellen Press.

Erlanger, Rodolphe d'. 1930. *La musique arabe.* Vol. 1. Paris: Paul Geuthner.

Erlanger, Rodolphe d'. 1935. *La musique arabe.* Vol. 2. Paris: Paul Geuthner.

Erlmann, Veit. 1985. Model, variation and performance: Ful'be praise-song in northern Cameroon. *YTM* 17, 88–112.

Erlmann, Veit. 1987. Modèle, variation et exécution: Chants de louanges peuls (Cameroun). In *L'Improvisation dans les musiques de tradition orale,* edited by Bernard Lortat-Jacob, 85–94. Paris: SELAF.

Erlmann, Veit. 2010. *Reason and resonance: A history of modern aurality.* New York: Zone Books.

Erlmann, Veit. 2015. Resonance. In *Keywords in sound,* edited by David Novak and Matt Sakakeeny, 175–82. Durham, NC: Duke University Press.

Estreicher, Zygmunt. 1964. Le rythme des Peuls bororo. *Colloques de Wégimont* 4, *Ethnomusicologie* 3, 185–228.

Estreicher, Zygmunt. 1974. Le sous-entendu, facteur de la forme musicale. *Schweizer Beiträge zur Musikwissenschaft,* ser. 3, 2, 133–56.

Euba, Akin. 1990. *Yoruba Drumming: The Dùndún Tradition.* Bayreuth African Studies, 21–22. Bayreuth: Breitinger.

Euba, Akin, and Cynthia Tse Kimberlin, eds. 1995. *Intercultural music I.* Bayreuth African Studies, 29. Bayreuth: Breitinger.

Euclid. 1947. *The Elements,* edited and translated by T. L. Heath. Annapolis: St. John's College Press.

Evans, David. 1978. African elements in twentieth-century United States Black folk music. *Jazzforschung* 10, 85–110.

Evans, David. 1981. African elements in twentieth-century United States Black folk music. In International Musicological Society, *Report of the Twelfth Congress, Berkeley 1977,* edited by Daniel Heartz and Bonnie C. Wade, 54–66. Kassel: Bärenreiter.

Everett, Walter. 2004. Making sense of rock's tonal systems. *MTO* 10/4. Online at mtosmt.org.

Ewing, Katherine Pratt. 2007. *Arguing sainthood: Modernity, psychoanalysis, and Islam.* Durham, NC: Duke University Press.

Fabian, Johannes. 1983. *Time and the other: How anthropology makes its object.* New York: Columbia University Press.

Fabian, Johannes. 1990. *Power and performance: Ethnographic explorations through proverbial wisdom and theater in Shaba, Zaire.* Madison: University of Wisconsin Press.

Fārābī, Abū Naṣr al-. 1967. *Kitāb al-mūsīqā al-kabīr* [Great book on music]. Cairo: Dār al-Kātib al-'Arabī.

Ghaṭṭās 'Abd al-Malik Khashaba and Muḥammad Aḥmed al-Ḥifnī. Cairo: Dār al-Kātib al-'Arabī. French translation in Rodolphe d'Erlanger, *La musique arabe* I and II. Paris: Paul Geuthner, 1930 and 1935.

Farhat, Hormoz, and Hūmān As'adi. 2005. *Descriptive analysis of the dastgāh of Māhur by Ostād Nur'ali Borumand.* Tehran: Māhūr. Four CDs from original recordings by Farhat with notes by As'adi.

Farmer, Henry George. 1929. *A history of Arabian music to the XIIIth century.* London: Luzac.

Fātemi, Sāsān. 2003. *Ritm-e kudakān dar Irān* [Nursery rhythms in Iran]. Tehran: Māhūr.

Fatone, Gina A. 2010. "You'll break your heart trying to play it like you sing it": Intermodal imagery and the transmission of Scottish classical bagpiping. *EM* 54/3, 395–424.

Faudree, Paja. 2012. Music, language, and texts: Sound and semiotic ethnography. *Annual Review of Anthropology* 41, 519–36.

Feld, Steven. 1981. "Flow like a waterfall": The metaphors of Kaluli musical theory. *YTM* 13, 22–47.

Feld, Steven. 1982. *Sound and sentiment: Birds, weeping, poetics, and song in Kaluli expression.* University of Pennsylvania Publications in Conduct and Communication. Philadelphia: University of Pennsylvania Press.

Feld, Steven. 1986a. Sound as a symbolic system: The Kaluli drum. In *Explorations in ethnomusicology: Essays in honor of David P. McAllester*, edited by Charlotte J. Frisbie, 147–58. Detroit: Information Coordinators.

Feld, Steven. 1986b. Orality and consciousness. In *The oral and the literate in music*, edited by Tokumaru Yosihiko and Yamaguti Osamu, 18–28. Tokyo: Academia Music.

Feld, Steven. 1987. "Dialogic editing": Interpreting how Kaluli read *Sound and sentiment. Cultural Anthropology* 2/2, 190–210.

Feld, Steven. 1996. Waterfalls of song: An acoustemology of place resounding in Bosavi, Papua New Guinea. In *Senses of place*, edited by S. Feld and K. Basso, 91–135. Santa Fe: School of American Research Press.

Feld, Steven. 2015. Acoustemology. In *Keywords in sound*, edited by David Novak and Matt Sakakeeny, 12–21. Durham, NC: Duke University Press.

Feld, Steven, and Aaron A. Fox. 1994. Music and language. *Annual Review of Anthropology* 23, 25–53.

Feld, Steven, Aaron A. Fox, Thomas Porcello, and David Samuels. 2004. Vocal anthropology: From the music of language to the language of song. In *A companion to linguistic anthropology*, edited by Alessandro Duranti, 321–26. Malden: Blackwell.

Fernández-Armesto, Felipe. 2019. *Our of our minds: What we think and how we come to think it.* Berkeley: University of California Press.

180 REFERENCES

Ferrarini, Lorenzo, and Nicola Scaldaferri. 2020. *Sonic ethnography: Identity, heritage and creative research practice in Basilicata, southern Italy.* Manchester: Manchester University Press. Open access.

Fiagbedzi, Nissio. 1980. A preliminary inquiry into inherent rhythms in anlo dance drumming. *Journal of the Performing Arts* (University of Ghana, Legon) 1/1, 83–92.

Fink, Robert, Melinda Latour, and Zachary Wallmark, eds. 2018. *The relentless pursuit of tone: Timbre in popular music.* New York: Oxford University Press.

Finnegan, Ruth. 1990. What is orality—if anything? *Byzantine and Modern Greek Studies* 14, 130–49.

Foley, John Miles. 1988. *The theory of oral composition: History and methodology.* Folkloristics. Bloomington: Indiana University Press.

Forkel, Johann Nikolaus. 1802 [1968]. *Ueber Johann Sebastian Bachs Leben, Kunst und Kunstwerke,* edited by Walther Vetter. Kassel: Bärenreiter. First published Leipzig: Hoffmeister & Kühnel. English translation in David and Mendel, eds. 1966, 293–356.

Fossum, David C. 2015. Westernizing reform and indigenous precedent in traditional music: Insights from Turkmenistan. *EM* 59/2, 202–26.

Fraser, Wilmot Alfred. 1983. *Jazzology: A study of the tradition in which jazz musicians learn to improvise.* Ph.D. dissertation, University of Pennsylvania.

Freud, Sigmund. 1920. *Jenseits des Lustprimzips.* Vienna: Internationaler Psychoanalytischer Verlag G.M.B.H.

Friedson, Steven M. 1996. *Dancing prophets: Musical experience in Tumbuka healing.* CSE.

Frolova-Walker, Marina. 1998. "National in form, socialist in content": Musical nation-building in the Soviet republics. *Journal of the American Musicological Society* 51/2, 331–71.

Fujita Takanori. 2019. Layers and elasticity in the rhythm of Noh songs: "Taking komi" and its social background. In *Thought and play in musical rhythm,* edited by R. K. Wolf, S. Blum, and C. F. Hasty, 212–31. New York: Oxford University Press.

Gallope, Michael. 2010. The sound of repeating life: Ethics and metaphysics in Deleuze's philosophy of music. In *Sounding the virtual: Gilles Deleuze and the theory and philosophy of music,* edited by Brian Hulse and Nick Nesbitt, 77–102. Hampshire: Ashgate.

Garfias, Robert. 2014. The Demise of the gurukula system in Asia and the condition of music tradition in the post-industrial era. Keynote address, Society for Asian Music, Pittsburgh, November 14.

Gay, Leslie C., Jr. 1991. Commitment, cohesion, and creative process: A study of New York City rock bands. Ph.D. dissertation, Columbia University.

Gay, Leslie C., Jr. 1998. Acting up, talking tech: New York rock musicians and their metaphors of technology. *EM* 42/1, 81–98.

Gelbart, Matthew. 2019. Scale. In *CCMT,* 78–105.

REFERENCES 181

Gellner, Ernest. 1989. *Plough, sword and book: The structure of human history*. Chicago: University of Chicago Press.

Germann, Nadja. 2020. How do we learn? Al-Fārābī's epistemology of teaching. In *Knowledge and education in classical Islam: Religious learning between continuity and change*, edited by S. Günther, 1, 147–85. Leiden: Brill.

Gerstin, Julian. 1998. Interaction and improvisation between dancers and drummers in Martinican *bèlè*. *Black Music Research Journal* 18/1–2, 121–65.

Ghosh, Manomohan, trans. 1961 *The Nāṭyaśāstra, a treatise on Hindu dramaturgy and histrionics ascribed to Bharata-Muni. Vol. II (chapters XXVIII–XXXVI) completely translated for the first time from the original Sanskrit with an introduction and various notes*. Calcutta: The Asiatic Society.

Giannattasio, Francesco. 1985. Suonare a bocca. Elementi di 'teoria e solfeggio' dei suonatori di launeddas sardi. In *Forme e comportamenti della musica folklorica italiana: Etnomusicologia e didattica*, edited by Giovanni Giuriati, 203–30. Milan: Edizioni Unicopli.

Giannattasio, Francesco. 1987. Systèmes d'improvisation dans les musiques d'Italie du sud. In *L'Improvisation dans les musiques de tradition orale*, edited by Bernard Lortat-Jacob, 239–50. Paris: SELAF.

Giannattasio, Francesco. 1990. Theory or concepts? Some questions raised by a research on Somali music. In International Musicological Society. *Atti del XIV congresso della Società Internazionale de Musicologia: Trasmissione e recezione delle forme di cultura musicale*, I, *Round Tables*, edited by A. Pompilio, D. Restani, L. Bianconi, and F. Alberto Gallo, 221–27. Turin: E.D.T.

Giannattasio, Francesco. 1992. *Il concetto di musica. Contributi e prospettive della ricerca etnomusicologica*. Rome: La Nuova Italia Scientifica.

Giannattasio, Francesco. 2017. Perspectives on a 21st-century comparative musicology: An introduction. In *Perspectives on a 21st century comparative musicology*, edited by F. Giannattasio and G. Giuriati, 10–28. Udine: Nota.

Giannattasio, Francesco, and Giovanni Giuriati, eds. 2017. *Perspectives on a 21st century comparative musicology: Ethnomusicology or transcultural musicology?* Udine: Nota.

Giddens, Anthony. 1984. *The constitution of society: Outline of the theory of structuration*. Berkeley: University of California Press.

Gill, Denise. 2017. *Melancholic modalities: Affect, Islam, and Turkish classical musicians*. New York: Oxford University Press.

Gillespie, Dizzy, and Al Fraser. 1979. *To be, or not . . . to bop. Memoirs*. Garden City, NY: Doubleday.

Gimm, Martin. 1995. China, V. Qin- und Han-Dynastie. In *MGG 2, Sachteil*, 2, 711–17.

Gjerdingen, Robert J., and Janet Bourne. 2015. Schema theory as a constructive grammar. *MTO* 21/2. Online at mtosmt.org.

Gluck, Carol. 2011. The end of elsewhere: Writing modernity now. *American Historical Review* 116/3, 676–87.

182 REFERENCES

Gourlay, Kenneth A. 1972. The practice of cueing among the Karimojon of north-east Uganda. *EM* 16/2, 240–46.

Gourlay, Kenneth A. 1984. The non-universality of music and the universality of non-music. *WoM* 26/2, 25–38.

Gregory, A. 1997. The roles of music in society: The ethnomusicological perspective. In *The social psychology of music*, edited by D. Hargreaves and A. North, 123–40. Oxford: Oxford University Press.

Greve, Martin. 2005. Hybrides Musikdenken im türkischen Nationalstaat. In *Musiktheoretisches Denken und kultureller Kontext*, edited by Dörte Schmidt, 149–70. Forum Musikwissenschaft, 1. Schliengen: Edition Argus.

Griaule, Marcel. 1965 [1948]. *Conversations with Ogotemmêli: An introduction to Dogon religious ideas.* London: Oxford University Press. Translation of *Dieu d'eau: entretiens avec Ogotemmêli*, Paris: Editions du Chêne, 1948.

Gritten, Anthony, and Elaine King, eds. 2011. *New perspectives on music and gesture.* SEMPRE Studies in the Psychology of Music. Farnham and Burlington, VT: Ashgate.

Grupe, Gerd. 2004. *Die Kunst des Mbira-Spiels = The art of mbira playing: harmonische Struktur und Patternbildung in der Lamellaphonmusik der Shona in Zimbabwe.* Musikethnologische Sammelbände, 19. Tutzing: Hans Schneider.

Guignard, Michel. 1975. *Musique, honneur et plaisir au Sahara. Étude psychosociologique et musicologique de la société maure.* Bibliothèque d'Études Islamiques, 3. Paris: Paul Geuthner. Accompanying phonorecord.

Gulik, Robert Hans van. 1969. *The lore of the Chinese lute.* Second edition. Rutland, VT: Charles E. Tuttle and Tokyo: Sophia University.

Gushee, Lawrence. 1973. Questions of genre in Medieval treatises on music. In *Gattungen der Musik in Einzeldarstellungen: Gedenkschrift Leo Schrade*, edited by Wulf Arlt, 365–433. Bern: Francke.

Gutzwiller, Andreas. 1974. *Shakuhachi: Aspects of history, practice and teaching.* Ph.D. dissertation, Wesleyan University.

Gutzwiller, Andreas. 1983. *Die Shakuhachi der Kinko-Schule.* Studien zur traditionellen Musik Japans, 5. Kassel: Bärenreiter.

Gutzwiller, Andreas, and Gerald Bennett. 1991. The world of a single sound: Basic structure of the music of the Japanese flute shakuhachi. *Musica asiatica* 6, 36–59.

Ha Gyangtian and Slavs and Tatars, eds. 2021. *The contest of the fruits.* Cambridge, MA: MIT Press.

Hacıbäyli, Üzeyir. 1945 [1985]. *Osnovy azerbaĭdzhanskoĭ narodnoĭ muzyki.* Baku: Izd-vo AN Azerbaĭdzhanskoĭ SSR. English translation, *Principles of Azerbaijan folk music.* Baku: Yazichi, 1985.

Haefer, J. Richard. 1981. Musical thought in Papago culture. Ph.D. dissertation, University of Illinois at Urbana-Champaign.

REFERENCES 183

Halberstam, Jack. 2013. The wild beyond: With and for the undercommons. In Stefano Harney and Fred Moten, *The undercommons: Fugitive planning and Black study*, 3–12. Brooklyn: Autonomedia.

Harnoncourt, Nikolaus. 1982. *Musik als Klangrede: Wege zu einem neuen Musikverständnis*. Salzburg and Vienna: Residenz Verlag. English translation by Mary O'Neill, *Baroque music today: Music as speech. Ways to a new understanding of music*. Portland, OR: Amadeus Press, 1988.

Harris, Marvin. 1968. *The rise of anthropological theory A history of theories of culture*. New York: Thomas Y. Crowell.

Harris, Marvin. 1976. History and significance of the emic/etic distinction. *Annual Review of Anthropology* 5, 329–50.

Harris, Rachel. 2008. *The making of a musical canon in Chinese Central Asia: The Uyghur twelve muqam*. SOAS Musicology Series. Aldershot: Ashgate.

Hassan, Schéhérazade Qassim. 2002. The Iraqi maqām and its transmission. In *GEWM* 6, 311–16.

Hassan, Schéhérazade Qassim. 2004. Tradition et modernisme: Le cas de la musique arabe au Proche-Orient. *L'Homme* 171–72, 353–70.

Hassan, Schéhérazade Qassim. 2008. Terminology, concepts and classification of the Iraqi maqam. In *Intercultural comparison of maqām and related phenomena: Proceedings of the fifth meeting of the ICTM Study Group "maqām"*, *Samarkand, 26–30 August 2001*, edited by Jürgen Elsner and Gisa Jänichen, 101–14. Berlin: trafo.

Hassanpour, Amir. 2020. *Essays on Kurds: Historiography, orality, and nationalism*. Kurdish People, History, and Politics, 1. New York: Peter Lang.

Hatten, Robert S. 1994. *Meaning in Beethoven's music: Markedness, correlation, and interpretation*. Musical Meaning and Interpretation. Bloomington: Indiana University Press.

Heartz, Daniel. 1981. *Report of the Twelfth Congress, Berkeley 1977*, edited by Daniel Heartz and Bonnie C. Wade, 776–78. Kassel: Bärenreiter.

Heimarck, Brita Renée. 1999. Balinese discourses on music: Musical modernization in the ideas and practices of shadow play performers from Sukawati, and the Indonesian College of the Arts. Ph.D. dissertation, Cornell University.

Heimarck, Brita Renée. 2003. *Balinese discourses on music and modernization: Village voices and urban views*. Current Research in Ethnomusicology, 5. New York: Routledge.

Henrich, Joseph. 2020. *The weirdest people in the world: How the West became psychologically peculiar and particularly prosperous*. New York: Farrar, Straus & Giroux.

Herbst, Anri, Meki Nzewi, and Kofi Agawu, eds. 2003. *Musical arts in Africa: Theory, practice, and education*. Pretoria: Unisa Press.

Herzfeld, Michael. 2004. *The body impolitic: Artisans and artifice in the global hierarchies of value*. Chicago: University of Chicago Press.

184 REFERENCES

Herzog, George. 1938. Music in the thinking of the American Indian. *Peabody Bulletin*, May, 1–5.

Herzog, George. 1945. Drum signaling in a West African tribe. *Word* 1, 217–38.

Hicks, Andrew. 2017. *Composing a world: Harmony in the Medieval Platonic cosmos.* New York: Oxford University Press.

Hijleh, Mark. 2012. *Towards a global music theory. Practical concepts and methods for the analysis of music across human cultures.* SOAS Musicology Series. Farnham: Ashgate.

Hodges, Donald A. 2019. Music through the lens of cultural neuroscience. In *The Oxford handbook of music and the brain*, edited by M. H. Thaut and D. A. Hodges, 19–41. New York: Oxford University Press.

Hood, Mantle. 1963. Music, the unknown. In *Musicology*, edited by F. Ll. Harrison, M. Hood, and C. V. Palisca, 215–326. The Princeton Series: Humanistic Scholarship in America. Englewood Cliffs, NJ: Prentice-Hall.

Hood, Mantle. 1971. *The ethnomusicologist.* New York: McGraw-Hill.

Hopkins, A. G. 2018 *American empire: A global history.* Princeton: Princeton University Press.

Hopkins, Pandora. 1982. Aural thinking. In *Cross-cultural perspectives on music*, edited by Robert Falck and Timothy F. Rice, 143–61. Toronto: University of Toronto Press.

Hornbostel, E. M. von. 1904. Melodischer Tanz. Eine musikpsychologische Studie. *Zeitschrift der Internationalen Musikgesellschaft* 5/12, 482–88. Reprinted in Hornbostel, *Tonart und Ethos. Aufsätze zur Musikethnologie und Musikpsychologie*, edited by Christian Kaden, 76–85. Leipzig: Reclam, 1986. Reprinted with English translation in *Hornbostel Opera Omnia*, edited by Klaus P. Wachsman, Dieter Christensen, and Hans-Peter Reinecke. Vol. 1, 203–15. The Hague: Nijhoff.

Hornbostel, E. M. von. 1909. Wanyamwezi-Gesänge. *Anthropos* 4, 781–800, 1033–53 and 8p. of notations.

Hornbostel, E. M. von. 1910. Über vergleichende akustische und musikpsychologische Untersuchungen. *Zeitschrift für angewandte Psychologie und psychologische Sammelforschung* 3, 465–87.

Hornbostel, E. M. von. 1913. Melodie und Skala. *Jahrbuch der Musikbibliothek Peters* 19, 11–23. Reprinted in Hornbostel, *Tonart und Ethos. Aufsätze zur Musikethnologie und Musikpsychologie*, edited by Christian Kaden, 59–75. Leipzig: Reclam, 1986.

Hornbostel, E. M. von. 1925. Die Einheit der Sinne. *Melos* 5 [*recte* 4]/6, 290–97. Translated by Elisabeth Koffka and Warren Vinton as "The unity of the senses," *Psyche* 28 (1927), 83–89.

Hornbostel, E. M. von. 1929. Tonart und Ethos. In *Musikwissenschafliche Beiträge. Festschrift für Johannes Wolf zu seinem sechzigsten Geburtstage*, edited by W. Lott, H. Osthoff, and W. Wolffheim, 73–78. Berlin: Breslauer. Reprinted in Hornbostel, *Tonart und Ethos. Aufsätze zur Musikethnologie*

REFERENCES 185

und Musikpsychologie, edited by Christian Kaden, 104–11. Leipzig: Reclam, 1986.

Hornbostel, E. M. von. 1975. *Hornbostel Opera Omnia*, edited by Klaus P. Wachsman, Dieter Christensen and Hans-Peter Reinecke. Vol. 1. The Hague: Nijhoff.

Hountondji, Paulin J. 1983 [1976]. *African philosophy: Myth and reality*, translated by Henri Evans with Jonathan Rée. Bloomington: Indiana University Press. First published in French, *Vers une philosophie africaine*. Paris: François Maspéro, 1976.

Hoyningen-Huene, Paul. 2013. *Systematicity—the nature of science*. Oxford: Oxford University Press.

Hughes, David W. 1991. Grammars of non-Western musics: A selective survey. In *Representing musical structure*, edited by P. Howell, R. West, and I. Cross, 327–62. London: Academic Press.

Hughes, David W. 2000. No nonsense: the logic and power of acoustic-iconic mnemonic systems. *British Journal of Ethnomusicology* 9/2, 93–120.

Hulse, Brian, and Nick Nesbitt., eds, 2010. *Sounding the virtual: Gilles Deleuze and the theory and philosophy of music*. Hampshire: Ashgate.

Huron, David. 2006. *Sweet anticipation: Music and the psychology of expectation*. Cambridge, MA: MIT Press.

Ibn Khaldun. 1961. *Muqaddimah*. In *Tarīkh al-allāma Ibn Khaldūn*, edited by Y. A. Dāghir. I, second edition. Beirut: Dār al-Kitāb al-Lubnanī.

Ibn Khaldun. 1967. *The Muqaddimah, an introduction to history*, translated by Franz Rosenthal. Second edition. Bollingen Series, 43. Princeton: Princeton University Press. 3 vols.

Impey, Angela. 2002. Culture, conservation and community reconstruction: Explorations in advocacy ethnomusicology and action research in northern KwaZulu. *YTM* 34, 9–24.

Ingold, Tim. 2011. *Being alive: Essays on movement, knowledge and description*. London and New York: Routledge.

Iyer, Vijay. 2019. Beyond improvisation. In *CCMT*, 760–79.

Jackendoff, Ray. 1992. What is a concept? In *Frames, fields, and contrasts: New essays in semantic and lexical organization*, edited by A. Lehrer and E. F. Kittay, 191–208. Hillsdale, NJ: Erlbaum.

Jacoby, Nori, Elizabeth Hellmuth Margulis, et al. 2020. Cross-cultural work in music cognition: Challenges, insights, and recommendations. *Music Perception* 37/3, 185–95.

Jäger, Ralf Martin. 1997. Notation, XI. Nichtwestliche Notationsformen, 2. Osmanische Notationsformen. *MGG 2 Sachteil*, 7, 386–97, 431.

Jairazbhoy, N. A. 1971. *The rāgs of north Indian music: Their structure and evolution*. Middletown, CT: Wesleyan University Press.

Jairazbhoy, N. A. 2008. What happened to Indian music theory? Indo-Occidentalism? *EM* 52/3, 349–77.

186 REFERENCES

Jairazbhoy, N. A., and A. W. Stone. 1963. Intonation in present-day North Indian classical music. *Bulletin of the School of Oriental and African Studies* 26/1, 119–32.

James, William. 1987a [1907]. *Pragmatism: A new name for some old ways of thinking*. In James, *Writings 1902–1910*. New York: Library of America, 479–624. First published New York and London: Longmans, Green, and Co., 1907.

James, William. 1987b [1909]. *A pluralistic universe*. In James, *Writings 1902–1910*. New York: Library of America, 625–819. First published New York and London: Longmans, Green, and Co., 1909.

Janata, P., J. L. Birk, J. D. Van Horn, M. Leman, B. Tillmann, and J. J. Bharucha. 2002. The cortical topography of tonal structures underlying Western music. *Science* 298/5601 (December 13), 2167–70.

Jäncke, Lutz. 2019. Music and memory. In *The Oxford handbook of music and the brain*, edited by M. H. Thaut and D. A. Hodges, 237–62. New York: Oxford University Press.

Johnson, Mark L., and Steve Larson. 2003. "Something in the way she moves": Metaphors of musical motion. *Metaphor & Symbol* 18/2, 63–84. Reprinted in Larson 2012, 61–81.

Johnston, Ben. 1974. Music theory. *Encyclopedia Britannica*, fifteenth edition, 12, 746–49. Reprinted in Johnston, *Maximum clarity and other writings on music*, edited by Bob Gilmore, 53–61. Urbana: University of Illinois Press. Reprinted 2006.

Jousse, Marcel. 1924. Le style orale rythmique et mnémotechnique chez les verbo-moteurs. *Archives de philosophie* 4, 1–240. Published separately, Paris: Gabriel Beauchesne, 1925. English translation by Edgard Sienaert and Richard Whitaker, *The oral style*. The Albert Bates Lord Studies in Oral Tradition, 6. New York and London: Garland, 1990.

Juslin, Patrik N., and John A. Sloboda, eds. 2010. *Handbook of music and emotion: Theory, research, applications*. Oxford: Oxford University Press.

Kaden, Christian. 1997. Musiksoziologie. *MGG 2, Sachteil*, 6, 1618–58.

Kapchan, Deborah, ed. 2017. *Theorizing sound writing*. Middletown, CT: Wesleyan University Press.

Karlgren, Bernhard. 1950. *The book of documents: The shu king*. Göteborg: Elanders Boktryckeri Aktiebolag.

Karomatov, Faizullah. 1983. Uzbek instrumental music, translated by Tom Djijiak, Theodore Levin, and Mark Slobin. *AsM* 15/1, 11–53.

Karomatov, F. M., and I. Radjabov. 1981. Introduction to the šašmaqam, translated by Theodore Levin. *AsM* 13/1, 97–118. First published in Russian and Uzbek as the introduction to Iu. Razhabii and F. M. Karamatov, *Shashmaqom*, vol. 1, Tashkent, 1966.

Kartomi, Margaret J. 1990. *On concepts and classifications of musical instruments*. CSE.

REFERENCES 187

Kartomi, Margaret J. 2012. *Musical journeys in Sumatra*. Urbana: University of Illinois Press.

Katz, Israel J., ed. 2015. *Henry George Farmer and the 1st International Congress of Arab Music (Cairo 1932)*. Islamic History and Civilization, Studies with Texts, 115. Leiden: Brill.

Katz, Max Gardner. 2010. Hindustani music history and the politics of theory. Ph.D. dissertation, University of California Santa Barbara.

Katz, Max. 2012. Institutional communalism in North Indian classical music. *EM* 56/2, 279–98.

Katz, Max. 2017. *Lineage of loss: Counternarratives of North Indian music.* Middletown, CT: Wesleyan University Press.

Katz, Ruth. 2003. *The Lachmann problem: An unsung chapter in comparative musicology, including unpublished letters and lectures of Robert Lachmann.* YUVAL Monograph Series, 12. Jerusalem: Hebrew University Magnes Press.

Kaufmann, Walter. 1967. *Musical notations of the Orient: Notational systems of continental East, South, and Central Asia.* Indiana University Humanities Series. Bloomington: Indiana University Press.

Kaufmann, Walter. 1976. *Musical references in the Chinese classics.* Detroit Monographs in Musicology, 5. Detroit: Information Coordinators.

Keating, Elizabeth, and Maria Egbert. Conversation as a cultural activity. In *A companion to linguistic anthropology*, edited by Alessandro Duranti, 169–96. Malden, MA: Blackwell.

Keil, Charles. 1979. *Tiv song: The sociology of art in a classless society.* Chicago: University of Chicago Press.

Keym, Stefan, and Hans-Joachim Hinrichsen, eds. 2020. *Dur versus Moll. Zur Geschichte der Semantik eines musikalischen Elementarkontrasts.* Vienna: Böhlau.

Khāleqi, Ruhollāh. 1967 [1346]. *Nazari be musiqi*, Vol. 2. Third printing. Tehran: Sherkat-e Chāpkhāne-he Ferdowsi.

Khoshzamir, Mojtaba. 1979. Ali Naqi Vaziri and his influence on music and music education in Iran. Ph.D. dissertation, University of Illinois at Urbana-Champaign.

Kilmer, Anne Draffkorn. 1997. Mesopotamien, II. Textquellen. *MGG 2, Sachteil*, 6, 134–43.

Kilmer, Anne Draffkorn. 2001. Mesopotamia. *NG 2*, 16, 480–87 and *OMO*.

Kippen, James. 1988. *The Tablā of Lucknow: A cultural analysis of a musical tradition.* Cambridge Studies in Ethnomusicology. Cambridge: Cambridge University Press. Accompanying audiocassette.

Kippen, James. 2006. *Gurudev's drumming legacy: Music, theory and nationalism in the* Mrdang aur Tablā Vādanpaddhati *of Gurudev Patwardhan.* SOAS Musicology Series. Aldershot: Ashgate.

Kippen, James. 2008. Working with the masters. In *Shadows in the field: New perspectives for fieldwork in ethnomusicology*, edited by Gregory

188 REFERENCES

Barz and Timothy J. Cooley, second edition, 125–40. New York: Oxford University Press.

Kittay, Eve Feder. 1987. *Metaphor: Its cognitive force and linguistic structure.* Oxford: Clarendon Press. 1990 edition in *OSO.* DOI: 10.1093/acprof:oso/9780198242468.003.0007.

Kittay, Eve Feder. 1992. Semantic fields and the individuation of content. In *Frames, fields, and contrasts: New essays in semantic and lexical organization,* edited by A. Lehrer and E. F. Kittay, 229–52. Hillsdale, NJ: Erlbaum.

Klee, Paul. 1964 [1956]. *Das bildnerische Denken. Schriften zur Form- und Gestaltungslehre,* edited by Jürg Spiller. Basel and Stuttgart: B. Schwabe.

Klee, Paul. 1961. *Notebooks. Volume 1, The thinking eye,* edited by Jürg Spiller, translated by Ralph Mannheim. London: Lund Humphries.

Kobayashi, Eriko. 2003. Hindustani classical music reform movement and the writing of history, 1900s to 1940s. Ph.D. dissertation, University of Texas.

Kongo, Zabana, and Jeffrey Robinson. 2003. Improvisation. In *Musical arts in Africa: Theory, practice, and education,* edited by Anri Herbst, Meki Nzewi, and Kofi Agwu, 95–117. Pretoria: Unisa Press.

Koskoff, Ellen. 1988. Cognitive strategies in rehearsal. *SRE* 7, 59–68.

Kresánek, Jozef. 1977. *Základy hudobného myslenia* [Fundamentals of musical thinking]. Bratislava: Opus. Summaries in English and German, 328–39.

Kubik, Gerhard. 1960. The structure of Kiganda xylophone music. *AfM* 2/3, 6–30.

Kubik, Gerhard. 1962. The phenomenon of inherent rhythms in East and Central African instrumental music. *AfM* 3/1, 33–42, with corrigenda 4/4, 136–37.

Kubik, Gerhard. 1968. *Mehrstimmigkeit und Tonsysteme in Zentral und Ostafrika.* Vienna: Hermann Böhlaus Nachfolger.

Kubik, Gerhard. 1969. Composition techniques in Kiganda xylophone music. *AfM* 4/3, 22–72.

Kubik, Gerhard. 1972a. Oral notation of some West and Central African time-line patterns. *Review of Ethnology* 3, 169–76.

Kubik, Gerhard. 1972b. Letter to Peter Cooke. *AfM* 5/2, 114–15.

Kubik, Gerhard. 1983. Die Amadinda-Musik von Buganda. In *Musik in Afrika,* edited by Artur Simon, 139–65. Berlin: Museum für Völkerkunde. Revision of an article first published in *Musik als Gestalt und Erlebnis: Festschrift Walter Graf,* 109–37 (1970).

Kubik, Gerhard. 1990. Drum patterns in the *batuque* of Benedito Caxias. *Latin American Music Review* 11/2, 115–181.

Kubik, Gerhard. 1991. Theorie, Aufführungspraxis und Kompositionstechniken der Hofmusik von Buganda. *Hamburger Jahrbuch der Musikwissenschaft* 11, 23–162.

Kubik, Gerhard. 1994. *Theory of African music,* Vol. 1. Intercultural Music Studies, 7. Wilhelmshaven: Florian Noetzel. Reprinted in CSE, 2010.

REFERENCES 189

Kubik, Gerhard. 1996. Emics and etics: Theoretical considerations. *AfM* 7/ 3, 3–10.

Kubik, Gerhard. 1999. *Africa and the blues*. Jackson: University Press of Mississippi.

Kubik, Gerhard. 2010. *Theory of African music*, Vol. 2. CSE.

Kuckertz, Josef. 1970. *Form und Melodiebildung der karnatischen Musik Südindiens im Umkreis der vorderorientalischen und der nordindischen Kunstmusik.* Wiesbaden: Harrassowitz. English summary.

Kunst, Jaap. 1959. *Ethnomusicology: A study of its nature, its problems, methods and representative personalities to which is added a bibliography.* Third edition. The Hague: Nijhoff.

Kunst, Jaap. 1973. *Music in Java: Its history, its theory and its technique.* Third edition, edited by E. L. Heins. The Hague: Nijhoff. First edition, 1949.

Kurth, Ernst. 1917. *Grundlagen des linearen Kontrapunkts. Einführung in Stil und Technik von Bach's melodischer Polyphonie.* Bern: Max Drechsel.

Kyagambiddwa, Joseph. 1956. *African music from the source of the Nile.* New York: Praeger.

Labussière, Annie. 1976. Rythme enfantin, pentatonismes et giusto syllabique dans les créations mélodiques des enfants. *RdM* 62/1, 25–85.

Lachmann, Robert. 1929. *Musik des Orients.* Breslau: Jedermanns Bücherei.

Lakoff, George, and Mark Johnson. 1980. *Metaphors we live by.* Chicago: University of Chicago Press.

Lambert, Jean. 2007. Retour sur le congrès de musique arabe du Caire de 1932. Identité, diversité, acculturation: les prémisses d'une mondialisation. Paper presented at Congrès de Musiques dans le monde de l'Islam, Assilah, Morocco, August 8–13, 2007.

Lambert, Jean, and Pascal Cordereix. 2015. *Congrès de musique arabe du Caire / The Cairo Congress of Arab Music.* Paris: Bibliothèque Nationale de France. 18 CDs with booklet in French, English, and Arabic.

Lannoy, Michel de. 1987. L'improvisation comme conduite musicale: Sur un chant senoufo de Côte d'Ivoire. In *L'Improvisation dans les musiques de tradition orale,* edited by B. Lortat-Jacob, 105–18. Paris: SELAF.

Larson, Steve. 2005. Composition versus improvisation. *Journal of Music Theory* 49/2, 241–75.

Larson, Steve. 2012. *Musical forces: Motion, metaphor, and meaning in music.* Musical Meaning and Interpretation. Bloomington: Indiana University Press.

Lauer, Helen, and Kofi Anyidoho, eds. 2012. *Reclaiming the human sciences through African perspectives.* 2 vols. Accra: Sub-Saharan Publishers. Open access through EBook Central.

Lê Tuân Hùng. 1994. The dynamics of change in *Huê* and *tài tu* music. In *Musiccultures in contact: Convergences and collisions,* edited by M. J. Kartomi and S. Blum, 233–49. Sydney: Currency Press and Basel: Gordon and Breach.

190 REFERENCES

Lee Tong Soon. 1998. Performing Chinese street opera and constructing national culture in Singapore. Ph.D. dissertation, University of Pittsburgh.

Lee Tong Soon. 2004. Chinese street opera performance and the shaping of cultural aesthetics in contemporary Singapore. *YTM* 34, 139–61.

Lee Tong Soon. 2009. *Chinese street opera in Singapore.* Urbana: University of Illinois Press.

Lee Tong Soon, ed. 2021. *Routledge handbook of Asian Music: Cultural intersections.* London and New York: Routledge.

Lehrer, Adrienne. 1983. *Wine and conversation.* Bloomington: Indiana University Press.

Levin, Theodore C. 1984. The music and tradition of the Bukharan shashmaqām in Soviet Uzbekistan. Ph.D. dissertation, Princeton University.

Levin, Theodore C. 1996. *The hundred thousand fools of God: Musical travels in Central Asia (and Queens, New York).* Bloomington: Indiana University Press. Accompanying CD.

Levin, Theodore C. 2002. Making Marxist-Leninist music in Uzbekistan. In *Music and Marx: Ideas, practice, politics,* edited by Regula B. Qureshi, 190–203. New York and London: Routledge.

Levin, Theodore, and Valentina Süzükei. 2006. *Where rivers and mountains sing: Sound, music, and nomadism in Tuva and beyond.* Bloomington: Indiana University Press. Accompanying CD and DVD.

Lévi-Strauss, Claude. 1962. *La pensée sauvage.* Paris: Plon.

Lévi-Strauss, Claude. 1966 [1950]. Introduction à l'oeuvre de Marcel Mauss. In Mauss, *Sociologie et anthropologie,* ix–lii. Paris: Presses Universitaires de France.

Lewis, George E. 2008. *A power stronger than itself: The AACM and American experimental music.* Chicago: University of Chicago Press.

Light, Nathan. 2008. *Intimate heritage: Creating Uyghur muqam song in Xinjiang.* Halle Studies in the Anthropology of Eurasia, 19. Berlin: Lit.

Lochhead, Judy. 2011. Music theory and philosophy. In *The Routledge companion to philosophy and music,* edited by Theodore Gracyk and Andrew Kania, 506–16. New York: Routledge.

Lochhead, Judy. 2016. *Reconceiving structure in contemporary music: New tools in music theory and analysis.* New York: Routledge.

Locke, David. 1978. The music of Atsiagbeko. Ph.D. dissertation, Wesleyan University.

Locke, David. 2019. An approach to musical rhythm in Agbadza. In *Thought and play in musical rhyrhm,* edited by R. K. Wolf, S. Blum, and C. F. Hasty, 100–45. New York: Oxford University Press.

Locke, David, with Godwin Agbeli. 1992. *Kpegisu, a war-drum of the Ewe.* Tempe, AZ: White Cliffs Media.

Lomax, Alan. 1968. *Folk song style and culture.* Washington, D.C.: American Association for the Advancement of Science.

REFERENCES 191

Lomax, John and Alan. 1947. *Folk song U.S.A.* New York: Duell, Sloane and Pearce.

Lord, Albert Bates. 1991 *Epic singers and oral tradition.* Myth and Poetics. Ithaca: Cornell University Press.

Lortat-Jacob, Bernard. 1987. Improvisation: Le modèle et ses réalisations. In *L'Improvisation dans les musiques de tradition orale,* edited by B. Lortat-Jacob, 45–59. Paris: SELAF.

Lortat-Jacob, Bernard. 1996. *Canti di passione, Castelsardo, Sardegna.* Translated by Piero Fattaccio and Bachisio Masia. Lucca: Libreria Musicale Italiana. Accompanying CD.

Lortat-Jacob, Bernard. 1998a. *Chants de passion: Au coeur d'une confrérie de Sardaigne.* La voie esthétique. Paris: Editions du Cerf. Accompanying CD.

Lortat-Jacob, Bernard. 1998b. Prononcer en chantant: analyse musicale d'un texte parlé. *L'Homme* 146, 87–112.

Lukaniuk, Bogdan. 2010. On the History of the Term *ethnomusicology. Folklorica: Journal of the Slavic and East European Folklore Association* 15, 129–54.

Macchiarella, Ignazio. 2009. *Cantare a cuncordu: Uno studio a più voci.* Second edition, revised. Udine: Nota. Accompanying CD.

Macchiarella, Ignazio. 2011. Dialogismi musicali. *Studi e ricerche* 4, 139–43.

Macchiarella, Ignazio. 2012. Theorizing on multipart music making. In *Multipart music. A specific mode of musical thinking, expressive behavior and sound. Papers from the First Meeting of the ICTM Study Group on Multipart Music (Sept. 15–20, 2010), Cagliari, Sardinia,* 7–22. Udine: Nota.

Macchiarella, Ignazio. 2014. Exploring micro-worlds of music meanings. *el oído pensante* 1/2. *Portal de Publicaciones Científicas y Técnicas.* http://ppct.caicyt.gov.ar/index.php/oidopensante.

Maceda, José. 1974. Drone and melody in Philippine musical instruments. In *Traditional drama and music of Southeast Asia,* edited by M. Taib Osman, 246–73. Kuala Lumpur: Kementerian Pelajaran Malaysia.

Maceda, José. 1979. A search for an old and a new music in Southeast Asia. *Acta Musicologica* 51/1, 160–68.

Maceda, José. 1981. Sources of musical thought in Southeast Asia. In *Final Report, Third Asian Composers' League Conference-Festival, October 12–18, 1975, Manila, Philippines,* 63–66.

Maceda, José. 1986. A concept of time in a music of Southeast Asia (a preliminary account). *EM* 30/1, 11–53.

Maceda, José. 1990. In search of a source of pentatonic hemitonic and anhemitonic scales in Southeast Asia. *Acta musicologica* 62/2-3, 192–223.

Mâche, François-Bernard. 2001. *Musique au singulier.* Paris: Odile Jacob.

Madian, Azza Abd al-Hamid. 1992. Language-music relationships in Al-Farabi's "Grand book of music". Ph.D. dissertation, Cornell University.

Magrini, Tullia. 1989. The group dimension in traditional music. *WoM* 31/2, 52–78.

192   REFERENCES

Magrini, Tullia. 1993. Analisi fra suono e uomo. Riflessioni su alcune tradizioni vocali italiane. In *Antropologia delle musica e culture mediterranee*, edited by Tullia Magrini, 165–81. Bologna: Il Mulino.

Magrini, Tullia. 1998. Improvisation and group interaction in Italian lyrical singing. In *In the course of performance: Studies in the world of musical improvisation*, edited by Bruno Nettl with Melinda Russell, 169–98. CSE.

Malamusi, Moya Aliya. 1994. Rise and development of a Chileka guitar style in the 1950s. In *For Gerhard Kubik: Festschrift on the occasion of his sixtieth birthday*, edited by A. Schmidhofer and D. Schüller, 7–72. Vergleichende Musikwissenschaft, 3. Frankfurt am Main: Peter Lang.

Malin, Yonatan. 2019. Ethnography and analysis in the study of Jewish music. AAWM 7.2, *Special issue on ethnography and analysis*, edited by Yonathan Malin. www.aawmjournal.com.

Malm, William P. 1959. *Japanese music and musical instruments*. Rutland, VT and Tokyo: Charles E. Tuttle.

Malm, William P. 1971. The modern music of Meiji Japan. In *Tradition and modernization in Japanese culture*, edited by Donald H. Shively, 257–300. Princeton: Princeton University Press.

Malm, William P. 1986. *Six hidden views of Japanese music*. The Ernest Bloch Lectures. Berkeley and Los Angeles: University of California Press.

Marchand, Trevor. 2008. Muscles, morals and mind: Craft apprenticeship and the formation of person. *British Journal of Educational Studies* 56/3, 245–71.

Marcu, George. 1983. Un sistem identic de executie polifonică a cîntecelor populare, întîlnit la unele populare din peninsula balcanică. *Revista de etnografie și folclor* 13, 545–54.

Marcus, Scott. 1989. Arab music theory in the modern period. Ph.D. dissertation, University of California, Los Angeles.

Marcus, Scott. 1992. Modulation in Arab music: Documenting oral concepts, performance rules, and strategies. *EM* 36/2, 171–95; https://doi.org/10.2307/851913.

Marett, Allan, Linda Barwick, and Lysbeth Ford. 2013. *For the sake of a song: Wangga songmen and their repertories*. The Indigenous Music of Australia, Book 2. Sydney: Sydney University Press.

Markoff, Irene. 1986. Musical theory, performance and the contemporary *bağlama* specialist in Turkey. Ph.D. dissertation, University of Washington.

Martin, Henry. 1997. Jazz theory: An overview. *Annual Review of Jazz Studies* 8, 1–17.

Massoudieh, Mohammad Taghi. 1996. *Manuscrits persans concernant la musique*. Répertoire International des Sources Musicales, Bxii. Munich: G. Henle.

Mathiesen, Thomas J. 2002. Greek music theory. In *The Cambridge history of western music theory*, edited by Thomas Christensen, 109–35. Cambridge: Cambridge University Press.

REFERENCES 193

Mauss, Marcel. 1966. Les techniques du corps. In Mauss, *Sociologie et anthropologie*, 363–86. Paris: Presses Universitaires de France. First published in *Journal de psychologie* 32/3–4, 1936.

Mauss, Marcel. 1973. Techniques of the body. Translated by Ben Brewster. *Economy and Society* 2/1, 70–88. Reprinted in *Beyond the body proper: Reading the anthropology of material life*, edited by M. Lock and J. Farquhar, 50–68. Durham, NC: Duke University Press, 2007.

Mauss, Marcel. 1974. *Oeuvres, 2. représentations collectives et diversité des civilisations*. Paris: Editions de Minuit.

Mavromatis, Panayotis. 2005. The echoi of modern Greek church chant in written and oral transmission: A computational model and its cognitive implications. Ph.D. dissertation, University of Rochester.

Mavromatis, Panayotis. 2006. A hidden Markov model of melody production in Greek chant. *Computing in Musicology* 14, 93–112.

May, Elizabeth. 1963. *The influence of the Meiji period on Japanese children's music*. Berkeley and Los Angeles: University of California Press.

McAllester, David P. 2006. Reminiscences of the early days. *EM* 50/2, 199–203.

McClary, Susan. 2019. Mode. In *CCMT*, 61–77.

Meintjes, Louise. 2003. *Sound of Africa! Making music Zulu in a South African studio*. CSE.

Merchant Henson, Tanya. 2006. Constructing musical tradition in Uzbek institutions. Ph.D. dissertation, University of California, Los Angeles.

Merchant, Tanya. 2021. Imagined homogeneity: *Maqom* in Soviet and Uzbek national projects. In *Routledge handbook of Asian Music: Cultural intersections*, edited by Lee Tong Soon, 221–40. London and New York: Routledge.

Merriam, Alan P. 1964. *The anthropology of music*. Evanston: Northwestern University Press.

Merriam, Alan P. 1969. The ethnographic experience: Drum-making among the Bala (Basongye). *EM* 13/1, 74–100. Reprinted in Merriam, *African music in perspective*. New York: Garland, 1982, 191–222.

Merriam, Alan P. 1981. African musical rhythm and concepts of time-reckoning. In *Music east and west: Essays in honor of Walter Kaufmann*, edited by Thomas L. Noblitt. New York: Pendragon. Reprinted in Merriam, *African music in perspective*. New York: Garland, 1982, 443–61.

Mersenne, Marin. 1936 [1636]. *Harmonie universelle, contenant la théorie et la pratique de la musique*. Paris: Centre National de la Recherche Scientifique. 3 vols. Facsimile of work first published in Paris, 1636.

Messiaen, Olivier. 1994. *Traité de rythme, de couleur, et d'ornithologie (1949–1992)*. Tome I. Paris: Alphonse Leduc.

Meyer, Leonard B. 1989. *Style and music: Theory, history, and ideology*. Studies in the Criticism and Theory of Music. Philadelphia: University of Pennsylvania Press.

Miller, Richard C. 2004. Music and musicology in the engineering of national identity in Meiji Japan: Modernization strategies of the Music

194 REFERENCES

Investigation Committee, 1870–1900. Ph.D. dissertation, University of Wisconsin-Madison.

Million, Dian. 2014. There is a river in me: Theory from life. In *Theorizing native studies*, edited by Audra Simpson and Andrea Smith, 31–42. Durham, NC: Duke University Press.

Ministère de l'Instruction Publique, Royaume d'Egypte. 1934. *Recueil des travaux du Congrès de musique arabe qui s'est trouvé au Caire en 1932 (hég. 1350) sous le haut patronage de S.M. Foyad 1er, roi d'Égypte*. Cairo: Imprimerie nationale, Boulac.

Mishra, Pankaj. 2012. *From the ruins of empire: The intellectuals who remade Asia*. New York: Farrar, Straus and Giroux.

Mitchell, Frank. 1978. *Navajo Blessingway singer: The autobiography of Frank Mitchell*, edited by Charlotte J. Frisbie and David P. McAllester. Tucson: University of Arizona Press.

Moisala, Pirrko, Taru Leppänen, Milla Tiainen, and Hanna Väätäinen, eds. 2017. *Musical encounters with Deleuze and Guattari*. Bloomsbury Sound Series. London: Bloomsbury Academic.

Molino, Jean. 1988. Musicologies et ethnomusicologie: vers un renouvellement des questions et une unification des méthodes." *Analyse musicale* 11, 9–15.

Monts, Lester. 1990. *An annotated glossary of Vai musical language and its social contexts*. Ethnomusicologie, 3. Paris: Peeters and SELAF.

Mora, Manolete. 1987. The sounding pantheon of nature: T'boli instrumental music in the making of an ancestral symbol. *Acta Musicologica* 65, 187–212.

Mora, Manolete. 2005a. *Myth, mimesis and magic in the music of the T'boli, Philippines*. Mindanao Studies Series. Quezon City: Ateneo de Manila University Press.

Mora, Manolete. 2005b. Mind, body, spirit, and soul: A Filipino epistemology of adeptness in musical performance. *AsM* 36/2, 81–95.

Moreno, Jairo. 2004. *Musical representations, subjects, and objects: The construction of musical thought in Zarlino, Descartes, Rameau, and Weber*. Musical Meaning and Interpretation. Bloomington: Indiana University Press.

Morgenstern, Ulrich, and Ardian Ahmedaja, eds. 2022. *Playing multipart music. Solo and ensemble traditions in Europe*. European Voices, 4. Vienna and Cologne: Böhlau.

Moro, Pamela. 2004. Constructions of nation and the classicisation of music: Comparative perspectives from Southeast and South Asia. *Journal of Southeast Asia Studies* 35/2, 187–211.

Music Educators National Conference. 1985. *Becoming human through music. The Wesleyan Symposium on the Perspectives of Social Anthropology in the Teaching and Learning of Music, August 6–10, 1984, Wesleyan University, Middletown, Connecticut*. Reston, VA: Music Educators National Conference.

Nattiez, Jean-Jacques. 1987. *Musicologie générale et sémiologie*. Paris: Christian Bourgois.

REFERENCES 195

Nattiez, Jean-Jacques. 1990. *Music and discourse: Toward a semiology of music.* Partial translation of Nattiez 1987 by Carolyn Abbate. Princeton: Princeton University Press.

Neal, Jocelyn R. 2018. The twang factor in country music. In *The relentless pursuit of tone: Timbre in popular music*, edited by R. Fink, M. Latour, and Z. Wallmark, 43–64. New York: Oxford University Press.

Needham, Joseph, and Kenneth Girdwood Robinson. 1962. Sound (acoustics). In Needham, *Science and civilisation in China*, 4/1, 126–228. Cambridge: Cambridge University Press.

Nelson, David P. 2008. *Solkattu manual: An introduction to the rhythmic language of South Indian music.* Middletown, CT: Wesleyan University Press.

Nesbitt, Nick. 2010. Critique and clinique: From sounding bodies to the musical event. In *Sounding the virtual: Gilles Deleuze and the theory and philosophy of music*, edited by Brian Hulse and Nick Nesbitt, 159–79. Hampshire: Ashgate.

Nettl, Bruno. 1954. Notes on musical composition in primitive culture. *Anthropological Quarterly* 27/2, 81–90.

Nettl, Bruno. 1974. Thoughts on improvisation: A comparative approach. *Musical Quarterly* 60/1, 1–19.

Nettl, Bruno. 1983. *The study of ethnomusicology: Twenty-nine issues and concepts.* Urbana: University of Illinois Press.

Nettl, Bruno. 1989. *Blackfoot musical thought: Comparative perspectives.* Kent, OH: Kent State University Press.

Nettl, Bruno. 1998. Introduction: An art neglected in scholarship. In *In the course of performance: Studies in the world of musical improvisation*, edited by Bruno Nettl with Melinda Russell, 1–23. CSE.

Nettl, Bruno. 2005. *The study of ethnomusicology: Thirty-one issues and concepts.* Urbana: University of Illinois Press.

Nettl, Bruno. 2006. Was ist Musik? Ethnomusikologische Perspective. In *Musik—Zu Begriff und Konzepten*, edited by Michael Beiche and Albrecht Riethmüller, 9–18. Wiesbaden: Franz Steiner.

Nettl, Bruno. 2015. *The study of ethnomusicology: Thirty-three discussions.* Urbana: University of Illinois Press.

Neubauer, Eckhard. 1994. Die acht "Wege" der arabischen Musiklehre und der Oktoechos. *Zeitschrift für Geschichte der arabisch-islamischen Wissenschaften* 9, 373–414.

Neubauer, Eckhard. 1998. *Arabische Musiktheorie von den Anfängen bis zum 6./12.Jahrhundert. Studien, Übersetzungen und Texte in Faksimile.* Publications of the Institute for the History of Arabic-Islamic Science: The Science of Music in Islam, 3. Frankfurt: Institute for the History of Arabic-Islamic Science.

Neubauer, Eckhard, 2004–5. Die Euklid zugeschriebene "Teilung des Kanon" in arabischer Übersetzung. *Zeitschrift für Geschichte der arabisch-islamischen Wissenschaften* 16, 309–85.

196 REFERENCES

Neuman, Daniel M. 1980. *The life of music in north India: The organization of an artistic tradition*. Detroit: Wayne State University Press.

Neuman, Daniel M. 1985. Indian music as a cultural system. *AsM* 17/1, 98–113.

Newen, Albert, Leon De Bruin, and Shaun Gallagher, eds. 2018. *The Oxford handbook of 4E cognition*. New York: Oxford University Press.

Ngũgĩ wa Thiong'o. 2012. *Globalectics: Theory and the politics of knowing*. The Wellek Library Lectures in Critical Theory. New York: Columbia University Press.

Nijenhuis, Emmie te. 1974. *Indian music, history and structure*. Handbuch der Orientalistik, 2/6. Leiden: Brill.

Nijenhuis, Emmie te. 1977. *Musicological literature*. A History of Indian Literature, 6/1. Wiesbaden, Harrassowitz.

Niranjana, Tejaswini. 2020. *Musicophilia in Mumbai: Performing subjects and the metropolitan unconscious*. Durham, NC: Duke University Press. (Duke e-book)

Nketia, J. H. Kwabena. 1974. *The music of Africa*. New York: Norton.

Nketia, J. H. Kwabena. 1989. Musical interaction in ritual events. *Concilium: Révue international de théologie* 1989/2, 111–24.

Norris, H. T. 1968. Sẖinqīṭī *folk literature and song*. Oxford Library of African Literature. Oxford: Clarendon Press.

Novak, David, and Matt Sakakeeny, eds. 2015. *Keywords in sound*. Durham, NC: Duke University Press.

Nzewi, Meki. 1997. *African music: Theoretical content and creative continuum: The culture-exponent's definitions*. Olderhausen: Institut für Didaktik populärer Musik.

Nzewi, Meki. 2007a. *A contemporary study of musical arts informed by African indigenous knowledge systems*, 1. *The root—Foundation*. Pretoria: Centre for Indigenous African Instrumental Music and Dance (Ciimda).

Nzewi, Meki. 2007b. *A contemporary study of musical arts informed by African indigenous knowledge systems*, 3. *The foliage: Consolidation*. Pretoria: Centre for Indigenous African Instrumental Music and Dance (Ciimda).

Nzewi, Meki and O'Dyke Nzewi. 2007. *A contemporary study of musical arts: informed by African indigenous knowledge systems*, 5. *Theory and practice of modern African classical drum music*. Pretoria: Centre for Indigenous African Instrumental Music and Dance (Ciimda). 3 vols.

Ochoa Gautier, Ana María. 2014. *Aurality: Listening and knowledge in nineteenth-century Colombia*. Sign, Storage, Transmission. Durham, NC: Duke University Press.

O'Connell, John Morgan. 2000. Fine art, fine music: Controlling Turkish taste at the Fine Arts Academy in 1926. *YTM* 32, 117–42.

O'Connell, John Morgan. 2010. *Alabanda*: Brass bands and musical methods in Turkey. In *Giuseppe Donizetti Pascià: Traiettorie musicali e storiche tra Italia e Turchia/Giuseppe Donizetti Pasha: Musical and historical trajectories between Italy and Turkey*, edited by Federico Spinetti, 19–37. Bergamo: Fondazione Donizetti.

Odoyevsky, V. F. 1956. *Muzykal'no-literaturnoye naslediye*, edited by G. B. Bernandt. Moscow: Gos. Muzykal'noe izd.vo.

Ogawa Masafumi. 2000. Early nineteenth century American influences on the beginning of Japanese public music education: An analysis and comparison of selected music textbooks published in Japan and the United States. DMEd dissertation, Indiana University.

Oliveira Pinto, Tiago de. 1994. Cross-cultural communication: How do Brazilian berimbau players perceive an Angolan musical bow performance? In *For Gerhard Kubik: Festschrift on the occasion of his sixtieth birthday*, edited by A. Schmidhofer and D. Schüller, 469–78. Vergleichende Musikwissenschaft, 3. Frankfurt am Main: Peter Lang.

Ong, Walter. 1982. *Orality and literacy: The technologizing of the word*. London: Methuen.

Pandolfo, Stefania. 1997. *Impasse of the angels: Scenes from a Moroccan space of memory*. Chicago: University of Chicago Press.

Panopoulos, Panayotis, Nicola Scaldaferri, and Steven Feld. 2020. Resounding participatory ethnography: Ethnographic dialogue in dialogue. *Visual Anthropology Review* 36/2, 426–41.

Parker, William. 2011. *Conversations*. n.p.: RogueArt.

Parker, William. 2020. *The music of William Parker: Migration of silence into and out of the tone world*. Ten CDs with booklet.

Patel, Aniruddh D. 2008. *Music, language, and the brain*. New York: Oxford University Press.

Patel, Aniruddh D., and Steven M. Demorest. 2013. Comparative music cognition: Cross-species and cross-cultural studies. In *The psychology of music*, third edition, edited by D. Deutsch, 647–81. London: Academic Press.

Paulhan, Jean. 1913 [1939]. *Les hain-teny*. Paris: Gallimard. Reprinted 1939.

Peiris, Eshantha. 2018. Changing conceptualizations of rhythm in Sri Lankan up-country percussion: From rhythmic contours to metric cycles. *AAWM* 6/2. Online: mtosmt.org.

Perlman, Marc. 1994. Unplayed melodies: Music theory in postcolonial Java. Ph.D. dissertation, Wesleyan University.

Perlman, Marc. 1998. The social meanings of modal practices: Status, gender, history, and pathet in Central Javanese music. *EM* 42/1, 45–80.

Perlman, Marc. 2004. *Unplayed melodies: Javanese gamelan and the genesis of music theory*. Berkeley: University of California Press.

Perman, Anthony W. 2008. History, ethics, and emotion in Ndau performance in Zimbabwe: Local theoretical knowledge and ethnomusicological perspectives. Ph.D. dissertation, University of Illinois at Urbana-Champaign.

Perman, Tony. 2020. *Signs of the spirit: Music and the experience of meaning in Ndau ceremonial life*. Urbana: University of Illinois Press.

198 REFERENCES

Petrović, Ankica. 1977. Ganga: A form of traditional rural singing of Yugoslavia. Ph.D. dissertation, Queen's University of Belfast.

Petrović, Ankica. 1995. Perception of ganga. *WoM* 37/2, 60–71.

Phillips, John. 2006. Agencement/Assemblage. *Theory, Culture and Society* 23/ 2-3, 108–09.

Pian, Rulan Chao. 1967. *Sonq dynasty musical sources and their interpretation*. Harvard-Yenching Institute Monograph Series, 16. Cambridge, MA: Harvard University Press.

Pian, Rulan Chao. 1981. Modes, transposed scales, melody types and tune types. In International Musicological Society, *Report of the Twelfth Congress, Berkeley 1977*, edited by Daniel Heartz and Bonnie C. Wade, 776–78. Kassel: Bärenreiter.

Picken, Laurence. 1975. *Folk musical instruments of Turkey*. Oxford: Oxford University Press.

Picken, Laurence. 1977. The shapes of the *Shi Jing* song-texts and their musical implications. *Musica asiatica* 1, 85–109.

Pier, David G. 2015. *Ugandan music in the marketing era: The branded arena*. Houndmills, Basingstoke, Hampshire and New York: Palgrave Macmillan.

Pihl, Marshall R. 1994. *The Korean singer of tales*. Harvard-Yenching Institute Monograph Series, 37. Cambridge, MA: The Council on East Asian Studies, Harvard University.

Pike, Kenneth L. 1967. *Language in relation to a unified theory of the structure of human behavior*. Second, revised edition. Janua linguarum, series maior, 24. The Hague: Mouton.

Pirrotta, Nino, and Elena Povoledo. 1982 [1969]. *Music and theatre from Poliziano to Monteverdi*. Translated by Karen Bales. Cambridge Studies in Music. Cambridge: Cambridge University Press. First published as *Li due Orfei*, Turin: Eri, 1969.

Plato. 1982 [1914]. *Euthyphro, Apology, Crito, Phaedo, Phaedrus with an English translation by Harold North Fowler*. Loeb Classical Library, 36. Cambridge, MA: Harvard University Press and London: William Heinemann.

Pocorobba, Janet. 2019. *The fourth string: A memoir of sensei and me*. Berkeley: Stone Bridge Press.

Polak, Rainer. 2007. Performing audience. On the social constitution of focused interaction at celebrations in Mali. *Anthropos* 102/1, 3–18.

Polak, Rainer. 2012. Urban drumming: Traditional jembe celebration music in a West African city (Bamako). In *Hip Hop Africa: New African music in a globalizing world*, edited by Eric Charry, 261–81. Bloomington: Indiana University Press.

Polanyi, Michael. 1962 [1958]. *Personal knowledge: Towards a post-critical philosophy*. Corrected edition. Chicago: University of Chicago Press. First published 1958.

Porcello, Thomas. 1996. Sonic artistry: Music, discourse, and technology in the sound recording studio. Ph.D. dissertation, University of Texas at Austin.

REFERENCES 199

Porcello, Thomas. 2004. Talk about timbre in the recording studio. In *A companion to linguistic anthropology*, edited by Alessandro Duranti, 323–28. Malden: Blackwell.

Porter, Eric. 2002. *What is this thing called jazz? African American musicians as artists, critics, and activists*. Music of the African Diaspora, 6. Berkeley and Los Angeles: University of California Press.

Powers, Harold S. 1977. The structure of musical meaning: A view from Banares. *Perspectives of New Music* 14/2-15/1, 308–34.

Powers, Harold S. 1980a. India, subcontinent of. I. The region, its music and music history; II. Theory and practice of classical music. In *The new Grove dictionary of music and musicians*, edited by Stanley Sadie, 9, 69–141. London: Macmillan.

Powers, Harold S. 1980b. Mode, V. Mode as a musicological concept. In *The new Grove dictionary of music and musicians*, edited by Stanley Sadie, 12, 422–50. London: Macmillan.

Powers, Harold S. 1980c. Language models and musical analysis. *EM* 24/1, 1–60.

Powers, Harold S. 1981. Eastern and Western concepts of mode, Introduction: mode and modality. In International Musicological Society, *Report of the Twelfth Congress, Berkeley 1977*, edited by Daniel Heartz and Bonnie C. Wade, 501–03. Kassel: Bärenreiter.

Powers, Harold S. 1992a. Modality as a European cultural construct. In *Secondo convegno europeo di analisi musicale: Atti*, edited by Rossana Dalmonte and Mario Baroni, 207–19. Trent: Università degli Studi di Trento.

Powers, Harold S. 1992b. Reinterpretations of tradition in Hindustani music: Omkarnath Thakur versus Vishnu Narayan Bhatkhande. In *The traditional Indian theory and practice of music and dance*, edited by Jonathan Katz, 9–51. Leiden: Brill.

Powers, Harold S., revised by Richard Widdess. 2001. Mode, V.1, Introduction: Mode as a musicological concept. *NG 2* and *OMO*.

Powers, William K. 1980. Oglala song terminology. *SRE* 3/2, 23–41.

Pressing, Jeff. 1984. Cognitive processes in improvisation. In *Cognitive processes in the perception of art*, edited by Ray Crozier and Anthony Chapman, 345–63. Amsterdam: North Holland.

Putnam, Hilary. 1988. *Representation and reality*. Cambridge, MA: The MIT Press.

Qureshi, Regula Burckhardt. 1986. *Sufi music of India and Pakistan: Sound, context and meaning in qawwali*. Cambridge Studies in Ethnomusicology. Cambridge: Cambridge University Press.

Qureshi, Regula Burckhardt. 2007. *Master musicians of India: Hereditary sarangi players speak*. New York: Routledge.

Qureshi, Regula Burckhardt. 2009. Sīna ba sīna or "from father to son": Writing the culture of discipleship. In *Theorizing the local: Music, practice, and experience in South Asia and beyond*, edited by Richard K. Wolf, 165–83. New York: Oxford University Press.

Rahaim, Matthew. 2012. *Musicking bodies: Gesture and voice in Hindustani music*. Middletown, CT: Wesleyan University Press.

Rahn, Jay. 1983. *A theory for all music: Problems and solutions in the analysis of non-Western forms*. Toronto: University of Toronto Press.

Ramanujan, A. K. 1986. Two realms of Kannada folklore. In *Another harmony: New essays on the folklore of India*, edited by Stuart Blackburn and A. K. Ramanujan, 41–75. Berkeley: University of California Press.

Rameau, Jean-Philippe. 1726 [1965]. *Nouveau système de musique théorique et pratique*. Paris: Ballard. Facsimile reprint, New York: Broude, 1965.

Ramón y Rivera, Luis Felipe. 1980. *Fenomenología de la etnomúsica del area latinoamericana*. Caracas: Biblioteca INIDEF.

Rehding, Alexander, and Steven Rings, eds. 2019. *The Oxford handbook of critical concepts in music theory*. New York: Oxford University Press.

Reiche, Jens Peter. 1991. Der Aksak—ein rhythmisches Phänomen, neu definiert. *Hamburger Jahrbuch der Musikwissenschaft* 11, 225–30.

Revel-Macdonald, Nicole, and José Maceda. 1987. *Philippines: Musique des hautes-terres Palawan*. Collection du C.N.R.S. et du Musée de l'Homme. Paris: Le Chant du Monde. LP recording with notes, LDX 74 865; reissued on CD as Chant du Monde LDX 274865, 1992.

Rice, Timothy. 1980. Aspects of Bulgarian musical thought. *YTM* 12, 43–67.

Rice, Timothy. 1988. Understanding three-part singing in Bulgaria: The interplay of theory and experience. *SRE* 7, 43–57.

Rice, Timothy. 2003. Time, place, and metaphor in musical experience and ethnography. *EM* 47/2, 151–79. Reprinted in Rice, *Modeling ethnomusicology*. New York: Oxford University Press, 2017, 109–38.

Rice, Timothy. 2017. *Modeling ethnomusicology*. New York: Oxford University Press.

Ricoeur, Paul. 1975. *La métaphore vive. L'ordre philosophique*. Paris: Editions du Seuil.

Roach, Max. 1979. Statement. Liner note to LP, Max Roach Quartet, *Pictures in a frame*. Milan: Soul Note. SN 1003.

Robbins, James. 1989. Practical and abstract taxonomy in Cuban music. *EM* 33/3, 379–89.

Robertson, Carol. 1979. "Pulling the ancestors": Performance practice and praxis in Mapuche ordering. *EM* 23/3, 395–416.

Rohloff, Ernst. 1972. *Die Quellenhandschriften zum Musiktraktat des Johannes de Grocheio*. Leipzig: Deutsche Verlag für Musik.

Roongruang, Panya. 1999. Thai classical music and its movement from oral to written transmission, 1930–1942: Historical context, method, and legacy of the Thai music manuscript project. Ph.D. dissertation, Kent State University.

Rosch, Eleanor, and Carolyn B. Mervis. 1975. Family resemblances. *Cognitive Psychology* 7, 573–605.

REFERENCES 201

Rosse, Michael D. 1995. The movement for the revitalization of "Hindu" music in Northern India, 1860–1930: The role of associations and institutions. Ph.D. dissertation, University of Pennsylvania.

Rosse, Michael D. 2010. Music schools and societies in Bombay c. 1864–1937. In *Hindustani music: Thirteenth to twentieth centuries*, edited by Jop Bor, F. N. Delvoye, J. Harvey, and E. te Nijenhuis, 313–29. Delhi: Manohar.

Rouget, Gilbert. 1980. *La musique et la transe. Esquisse d'une théorie générale des relations de la musique et de la possession*. Paris: Gallimard. English translation by Brunhilde Biebuyck, *Music and trance: A theory of the relations between music and possession*. Chicago: University of Chicago Press, 1985.

Rouget, Gilbert. 1982. Qui étiez-vous André Schaeffner? *RdM* 68/1–2, 3–10.

Rouget, Gilbert. 1996. *Un roi africain et sa musique de cour. Chants et danses du palais à Porto-Novo sous le règne de Gbèfa (1948–1976)*. Paris: CNRS Editions.

Rouget, Gilbert. 2004. L'efficacité musicale: musiquer pour survivre. Le cas des Pygmées. *L'Homme* 171–72, 27–52. Translated as "Musical efficacy—musicking to survive. The case of the Pygmies," *YTM* 43 (2011), 89–121.

Rouget, Gilbert. 2006. *Musica reservata. Deux chants initiatiques pour le culte des vodoun au Bénin. Enregistrements, photographies, mises en page et texte*. Paris: Palais de l'Institut de France. Accompanying CD.

Rousseau, Jean-Jacques. 1995 [1768]. *Dictionnaire de musique*. Paris: Duchesne. Critical edition, *Oeuvres complètes*, 5, 603–1191. Paris: Gallimard.

Rousseau, Jean-Jacques. 1781 [1995]. *Essai sur l'origine des langues où il est parlé de la mélodie et de l'imitation musicale*. Critical edition, *Oeuvres complètes*, 5, 371–429. Paris: Gallimard.

Rovsing Olsen, Miriam. 2004. Le musical et le végétal: essai de décrytage. Exemple berbère de l'Anti-Atlas. *L'Homme* 171–72, 103–24.

Rovsing Olsen, Miriam. 2019. Rhythmic metamorphoses: Botanical process models on the Atlas Mountains of Morocco. In *Thought and play in musical rhythm*, edited by R. K. Wolf, S. Blum, and C. F. Hasty, 232–52. New York: Oxford University Press.

Rowell, Lewis. 1992. *Music and musical thought in early India*. CSE.

Russell, Bertrand. 1912. *The problems of philosophy*. New York: Henry Holt.

Russell, George. 1959 [1953]. *The Lydian chromatic concept of tonal organization*. Second edition. New York: Concept Publishing Co. First published 1953.

Ryle, Gilbert. 1949. *The concept of mind*. London: Hutchinson.

Sachs, Klaus-Jürgen. 1997. Musiktheorie. *MGG 2 Sachteil*, 6, 1714–35.

Sakata, Hiromi Lorraine. 1983. *Music in the mind: The concepts of music and musician in Afghanistan*. Kent, OH: Kent State University Press.

Sandell, Gregory J. 1990. Review of Cogan 1984. *Music Theory Spectrum* 12/2, 255–61.

Sapir, J. David. 1969. Diola-Fogny funeral songs and the native critic. *African Language Review* 8, 176–91.

202 REFERENCES

Saslaw, Janna. 1996. Forces, containers, and paths: The role of body-derived image schemas in the conceptualization of music. *Journal of Music Theory* 40/2, 217–43.

Saussy, Haun. 1993. *The problem of a Chinese aesthetic.* Stanford: Stanford University Press.

Saussy, Haun. 2016. *The ethnography of rhythm: Orality and its technologies.* Verbal Arts: Studies in Poetics. New York: Fordham University Press.

Sauveur, Joseph. 1701. *Principes d'acoustique et de musique, ou système generale des intervales des sons, et de son application à tous les systèmes et à tous les instrumens de Musique.* Paris: n.p. Two facsimile reprints: Geneva: Minkoff, 1973; *Joseph Sauveur: Collected writings on musical acoustics (Paris 1700–1713),* edited by Rudolf Rasch. Utrecht, 1984, 99–166.

Savage, Patrick E., and Steven Brown. 2013. Toward a new comparative musicology. *AAWM* 2/2. Online: mtosmt.org.

Sawa, George D. 1989. *Music performance practice in the early 'Abbāsid Era 132-320 A.H./750-932 A.D.,* Toronto: Institute of Mediaeval Studies.

Sawa, George D. 2009. *Rhythmic theories and practices in Arabic writings to 339AH/950CE.* Musicological Studies, 93. Ottawa: Institute of Mediaeval Music.

Scaldaferri, Nicola. 2021. *Wild songs, sweet songs: The Albanian epic in the collections of Milman Parry and Albert B. Lord.* Cambridge, MA: Milman Parry Collection of Oral Literature, Harvard University.

Scaldaferri, Nicola, and Steven Feld, eds. 2019. *When the trees resound: Collaborative media research on an Italian festival.* With photographs by Stefano Vaja and Lorenzo Ferrarini. Two accompanying CDs. Udine: Nota.

Schaeffner, André. 1936. *Origine des instruments de musique. Introduction ethnologique à l'histoire de la musique instrumentale.* Paris: Payot.

Schaeffner, André. 1946. La musique noire d'Afrique. In *La musique des origines à nos jours,* edited by Norbert Dufourq, 460–65. Paris: Larousse.

Schaeffner, André. 1951. *Les Kissi. Une société noire et ses instruments de musique.* Paris: Hermann.

Schaeffner, André. 1965, Rituel et pré-théâtre. In *Histoire des spectacles,* edited by Guy Dumur, 21–54. Encyclopédie de la Pléiade, 19. Paris: Gallimard.

Schechner, Richard. 2003. *Performance theory.* Revised edition. New York: Routledge.

Scherzinger, Martin. 2019. Temporalities. In *CCMT,* 234–70.

Schmidhofer, August, and Stefan Jena, eds. 2011. *Klangfarbe: vergleichend-systematische und musikhistorische Perspektiven.* Vergleichende Musikwissenschaft, 6. Frankfurt am Main: Peter Lang.

Schmidhofer, August, and Dietrich Schüller, eds. 1994. *For Gerhard Kubik: Festschrift on the occasion of his sixtieth birthday.* Vergleichende Musikwissenschaft, 3. Frankfurt am Main: Peter Lang.

REFERENCES 203

Schmidt, Dörte, ed. 2005. *Musiktheoretisches Denken und kultureller Kontext.* Forum Musikwissenschaft, 1. Schliengen: Edition Argus.

Schnabel, Artur. 1942. *Music and the line of most resistance.* Princeton: Princeton University Press.

Schneider, Albrecht. 2001. Sound, pitch, and scale: From "tone measurements" to sonological analysis in ethnomusicology. *EM* 45/3, 489–519.

Schofield, Katherine Butler. 2010. Reviving the Golden Age again: "Classicization," Hindustani music, and the Mughals. *EM* 54/3, 484–517.

Schulkin, Jay. 2013. *Reflections on the musical mind: An evolutionary perspective.* Princeton: Princeton University Press.

Seebass, Tilman. 1986. Between oral and written tradition: The origin and function of notation in Indonesia. In *The oral and the literate in music*, edited by Tokumaru Yosihiko and Yamaguti Osamu, 414–27. Tokyo: Academia Music.

Seebass, Tilman. 1990. *Theory* (English) and *Lehre* (German) versus *Teori* (Indonesian). In International Musicological Society, *Atti del XIV congresso della Società Internazionale di Musicologia, Bologna: Trasmissione e recezione delle forme di cultura musicale*, I, *Round Tables*, edited by A. Pompilio, D. Restani, L. Bianconi, and F. Alberto Gallo, 200–11. Turin: E.D.T.

Seeger, Anthony. 1979. What can we learn when they sing? Vocal genres of the Suyá Indians of central Brazil. *EM* 23/3, 373–94.

Seeger, Anthony. 1987. *Why Suyá sing: A musical anthropology of an Amazonian people.* Cambridge Studies in Ethnomusicology. Chicago: University of Chicago Press.

Seeger, Charles. 1976. Tractatus esthetico-semioticus: Model of the systems of human communication. In *Current thought in musicology*, edited by John W. Grubbs, 1–39. Austin: University of Texas Press. Reprinted in Seeger, *Studies in Musicology II: 1929–1979*, edited by Ann M. Pescatello, 335–66. Berkeley: University of California Press, 1994.

Şenay, Banu. 2020. *Musical ethics and Islam: The art of playing the ney.* Urbana: University of Illinois Press.

Shaffer, Aaron. 1981. A new musical term in ancient Mesopotamian music. *Iraq* 43/1, 79–83.

Shapin, Steven and Simon Schaffer. 2011. Up for air: Leviathan and the air-pump a generation later. In their *Leviathan and the air-pump: Hobbes, Boyle, and the experimental life*, new edition, xi–l. Princeton: Princeton University Press. First published 1985.

Shiloah, Amnon. 1979. *The theory of music in Arabic writings (c. 900–1900): Descriptive catalogue of manuscripts in libraries of Europe and the U.S.A.* Répertoire International des Sources Musicales, Bx. Munich: G. Henle.

Shiloah, Amnon. 2003. *The theory of music in Arabic writings (c. 900–1900): Descriptive catalogue of manuscripts in libraries of Egypt, Israel,*

204 REFERENCES

Morocco, Russia, Tunisia, Uzbekistan, and supplement to B X. Répertoire International des Sources Musicales, Bx-A. Munich: G. Henle.

Shim, Eunmi. 2007. *Lennie Tristano: His life in music.* Jazz Perspectives. Ann Arbor: University of Michigan Press.

Short, T. L. 2007. *Peirce's theory of signs.* Cambridge: Cambridge University Press.

Simon, Artur. 1994. Avi Pwasi, eine Musikerpersönlichkeit aus Borno in Interview und Selbstdarstellung. In *For Gerhard Kubik: Festschrift on the occasion of his sixtieth birthday,* edited by A. Schmidhofer and D. Schüller, 83–145. Vergleichende Musikwissenschaft, 3. Frankfurt am Main: Peter Lang.

Sindoesawarno. 1987. *Ilmu Karawitan,* translated by Martin F. Hatch as "Knowledge of gamelan music." In *Karawitan: Source readings in Javanese gamelan and vocal music,* edited by Judith Becker and Alan H. Feinstein, 2, 311–87. Michigan Papers on South and Southeast Asia, 30. Ann Arbor: Center for South and Southeast Asian Studies, University of Michigan.

Slawek, Stephen M. 1987. *Sitār technique in nibaddh forms.* Delhi: Motalal BAnarsidass.

Slawek, Stephen M. 1994. The study of performance practice as a research method: A South Asian example. *International Journal of Musicology* 3, 9–22.

Slawek, Stephen M. 2000. The classical master-disciple tradition. In *GEWM* 5, 457–67.

Slawek, Stephen M. 2007. Review of Bakhle 2005. *EM* 51/3, 506–12.

Slobin, Mark. 1976. *Music in the culture of northern Afghanistan.* Viking Fund Publications in Anthropology, 54. Tucson: University of Arizona Press.

Small, Christopher. 1998. *Musicking: The meanings of performing and listening.* Hanover, NH: University Press of New England.

Smoliar, Stephen. 1995. Review of Cogan 1984. *MTO* 1/3. Online: mtosmt.org.

Sohn-Rethel, Alfred. 1983. *Intellectual and manual labor: A critique of epistemology,* translated by Martin Sohn-Rethel. Critical Social Studies. Atlantic Highlands, NJ: Humanities Press. First published as *Geistige und körperliche Arbeit: Zur Theorie der gesellschaftlichen Synthesis.* Frankfurt am Main: Suhrkamp, 1970.

Song Bang-song. 1976. *Kwangdae ha:* A source material for the p'ansori tradition. *Korean Journal* 16/8, 24–32.

Sorce Keller, Marcello. 2010. Was ist Musik? Einige Gründe dafür, warum wir die 'Musik' nicht mehr als 'Musik' bezeichnen sollen. *Schweizer Jahrbuch für Musikwissenschaft* 30, 11–26.

Sorce Keller, Marcello. 2016. Linnaeus, zoomusicology, ecomusicology, and the quest for meaningful categories. *Muzikološki Zbornbik/Musicological Research* 52/2, 163–76. DOI: 10.4312/mz.52.2.163-176.

REFERENCES 205

Spinetti, Federico, ed. 2010. *Giuseppe Donizetti Pascià: Traiettorie musicali e storiche tra Italia e Turchia/Giuseppe Donizetti Pasha: Musical and historical trajectories between Italy and Turkey*. Bergamo: Fondazione Donizetti.

Spitzer, Michael. 2004. *Metaphor and musical thought*. Chicago: University of Chicago Press.

Steeves, Pauline F. 2018. Indigeneity. In *Oxford Bibliographies in Anthropology*, edited by John L. Jackson, Jr. New York: Oxford University Press. (consulted April 10, 2022).

Steiner, George. 2011. *The poetry of thought from Hellenism to Celan*. New York: New Directions.

Stenzl, Jürg. 1981. Musikterminologie und "Theorielose Musikkulturen": Zum Verhältnis von musikalischen "Termini" und musikalischen "Benennungen." In International Musicological Society, *Report of the Twelfth Congress, Berkeley 1977*, edited by Daniel Heartz and Bonnie C. Wade, 778–80. Kassel: Bärenreiter.

Sterne, Jonathan. 2003. *The audible past: Cultural origins of sound reproduction*. Durham, NC: Duke University Press.

Sterne, Jonathan. 2011. The theology of sound: A critique of orality. *Canadian Journal of Communications* 36/2, 207–25.

Stęszewski, Jan. 1972. Sachen, Bewusstsein und Benennungen in ethnomusikologischen Untersuchungen. *Jahrbuch für Volksliedforschung* 17, 131–70.

Stęszewski, Jan. 1992. Zur Geschichte des Terminus 'Ethnomusicology.' In *Von der Vielfalt musikalischer Kultur: Festschrift für Josef Kuckertz*, edited by Rüdiger Schumacher, 527–34. Anif/Salzburg: Verlag Ursula Müller-Speiser.

Stock, Jonathan P. J. 2002. Learning huju in Shanghai 1900–1950: Apprenticeship and the acquisition of expertise in a Chinese local operatic tradition. *AsM* 33/2, 1–42.

Stoia, Nicholas. 2013. The common stock of schemes in early blues and country music. *Music Theory Spectrum* 35/2, 194–234.

Stoia, Nicholas. 2021. *Sweet Thing: The history and musical structure of a shared American vernacular form*. Oxford Studies in Music Theory, New York: Oxford University Press.

Stokes, Martin. 1992. *The Arabesk debate. Music and musicians in modern Turkey*. Oxford Studies in Social and Cultural Anthropology. Oxford: Clarendon Press.

Stone, Ruth M. 1982. *Let the inside be sweet: The interpretation of music event among the Kpelle of Liberia*. Bloomington: Indiana University Press.

Stover, Chris. 2019. Contextual theory, or theorizing between the discursive and the material. AAWM 7.2, *Special issue on ethnography and analysis*, edited by Yonathan Malin.

Strumpf, Mitchel, William Anku, Kondwani Phwandaphwanda, and Nçebakazi Mnukwana, 2003. Oral composition. In Herbst, Nzewi, and Agawu, eds. 2003, 118–41.

206 REFERENCES

Strunk, Oliver, comp. 1950. *Source readings in music history from classical antiquity through the Romantic era.* New York: Norton.

Such, David G. 1985. Music, metaphor and values among avant-garde jazz musicians living in New York City. Ph.D. dissertation, University of California, Los Angeles.

Such, David G. 1993. *Avant-garde jazz musicians: Performing "out there."* Iowa City: University of Iowa Press.

Sudnow, David. 1978. *Ways of the hand: The organization of improvised conduct.* Cambridge, MA: Harvard University Press.

Sudnow, David. 2001. *Ways of the hand: A rewritten account.* Cambridge, MA: MIT Press.

Sumarsam. 1995. *Gamelan: Cultural interaction and musical development in central Java.* CSE.

Sumarsam. 2013. *Javanese gamelan and the West.* Eastman/Rochester Studies in Music. Rochester: University of Rochester Press.

Sunardi, Christina. 2017. Talking about mode in Malang, East Java. *AsM* 48/2, 62–89.

Sykes, Jim. 2018. *The musical gift: Sonic generosity in post-war Sri Lanka.* Critical Conjunctures in Music & Sound. New York: Oxford University Press.

Takahashi Chikuzan. 1991 [1983]. *The autobiography of Takahashi Chikuzan: Adventures of a tsugaru-jamisen musician,* translated and annotated by Gerald Groemer. Detroit Monographs in Musicology/Studies in Music, 10. Warren, MI: Harmonie Park Press. First published in Japanese as *Jiden: Tsugaru-jamisen hitoritabi,* 1983.

Taylor, Art. 1993. *Notes and tones: Musician to musician interviews.* Expanded edition. New York: Da Capo Press. First published New York: Coward, McCann & Geoghegan, 1982.

Taylor, Charles. 1994. The politics of recognition. In *Multiculturalism: Examining the politics of recognition,* edited by Amy Gutmann, 25–73. Princeton: Princeton University Press.

Tedlock, Barbara. 1980. Songs of the Zuni Kachina society: Composition, rehearsal, and performance. In *Southwestern Indian ritual drama,* edited by Charlotte J. Frisbie, 7–35. Albuquerque: University of New Mexico Press.

Tedlock, Barbara. 1986. Crossing the sensory domain in Native American aesthetics. In *Explorations in ethnomusicology,* edited by Charlotte J. Frisbie, 187–98. Detroit Monographs in Musicology, 9. Information Coordinators.

Tedlock, Barbara. 1992. *The beautiful and the dangerous: Encounters with the Zuni Indians.* New York: Viking.

Tenzer, Michael. 2000. *Gamelan gong kebyar: The art of twentieth-century Balinese music.* CSE.

Tenzer, Michael. 2003. José Maceda and the paradoxes of modern composition in Southeast Asia. *EM* 47/1, 65–96.

Tenzer, Michael, ed. 2006. *Analytical studies in world music.* New York: Oxford University Press.

Tenzer, Michael. 2011. Integrating music: Personal and global transformations. In *Analytical and cross-cultural studies in world music*, edited by M. Tenzer and J. Roeder, 357–87. New York: Oxford University Press.

Tenzer, Michael. 2019. Polyphony. In *CCMT*, 602–47.

Tenzer, Michael, and John Roeder, eds. 2011. *Analytical and cross-cultural studies in world music*. New York: Oxford University Press.

Thaut, M. H., and D. A. Hodges, eds. 2019. *The Oxford Handbook of Music and the Brain*. New York: Oxford University Press.

Thomas, Anne Elise. 2006. Developing Arab music: Institutions, individuals, and discourses of progress in Cairo, 1932–2005. Ph.D. dissertation, Brown University.

Thompson, Robert Farris. 1966. An aesthetic of the cool: West African dance. *African Forum* 2/2, 85–102.

Thompson, Robert Farris. 1973. An aesthetic of the cool. *African Arts* 7/1, 40–43, 64–67, 89–92.

Thrasher, Alan R. 2008. *Sizhu instrumental music of South China: Ethos, theory and practice*. Sinica Leidensia, 84. Leiden: Brill.

Thrasher, Alan R., ed. 2016. *Qupai in Chinese music: Melodic models in form and practice*. Routledge Studies in Ethnomusicology, 6. New York and London: Routledge.

Tilley, Leslie A. 2019. *Making it up together: The act of collective improvisation in Balinese music and beyond*. CSE.

Titon, Jeff Todd. 1977. *Early downhome blues: A musical and cultural analysis*. Music in American Life. Urbana: University of Illinois Press.

Tokumaru Yoshihiko, and Yamaguti Osamu, eds. 1986. *The oral and the literate in music*. Tokyo: Academia Music.

Tomkins, Silvan. 1962–92. *Affect, imagery, consciousness*. 4 vols. New York: Springer.

Tomlinson, Gary. 2015. *A million years of music: The emergence of human modernity*. New York: Zone Books.

Torp, Jörgen. 2013. Musical movement: Towards a common term for music and dance. *YTM* 45, 231–49.

Tracey, Andrew. 1961. Mbira music of Jege A. Tapera. *AfM* 2/4, 44–63.

Tracey, Andrew. 1989. The system of the mbira. In *Papers presented at the Seventh Symposium on Ethnomusicology (1988)*, 43–55. Grahamstown: International Library of African Music, Rhodes University.

Trân Văn Khê. 1962. *La musique vietnamienne traditionelle*. Annales du Musée Guimet, Bibliothèque d'Études, 66. Paris: Presses Universitaires de France.

Trân Văn Khê. 1966. Asia. In *La musica*, 1, *Enciclopedia storica*, edited by Alberto Basso, 199–240. Turin: Uniono Tipografico Editrice Torinese.

Trân Văn Khê. 1977. Present and Future Preservation and Presentation of Traditional Music. *WoM* 19/3–4, 62–75.

Trasoff, David. 2010. The all-India music conferences of 1916–1925: Cultural transformation and colonial ideology. In *Hindustani music: Thirteenth to*

208 REFERENCES

twentieth centuries, edited by Jop Bor, F. N. Delvoye, J. Harvey, and E. te Nijenhuis, 331–56. Delhi: Manohar.

Trebinjac, Sabine. 2000. *Le pouvoir en chantant, 1. L'art de fabriquer une musique chinoise*. Mémoires de la Société d'Ethnologie, 7. Nanterre: Société d'Ethnologie.

Treitler, Leo. 2003. *With voice and pen: Coming to know Medieval song and how it was made*. Oxford: Oxford University Press. Accompanying CD.

Tsao Pen-yeh. 1986. Training of *t'an-ts'u* performers: Processes of oral transmission in the perpetuation of the Su-chou singing narrative. In *The oral and the literate in music*, edited by Tokumaru Yosihiko and Yamaguti Osamu, 221–30. Tokyo: Academia Music.

Tsao Pen-yeh. 1988. *The music of Su-chou t'an tz'u: Elements of the Chinese southern singing-narrative*. Hong Kong: Chinese University Press.

Tsukada Kenichi. 1997. Drumming, onomatopoeia and sound symbolisme among the Luvale of Zambia. *Cultures sonores d'Afrique* 1, 349–93.

Tsui Ying-fai. 2002. The modern Chinese orchestra. In *GEWM* 7, 227–32.

Tsukada Kenichi. 2002. Luvale drumming and sound symbolism: An analysis by wavelet transform. Working Paper Series, 3. Hiroshima: Faculty of International Studies (Division of Culture), Hiroshima City University. Includes Asaf'yev 1930 and the second volume of 1947.

Tunstill, Guy. 1995. Learning Pitjantjatjara songs. In *The essence of singing and the substance of song: Recent responses to the Aboriginal performing arts and other essays in honour of Catherine Ellis*, edited by Linda Barwick, Allan Marett, and Guy Tunstill, 59–73. Oceania Monograph 46. Sydney: University of Sydney.

Turino, Thomas. 1990. Structure, context, and strategy in musical ethnography. *EM* 34/3, 399–412.

Turino, Thomas. 1993. *Moving away from silence: Music of the Peruvian Altiplano and the experience of urban migration*. CSE.

Turino, Thomas. 2015. On theory and models: How to make our ideas clear. In *This thing called music: Essays in honor of Bruno Nettl*, edited by Victoria Lindsay-Levine and Philip V. Bohlman, 378–90. Lanham, MD: Rowman & Littlefield.

Väätäinen, Hanna. 2017. Forming common notions in a kinetic research collaboration. In *Musical encounters with Deleuze and Guattari*, edited by P. Moisala, M. Tianinin, and H. Väätäinen, 205–22. Bloomsbury Sound Series. London: Bloomsbury Academic.

Vaziri, 'Alinaqi. 1964. Notation: Means of preservation or destruction of music not traditionally notated. In *The preservation of traditional forms of the learned and popular music of the orient and the occident. La preservation des formes traditionnelles de la musique savante et populaire dans les pays d'Orient et d'Occident*, edited by William K. Archer, 251–57. Urbana: Center for Comparative Psycholinguistics, Institute of Communications Research, University of Illinois.

REFERENCES 209

Vico, Giambattista. 1984 [1744]. *The New Science of Giambattista Vico*, translated by Thomas Goddard Bergin and Max Harold Fisch. Ithaca, NY: Cornell University Press.

Vigreux, Philippe, ed. 1992. *Musique arabe: le Congrès du Caire de 1932*. Cairo: CEDEJ.

Vogels, Raimund. 2004. Blau, kalt, rechts: Musikkonzepte und -terminologien als Spiegel intermodaler Ästhetik und holistischer Klangwahrnehmung in aussereuropäischen Kontext. In *Synästhesie in der Musik--Musik in der Synästhesie. Vorträge und Referate während der Jahrestagung 2002 der Gesellschaft für Musikforschung in Düsseldorf (25.-28. September 2002)*, edited by Volker Kalisch, 97–104. Essen: Die Blaue Eule.

Wachsmann, Klaus P. 1950. An equal-stepped tuning in a Ganda harp. *Nature* 165/4184, 40–41.

Wachsmann, Klaus P. 1957. A study of norms in the tribal music of Uganda. *Ethnomusicology Newsletter* 11, 9–16.

Wachsmann, Klaus P. 1970. Ethnomusicology in Africa. In *The African experience*, edited by J. N. Paden and E. W. Soja, 128–47. Evanston: Northwestern University Press.

Wachsmann, Klaus, and Russell Kay. 1971. The interrelations of musical instruments, musical forms and cultural systems in Africa. *Technology and culture* 12, 399–413.

Wade, Bonnie C. 2014. *Composing Japanese musical modernity*. CSE.

Wadley, Susan S. 1989. Choosing a path: Performance strategies in a North Indian epic. In *Oral epics in India*, edited by Stuart H. Blackburn, Peter J. Claus, Joyce B. Flueckiger, and Susan S. Wadley, 75–101. Berkeley: University of California Press.

Walton, Susan Pratt. 1987. *Mode in Javanese music*. Ohio University Monographs in International Studies, Southeast Asia Series, 79. Athens, Ohio: Center for International Studies, Ohio University.

Weber, Max. 1921. *Die rationalen und sozialen Grundlagen der Musik*. Tübingen: J.C.B. Mohr. Edited and translated by Don Martindale, Johannes Riedel and Gertrude Neuwirth as *The rational and social foundations of music*, Carbondale: Southern Illinois University Press, 1957.

Weber, Max. 1904 [1968]. Die "Objektivität" sozialwissenschaftlicher und sozialpolitischer Erkentnis. *Archiv für Sozialwissenschaft und Sozialpolitik* 19. Reprinted in Weber, *Gesammelte Aufsätze zur Wissenschaftslehre*, edited by Johannes Winckelmann, 146–214. Third edition. Tübingen: J.C.B. Mohr.

Weber, Max. 2012. *Collected methodological writings*, edited by Hans Henrik Braun and Sam Whimster, translated by Hans Henrik Braun. London and New York: Routledge.

Wegner, Ulrich. 1993. Cognitive aspects of *amadinda* xylophone music from Buganda: Inherent patterns reconsidered. *EM* 37/2, 201–41.

Weidman, Amanda J. 2006. *Singing the classical, voicing the modern: The postcolonial politics of music in South Asia*. Durham, NC: Duke University Press.

210 REFERENCES

Weidman, Amanda J. 2012. The ethnographer as apprentice: Embodying sociomusical knowledge in South India. *Anthropology and Humanism* 37/2, 214–35.

Weintraub, Andrew N. 1993. Theory in institutional pedagogy and "theory in practice" for Sundanese gamelan music. *EM* 37/1, 29–39.

Wellek, Albert. 1928–29. Das Farbenhören im Lichte der vergleichenden Musikwissenschaft. Urgeschichte des Doppelempfindens im Geistesleben der Orientalen. *Zeitschrift für Musikwissenschaft* 11, 470.

Wellesz, Egon. 1954. Musicology. In *Grove's Dictionary of music and musicians*, fifth edition, edited by Eric Blom, 5, 1020–28.

Whitehead, Alfred North. 1938. *Modes of thought*. New York: Macmillan.

Widdess, D. R. 1979. The Kudumiyāmalai inscription: A source of early Indian music in notation. *Musica Asiatica* 2, 115–50.

Widdess, Richard. 1995. *The rāgas of early Indian music: Modes, melodies, and musical notations from the Gupta period to c.1250.* Oxford Monographs on Music. Oxford: Clarendon Press.

Widdess, Richard. 2011. Dynamics of melodic discourse in Indian music: Budhaditya Mukherjee's *ālāp* in rāg *Pūriyā-Kalyān*. In *Analytical and cross-cultural studies in world music*, edited by M. Tenzer and J. Roeder, 187–224. New York: Oxford University Press.

Wierzbicka, Anna. 2014. *Imprisoned in English: The hazards of English as a default language.* Oxford: Oxford University Press.

Wilczek Frank. 2021. *Fundamentals: Ten keys to reality*. New York: Penguin.

Wilf, Eitan Y. 2014. *School for cool: The academic jazz program and the paradox of institutionalized creativity.* Chicago: University of Chicago Press.

Will, Udo. 1999. La baguette magique d'ethnomusicologie: re-penser la notation et l'analyse de la musique. *Cahiers de Musiques Traditionnelles* 12, 9–34.

Will, Udo, and Catherine Ellis. 1996. A re-analyzed Australian Western Desert song: Frequency performance and interval structure. *EM* 40/2, 187–222.

Wilson, Blake McDowell. 1995. *Ut oratoria musica* in the writings of Renaissance music theorists. In *Festa musicologica: Essays in honor of George J. Buelow*, edited by T. J. Mathiesen and B. V. Rivera, 341–68. Stuyvesant, NY: Pendragon Press.

Wilson, Peter Niklas. 1999. *Ornette Coleman: His life and music*. Berkeley: Berkeley Hills Books.

Wissler, Holly. 2009. From grief and joy we sing: Social and cosmic regenerative processes in the songs of Q'eros, Peru. Ph.D. dissertation, Florida State University.

Witmer, Robert, and James Robbins. 1998. A historical and critical survey of recent pedagogical materials for the teaching and learning of jazz. *Council for Research in Music Education Bulletin* 96, 7–29.

Wizārat al-Ma'ārif al-'umūmiyya, al-Mamlaka al-Misriyya. 1934. *Kitāb mu'tamar al-mūsīqá al-'arabiyah: al mashmūl bi-ri'āyat hadrat sāhib al-jalālah al-Malik Fuʿād al-Awwal, al-mun ʿaqid bi-madīnat al-Qāhirah, fi samat 1350 H (sanat 1932 M)*. Cairo: al-Maṭbaʿah al-Amīrīyah.

Wolf, Richard K. 2005. *The black cow's footprint: Time, space, and music in the lives of the Kotas of South India*. Delhi: Permanent Black. Also published Urbana: University of Illinois Press, 2006.

Wolf, Richard K. 2009. Varnams and vocalizations: The special status of some musical beginnings. In *Theorizing the local: Music, practice, and experience in South Asia and beyond*, edited by Richard K. Wolf, 239–63. New York: Oxford University Press.

Wolf, Richard K. 2014. *The voice in the drum: Music, language, and emotion in Islamicate South Asia*. Urbana: University of Illinois Press.

Wolf, Richard K. 2019. "Rhythm," "beat," and "freedom" in South Asian musical traditions. In *Thought and play in musical rhythm*, edited by R. K. Wolf, S. Blum, and C. F. Hasty, 314–36. New York: Oxford University Press.

Wolf, Richard K., Stephen Blum, and Christopher F. Hasty. 2019. Introduction. In *Thought and play in musical rhythm*, edited by R. K. Wolf, S. Blum, and C. F. Hasty, 1–19. New York: Oxford University Press.

Wong Chuen-fung. 2006. Peripheral sentiments: Encountering Uyghur music in Urumchi, China. Ph.D. dissertation, University of California, Los Angeles.

Wong, Deborah. 1991. The empowered teacher: Ritual, performance, and epistemology in contemporary Bangkok. Ph.D. dissertation, University of Michigan.

Wong, Deborah. 2001. *Sounding the center: History and aesthetics in Thai Buddhist performance*. CSE.

Woolner, Christina J. 2021. "Out of tune" and "out of time": Reflections of an oud apprentice in Somaliland. *EM* 65/2, 259–85.

Wright, Owen. 1978. *The modal system of Arab and Persian music AD 1250–1300*. London: Oxford University Press.

Wright, Owen. 2009. *Touraj Kiaras and Persian classical music: An analytical perspective*. SOAS Musicology Series. Farnham: Ashgate. Accompanying CD.

Yavorsky, Boleslav. 1908. *Stroyeniye muzikal'noy rechi*. Moscow.

Yekta Bey, Rauf. 1922. La musique turque. In *Encyclopédie de la musique et dictionnaires du Conservatoire. Première Partie*, 5, 2945–3064. Paris: Delagrave.

Youssefzadeh, Ameneh. 2002. *Les bardes du Khorassan iranienne: le bakhshi et son répertoire*. Travaux et mémoires de l'Institut d'études iraniennes, 6. Leuven and Paris: Peeters.

Yung, Bell. 1984. Choreographic and kinesthetic elements in performance on the Chinese seven-string zither. *EM* 28/3, 505–17.

Yung, Bell. 1996. The nature of Chinese ritual sound. In *Harmony and counterpoint: Ritual music in Chinese context*, edited by Bell Yung, Evelyn S. Rawski, and Rubie S. Watson, 13–31. Stanford: Stanford University Press.

212 REFERENCES

Yung, Bell, ed. 1997. *Celestial airs of antiquity: Music of the seven-string zither of China*. Recent Researches in the Oral Traditions of Music, 5. Madison, WI: A-R Editions.

Yung, Bell. 2009. Tsar Teh-yun at age 100: A life of qin music, poetry, and calligraphy. In *Lives in Chinese music*, edited by Helen Rees, 65–90. Urbana: University of Illinois Press.

Zak, Albin J. III. 2001. *The poetics of rock: Cutting tracks, making records.* Berkeley: University of California Press.

Zaminer, Frieder, ed. 1985–2006. *Geschichte der Musiktheorie.* Darmstadt: Wissenschaftliche Buchgesellschaft. 11 vols. to date.

Zanten, Wim van. 1986. The tone material of the kacapi in tembang Sunda in West Java. *EM* 30/1, 84–112.

Zbikowski, Lawrence. 2002. *Conceptualizing music: Cognitive structure, theory, and analysis.* AMS Studies in Music. New York: Oxford University Press.

Zbikowski, Lawrence. 2008. Metaphor and music. In *The Cambridge handbook of metaphor and thought*, edited by Raymond W. Gibbs Jr., 502–24. Cambridge: Cambridge University Press.

Zbikowski, Lawrence. 2017. *Foundations of musical grammar.* Oxford and New York: Oxford University Press.

Zemp, Hugo. 1971. *Musique dan: La musique dans la pensée et la vie sociale d'une société africaine.* Cahiers de l'Homme: Ethnologie-Géographie-Linguistique, n.s. 11. Paris: Mouton.

Zemp, Hugo. 1978. 'Are'are classification of musical types and instruments. *EM* 22/1, 37–67.

Zemp, Hugo. 1979. Aspects of 'Are'are musical theory. *EM* 23/1, 5–48.

Zemtsovsky, Izaly. 1993. Dialogie musicale. *Cahiers de musiques traditionnelles* 6, 23–27.

Zenz, Adrian. 2018. "Thoroughly reforming them towards a healthy heart attitude"—China's political re-education campaign in Xinjiang. *Central Asian Survey* https://www.tandfonline.com/doi/full/10.1080/02634 937.2018.1507997.

Zonis, Ella. 1964. Review of Barkeshli and Ma'rufi 1963. *EM* 8/3, 303–10.

Index of Names

For the benefit of digital users, indexed terms that span two pages (e.g., 52–53) may, on occasion, appear on only one of those pages.
Tables are indicated by an italic *t* following the page number.

Abdulla Mäjnun, 74–75
Abraham, Otto, 17
Afaq Husain Khan, 37
Agawu, Kofi, 8, 20, 84, 129, 139
Ahmad Bey, ruler of Tunisia, 69–70
All India Music Conferences, 66–67
Alter, Andrew, 38
Ames, David W., 125
Amoozegar, Farzad, 38–39
Ampene, Kwame, 91
Analytical Approaches to World Music, 22, 76–77
Arel, Hüseyin Sâdeddin, 73–74
Aristides Quintilianus, 79
Aristotle, 8, 26, 98
Aristoxenus, 79, 97
Arom, Simha, 56, 95–96, 105–6
Asaf'yev, Boris, 101
Asia Pacific Society for Ethnomusicology, 75–76
Association for the Advancement of Creative Musicians (AACM), 49–50
Austin, J.L., 108

Bach, Johann Sebastian, 19
Baily, John, 14, 40–41, 57*t*
Bakhle, Janaki, 66
Bakhtin, Mikhail, 15
Bartók, Béla, 17
Bateson, Gregory, 5–6, 45–46
Beliayev, Viktor M., 73–74
Bellah, Robert N., 11
Benamou, Marc, 82, 102, 110, 123, 126–127
Berliner, Paul F., 17–18, 19, 44
Bharata, 97

Bhatkhande, V.N., 66–67
Black, Max, 98–99
Blacking, John, 19, 79
Blake, Daniel, 49
Blumenberg, Hans, 98–99
Boethius, Anicius Manlius Severinus, 27
Bourdieu, Pierre, 18, 36
Brăiloiu, Constantin, 81
Brambats, Karl, 132–33
Brandom, Robert, 52
Braxton, Anthony, 49
Brinner, Benjamin, 19, 56–57, 57*t*, 58–59
Brown, Marion, 49
Brown, Steven, 11
Bruner, Jerome, 6
Buelow, George J., 126–127
Burranca, Dionigi, 111–12

Campbell, Patricia Shehan, 43
Centre d' Études et de Documentation Économique, Juridique et Sociale (CEDEJ), 64–65
Centre for Aboriginal Studies in Music (CASM), 44–46
Centre for Indigenous Instrumental Music and Dance of Africa (CIIMDA), 46
Certeau, Michel de, 29
Chailley, Jacques, 89
Charry, Eric, 35, 122
Ciucci, Alessandra, 118
Cogan, Robert, 115
Cohen, Dalia, 57*t*, 105
Coleman, Ornette, 49–50
Coltrane, John, 16
Congress of Arab Music, 64–66

214 INDEX OF NAMES

Cook, Nicholas, 100–1
Cook, Will Marion, 33–34
Cooke, Peter, 135–36
Coplan, David B., 55
Cronk, M. Sam, 123–24
Curwen, John, 84

Dahlhaus, Carl, 22, 55
Darwin, Charles, 126
Davis, Ruth F., 70, 72–73
Decolonizing Southeast Asian Sound
    Archives, 20
De Ferranti, Hugh, 42
Dehoux, Vincent, 106
Deleuze, Gilles, 78, 102
Descartes, René, 98–99
DeWoskin, Kenneth, 117
Dharwadker, Vinay, 126–27
Diamond, Beverley, 124
Donald, Merlin, 6
Donizetti, Giuseppe, 69–70
Dor, George, 140
Douglas, Gavin, 9
Dowling, W. Jay, 107
Dreyfus, Hubert L. 49

Eisenstadt, S.N., 61–62
Ellington, Duke, 33–34
Ellis, Alexander J., 69
Ellis, Catherine J., 42–46, 79, 106–7, 118,
    124
Elschek, Oskár, 93–94
El-Mahdi, Salah, 72–73
Emin Effendi, Mehmet Hacı, 70
Erlmann, Veit, 9, 93
Euba, Akin, 4, 91
Evans, David, 121

Fabian, Johannes, 2
Fārābī, Abu Nasr al-, 26–27, 111, 119
Farmer, Henry George, 65–66
Faudree, Paja, 11
Feld, Steven, 18–19, 52–53, 78, 125–26, 138
Finnegan, Ruth, 53
Forkel, Johann Niklaus, 19
Fortune, Sonny, 48
Fraser, Al (Wilmot Alfred), 48
Freud, Sigmund, 114

Friedson, Steven M., 11
Fu'ad, King of Egypt, 64–65
Fumon Yoshinori, 42
Fürniss, Susanne, 105–6

Gandharva Mahavidyalaya, 66
Garfias, Robert, 38
Gbèfa, King of Porto Novo, 92–93
Gelbart, Matthew, 22
Gerstin, Julian, 55–56, 131
Ghazāli, Abu Hāmid al-, 38–39
Giannattasio, Francesco, 3–4, 56, 94–95,
    111–12
Giddens, Anthony, 57t
Gillespie, Dizzy, 48
Giotto, 100
Giuriati, Giovanni, 3–4
Gluck, Carol, 61–62
Gourlay, Ken, 131
Greve, Martin, 63
Grocheio, Johannes de, 28
Grupe, Gerd, 93–94
Guattari, Félix, 78–79
Guignard, Michel, 79–80
Gushee, Lawrence, 31–32
Gutzwiller, Andreas, 42

Hacıbäyli, Üzeyir, 71
Hammel, Stephan, 22
Hanafi, al-Sheykh Jalāl al-, 116
Harris, Marvin, 83
Harris, Rachel, 62, 74–75
Hassan, Scheherazade Qassim, 32–33,
    64–66, 116
Heimarck, Britta, 63–64
Herzog, George, 7
Hifni, Mahmud Ahmad al-, 65
Hijleh, Mark, 76–77
Hodges, Donald A., 12
Hood, Mantle, 88, 89
Hornbostel, Erich Maria von, 3–4, 17, 54,
    69, 83–84, 99–100
Hughes, David W., 112
Humboldt, Alexander von, 114–115
Huron, David, 97

Ibn Khaldun, 28
Indonesian College of the Arts (STSI), 63–64

INDEX OF NAMES · 215

Institut de Recherche et de Coordination Acoustique/Musique (IRCAM), 32
Intercultural Institute for Comparative Music Studies (IICMS), 68
International Council for Traditional Music (ICTM)
  ICTM Dialogues, 20
  Study Group on Multipart Music, 132–33
  Study Group on Sound, Movement and the Sciences, 3
International Musicological Society (IMS)
  Berkeley Congress, 1977, 89–90
  Bologna Congress, 1987, 56
Isawa Shuji, 68, 76–77
Iyer, Vijay, 22, 91–92

Jackendoff, Ray, 86
Jairazbhoy, Nazir Ali, 38, 57–58, 105
James, William, 57*t*, 126
Jankouk, Ata-Allāh, 38–39
Jing, King of Zhou, 31–32
Johnson, Mark, 99–100
Johnston, Ben, 9
Jousse, Marcel, 91

Karamatov, Faizullah M., 73
Kartomi, Margaret J., 19, 104, 115–16
Katz, Max, 38, 66–67
Katz, Ruth, 57*t*, 105
Keil, Charles, 122, 124, 129
Khashimov, Abdulaziz, 74–75
Khushnawāz, Amir Jān, 41
King, Anthony V., 124–25
Kippen, James, 37–38
Kittay, Eve Feder, 98–99, 125–26
Klee, Paul, 19
Kresánek, Josef, 19
Kubik, Gerhard, 17–18, 83, 104–5, 110, 113, 136–37
K'ung Ying-ta, 139
Kunst, Jaap, 16–17
Kurth, Ernst, 101
Kyagambiddwa, Joseph, 135–36

Lachenmann, Helmut, 12
Lakoff, George, 99–100

Lannoy, Michel de, 95–96
Larson, Steve, 100
Lateef, Yusef, 49
Leibniz, Gottfried Wilhelm, 85–86
Lemaire, Alfred-Jean-Baptiste, 69–70
Lévi-Strauss, Claude, 18, 81–82
Levin, Theodore C., 73–74
Light, Nathan, 74–75
Limociyan, Hamparsum, 70
Ling Zhoujiu, 31–32
Lochhead, Judy, 26
Locke, David, 4, 18
Lomax, Alan, 12–13, 97–98
Lomax, John, 97–98
Lord, Albert Bates, 91
Lortat-Jacob, Bernard, 94–95, 133–34
Lotfi, Mohammad-Rezā, 38–39
Lomax, Alan, 12
Lowery, Robert, 48
Lu Chi, 117

Macchiarella, Ignazio, 109, 133
Maceda, José, 20, 52, 75–76, 121
Magrini, Tullia, 94–95, 130
Mahmud II, Ottoman Sultan, 69–70
Malm, William P., 122
Marchand, Trevor, 34–35
Marcu, George, 132–33
Marcus, Scott L., 33, 70
Markoff, Irene, 73
Martin, Henry, 47, 49
Mason, Luther Whiting, 69
Mauss, Marcel, 16, 18, 63
Meintjes, Louise, 140
Menezes Bastos, Rafael José, 17
Messiaen, Olivier, 116–117
Meyer, Leonard B., 55
Miller, Richard C., 68–69
Million, Dion, 5–6
Ministry of Culture, Department of Music and Popular Arts, Tunisia, 72–73
Ministry of Culture, National Folklore Research Department, Turkey, 32
Misra, Lalmani, 37
Monts, Lester B., 125
Moreno, Jaime, 9
Mora, Manolete, 121

216 INDEX OF NAMES

Moro, Pamela, 62
Moscow Conservatory, 53–54
Muhammad 'Ali, ruler of Egypt, 69–70
Mukasa, Temuseo, 104
Music Educators National Conference
(MENC), 42–43
Music Investigation Committee, Meiji
Japan, 68
Muyinda, Evaristo, 17, 134

Nabi Gol, 41
Naim, Baba, 140
Nasruddin Shah, ruler of Persia, 69–70
National Conservatory of Tunisia, 72–73
Nattiez, Jean-Jacques, 11
Nesbitt, Nick, 78
Nettl, Bruno, 94
Neuman, Daniel, 35–36
Ngũgĩ wa Thiong'o, 53
Niranjana, Tejaswini, 35
Nzewi, Meki, 10, 43–44, 46–47

Ochoa Gautier, Ana María, 53
O'Connell John Morgan, 71–72
Odoyevsky, Prince V.F., 53–54, 81
Ömär Akhun, 74–75
Ong, Walter, 53

Paluskar, V.D., 66–67
Pan-African Society for Musical Arts
Education (PASMAE), 10, 47
Parker, William, 76–77
Parkhurst, Bryan, 22
Parry, Milman, 91
Patel, Aniruddh D., 12
Paulhan, Jean, 91
Peiris, Eshantha, 63–64
Perlman, Marc, 14–15, 55, 102–3
Petrović, Ankica, 17, 132
Pian, Rulan Chao, 89–90
Pier, Dave, 138
Pike, Kenneth 82–83
Plato, 85, 117
Polak, Rainer, 130
Polanyi, Michael, 55
Polytechnic College, Tehran, 69–70
Porcello, Thomas, 113–14
Porter, Eric, 49

Powers, Harold S., 36, 57–58, 87–90
Powers, William K., 124
Putnam, Hilary, 88

Qureshi, Regula Burckhardt, 35, 36–37,
96, 108–109

Rahaim, Matt, 14, 33
Rameau, Jean-Philippe, 79
Ramón y Rivera, Luis Felipe, 27–28
Rashidiyya Institute, Tunis, 32, 72–73
Research Centre for European Multipart
Music, 132–33
Rice, Timothy, 93, 101
Roach, Max, 50
Robbins, James, 47–48, 57t
Robertson, Carol, 17–18
Rosen, Franziska von, 124
Rouget, Gilbert, 57t, 92–93, 137
Rovsing Olsen, Miriam, 99–100
Rowell, Lewis, 7, 126
Russell, George, 47
Ryle, Gilbert, 57t

Sabri Khan, 36–37
Saîd, Dilşad, 67
Salih Hoca, 34–35
Sangit Research Academy, Calcutta, 38
Sapir, J. David, 131–32
Saussure, Ferdinand de, 96
Saussy, Haun, 52–53, 91
Schaeffner, André, 130
Schechner, Richard, 138
Scherzinger, Martin, 22
Schnabel, Artur, 19
Schofield, Katherine Butler, 60
School of Imperial Military Band,
Istanbul, 69–70
Sèdémèkpon, 92–93
Seebass, Tilman, 56
Seeger, Anthony, 120
Şenay, Banu, 34–35
Shankar, Ravi, 37
Shiloah, Amnon, 15
Shulgi, King of Ur, 28
Sindoesawarno, 23
Slawek, Stephen M., 37, 83
Slobin, Mark, 140

INDEX OF NAMES 217

Smith, Wadada Leo, 49
Society for Asian Music, 38
Society for Ethnomusicology (SEM), 20–21
Sorce Keller, Marcello, 11
Spaulding, Esperanza, 49
Sri Ram Bharatiya Kala Kendra, New Delhi, 38
State Conservatory for Turkish Music, Istanbul, 72
Steiner, George, 110
Sterne, Jonathan, 6–7, 52–53
Stęszewski, Jan, 17
Stock, Jonathan, 39
Stoia, Nicholas, 97–98
Stone, Ruth M., 109, 131
Stover, Chris, 122
Stumpf, Carl, 3
Sudnow, David, 49
Sumarsam, 63

Takahashi Chikuzan, 41
Tashkent Conservatory, Department of Oriental Music, 73
Taylor, Frederick W., 100–1
Tedlock, Barbara, 117–18
Tenzer, Michael, 2, 21, 88
Thai Music Manuscript Project, 71, 74
Thakur, Omkarnath, 66–67
Thomas, Anne Elise, 65–66
Thrasher, Alan R., 88
Tilley, Leslie A., 94
Tokyo School of Music, 69
Tomkins, Sylvan, 126
Tomlinson, Gary, 84
Trân Văn Khê, 89
Trasoff, David, 66
Trebinjac, Sabine, 32, 74–75
Tsao Pen-yeh, 39–40
Tsukada Kenichi, 113

Tunstill, Guy, 45
Turdi Akhun, 74–75
Turino, Thomas, 16, 79, 130–31
Turkish Folklore Society, 73

Vatin, Jean-Claude, 64–65
Vaziri, 'Alinaqi, 71
Vico, Giambattista, 98–99
Vogels, Raimund, 118
Voisin, Frédéric, 106

Wachsmann, Klaus, 104
Wade, Bonnie C., 68
Wadley, Susan, 114
Wan Tongshu, 74–75
Weber, Max, 29, 101–2
Wegner, Ulrich, 135–36
Weidman, Amanda, 35
Whitehead, Alfred North, 78
Widdess, Richard, 67, 89, 97–98, 113
Wierzbicka, Anna, 85–86
Will, Udo, 12, 106–7
Wissler, Holly, 10
Witmer, Robert, 47–48
Wolf, Richard K., 13, 112–13
Wong Chuen-fung, 74–75
Wright, Owen, 92–93

Yavaşça, Alâeddin, 71–72
Yekta Bey, Rauf, 65
Young, Lester, 16
Yung, Bell, 19–20, 137t, 138

Zak, Albin, 140
Zanten, Wim van, 104
Zbikowski, Lawrence, 13, 14–15, 58–59, 102–3
Zemp, Hugo, 4, 17–18, 124–25
Zemtsovsky, Izaly, 53–54
Zirimu, Pio, 53

Index of Topics

For the benefit of digital users, indexed terms that span two pages (e.g., 52–53) may, on occasion, appear on only one of those pages.
Tables are indicated by an italic *t* following the page number.

acoustemology, 52–53. *See also* listening
aesthetics, 8, 9, 53, 88, 104, 117–18, 121, 132
   comparative, 126
   intermodal judgment, 117–8
analogy, 10, 34–35, 102, 108, 115
archives, 20, 61*t*, 110
assemblage, 40–41, 50–51, 78
aurality, *see* listening
authenticity, 61–62, 74–76

body, *see* techniques of the body

canonization, 60–61, 62, 72–73, 74–75
categories, categorization, 12, 18, 63–64,
     97, 102–3, 116, 124–25, 132. *See also*
   sound, categorization of
ceremony, 8, 35, 39–40, 114, 117, 120,
     121, 124, 131, 137–39
classification, 102–3
   of musical instruments, 116
   of musical knowledge, 26
classicization, 60–61, 62, 66–67
code and coding, 6, 96
cognition
   embodied, 3
   of musical experience, 4, 19, 84, 87, 97,
     108, 128
colonialism, 20–21, 83, 87–88, 129
complementarity, 15
   of constituents in performing arts, 19,
     39, 117, 120
   of modes of expression in pedagogies,
     15, 30, 33
composition
   in performance, 92, 96
   oral, 47, 90–91

pre-performance, 91
   processes of, 90–91, 92–93
concepts. *See also* models, conceptual
   expansion and internationalization of,
     21, 87–88
   foundational, 22, 25, 63–64
   in relation to linguistic expressions, 86
   musical, 3, 13–14
conversation as a cultural activity, 18, 34,
     36–37, 108, 110
cross-cultural studies, 4, 8, 12, 24, 28, 89, 110
cultural practices, 22, 28, 76, 129–30
   eradication of, 32

dance, 10, 11, 46, 55–56, 61*t*, 63–64, 79,
     126–127, 130–31, 139–140
decolonizing, 20–21, 44–45, 60
drama, 8, 10, 41, 117, 138

emotions, 13, 18, 114, 115, 119, 126–127, 140
ethnotheory, 18
ethics, 1–2, 9, 34–35, 38–39, 51, 87*t*, *See
   also* responsibilities
ethos, 57–58, 88, 119
evolution, 1–2, 6

feedback interviews, 109
figure and ground 120–21
frequencies, measurement of, 16, 106–7

genres of speech, writing, or
     performance, 15, 31–32, 34–35, 37,
     82, 92, 120, 129–30
gestures, 52, 84, 114, 126, 131, 134, 139
grammar, musical, 98, 134. *See also* logic,
     musical

220 INDEX OF TOPICS

group plan, 94–95, 120, 130

habitus, 16
heritage, musical, 20, 31t, 45, 61t, 61–62, 72–73, 74–75
hybridization and hybridity, cultural, 1–2, 63, 68

ideal type, 101–2
imperialism, 60, 83–84, 87–88
improvisation
    in education, 43, 47
    processes of, 91–92, 94–96
instinct, 27, 135–36
instruments, musical
    as external memory devices, 6–7
    classification of, 116
    construction of, 22, 24, 30
intercultural contacts, 4, 50, 63, 75, 83, 86–88
interlocking parts, 134–37

knowledge, musical, 30
    organization and recognition of, 35, 40–41
    tacit, 55

learning
    kinesthetic modes of, 48
    stages of, 32–33, 39–40, 41, 45–46, 48
legitimization, 31t, 73
lexicography, 86
listening, 20, 48, 53–54, 76, 131
logic, musical, 33–34, 41, 48

markedness, 90–91, 120–21
mathematics, 8, 58–59, 100
memory, 6–7, 39, 55–56
metaphors, 98, 100–1, 125–26
    absolute, 98–99
    conceptual, 99–100
mimesis, 6, 129–30
mode
    concepts of, 85, 87–90
    of thinking and theorizing, 6, 26, 43–44, 49–50, 57t
models
    conceptual, 14, 24, 97, 139–40

generative, 97, 139
    of interaction in musicking, 49–50, 96, 131–32, 140
    musicological, 93
    of melody, 13–14, 74–75, 97
    representational and operational, 40–41
modernization, 60–62, 61t, 76–77
movement, 1, 3, 4, 6–7, 8, 11, 13–15, 33, 41, 53, 82, 99–100, 108, 109t, 110, 114–115, 126–27, 131
multimedia ethnography, 25, 138
multipart vocalizing, 132–34
music cognition, 3, 4, 84, 87–88, 128
musicology
    comparative, 1–2, 3–4, 69
    systematic, 18–19
    transcultural, 4
musilanguage, 11

national music
    in Afghanistan, 40–41
    in China, 32
    in Japan, 69
neuroscience, 12, 14–15
notation, musical, 54, 61t, 68, 70, 71, 72–73, 74–75, 83
    limitations of Western, 12, 62
    non-graphic or "oral", 128
    supplements to, 54, 71–72

options, 1, 5, 13, 25, 26, 49–50, 82, 93–94, 109t
orature, 53
orality, 52–53, 59

paradigms, 6, 116
peasant music, 16–17, 81–82
performance events, preparation
    of, 42. See also composition, pre-performance
physics, 100, 101
preservation, 65, 68, 72–73
progress, ideologies of, 75, 76–77, 100

rationalization, 29, 57–58
regulation, 28, 66–67, 83
researchers, roles of, 16–21, 35

INDEX OF TOPICS   221

renewal and revitalization, 60–61, 65
resources, musical, 5, 25, 29, 81, 86–87, 87t, 90, 97–98, 126
responsibilities, 9, 24, 33, 82, 109t, 134
rhythm, 38–39, 41, 45, 63–64, 79, 80t, 81, 90, 91, 100–1, 110, 116, 124, 135–36, 137t, 139–40
ritual, 8, 11, 17, 34–35, 38–39, 51, 79, 121, 137t, 137–139

scales, musical, 52, 65–67, 69, 70–71, 89, 105, 106, 107, 115
schema, schemata, 95–96, 97, 135–36
scheme
   conceptual, 17–18. *See also* model, conceptual
   of songs, 97–98
semantic fields, 88, 125–26
semiotics, 88, 137
solmization, 68, 70, 83, 111–12
sound
   categorization of, 12
   production of, 7, 37, 41
sound studies, 11
subjectivity, 9–10
synesthesia, 10, 118
systems, 80t
   acoustic-iconic mnemonic, 112
   acoustic-musicological, 17–18
   auditory, 12
   cognitive, 14, 78
   cueing, 122–23
   cultural, 79, 83
   memory, long term and short term, 55–56
   modal, 79, 89
   musical, 79, 94–95
   of knowledge production and storage, 23

of syllables, 112–14. *See also* solmization
   phonemic, 78, 82–83
   rhythmic, 79, 81–82
   tonal, 1, 7, 16–18, 79, 83
systematization, 23, 64–65, 66–67

techniques of the body, 16, 25, 36
theory
   aims and motivations of, 22
   as shaped by goals of institutions, 31–32
   attributes that may enhance values of, 31t
   communication of, 24, 33, 36, 37
   contexts for, 88
   definitions of, 9, 78
   explicit and implicit, 38, 52, 55, 56, 57–58
   for all music, 76–77
   indigenous, 18
   in relation to practice, 26–29
   oral and written, 52, 56
   social, 9, 24
   uses of, 31t
thinking, musical, 19, 37
timbre, 23, 115
transmission, 32–33, 35, 36–37, 52, 59, 64–65
tunings and temperament
   equal-stepped, 71, 104–5
   fixed, 16–17
   models of, 69, 104
typology, 116
   of music, 28
   of names for sounds, 111

universals, 53, 59, 76–77, 129